Labour in transition; a survey of British industrial history since 1914

William Aylott Orton

LABOUR IN TRANSITION.

LABOUR IN TRANSITION

A SURVEY OF BRITISH INDUSTRIAL
HISTORY SINCE 1914

BY

WILLIAM AYLOTT ORTON

B.A. *Cantab.*, M.Sc. *London.*

LONDON

PHILIP ALLAN & CO.,

QUALITY COURT, CHANCERY LANE

First published in October, 1921.

LONDON:
PRINTED BY THE ABBEY PRESS LTD.,
32 & 34, GREAT PETER STREET, WESTMINSTER, S.W.1.

Vouchsafe to those that have not read the story,
That I may prompt them: and of such as have,
I humbly pray them to admit th' excuse
Of time, of numbers, and due course of things,
Which cannot in their huge and proper life
Be here presented.

SHAKESPEARE,
King Henry the Fifth.

CONTENTS.

PART TWO.

JULY, 1915—DECEMBER, 1917.

PART FOUR.

JANUARY, 1919—JULY, 1921.

PROLOGUE.

Of social affairs, it has been said, war does but accelerate tendencies already in existence. In the long run, and on the national scale, the statement is probably true ; and even in the short run, and on the scale of the individual groups and sections of a complex community, it holds good in so far as the sudden assertion of an exacting national purpose demands the utmost of whatever serves, or can be made to serve it, while imposing a drastic test on all social dispositions. It is with the historic application of that test, more especially to the industrial groups of the community, that the following chapters deal. In the result, the numerical and the psychological strength, the functions, the inter-relations, the political status of those groups have been profoundly altered ; and in this respect alone, to speak of no other, we are a fundamentally changed society. " Things will be different after the war," we used to say six years ago. They are, with a vengeance. This book is an attempt to explain how and why.

To this attempt some broad picture of the society over which the storm burst in 1914 is a necessary preface. It was a society, prosperous as modern societies go, of some 28 million more or less educated adults, of whom 8 million men were parliamentary voters—the first full-grown generation in which some degree of education was practically universal : a fact not without significance in regard to the quality of its institutions, its recreations, and its press. It was a society with individualism in its very blood, gregarious only within narrow limits, organising itself rather according to the fortuitous pressure of circumstance than according to any preconceived plan ; moved more by personalities and events than by principles and ideals, amenable to tradition and custom rather than to system and coercion, possessed to an extraordinary degree, though less than half-consciously, with a sort of historic sense of continuity, so that while in its political and legal organisation it had achieved no small measure of at least nominal democracy, its education, its churches (except those of the Catholic faith), its amusements, its manners, and even its dress, tended still to conform, as it were in spite of themselves, to a social framework that was becoming increasingly an anachronism.

The survival of this framework, while making within certain limits for social stability, served to disguise from the general consciousness amazing inequalities of wealth and liberty. In its higher or narrower stages the functions of economic ascendancy were being strained, with a good deal of tacit consent and some success, to fill the space formerly occupied by those of an aristocracy ; while strictly within the lower or broader stages there had been growing up for near a century a sullen " class-consciousness " founded, for what it was worth, almost entirely on a community of economic disabilities. To this extent at least the permeation of the old framework by the modern economic system—" capitalist " system as it is called by its opponents—had dried out the cement that held the fabric together ; and it had been repeatedly asserted, and by some believed, that a good jerk from below would bring it all tumbling. The permeation had had other consequences It had proved necessary to mitigate by statutory regulation—by Trade Boards, by Factory Acts, by various species of insurance—the incidence of the system on those least favourably situated ; and by the action of associations nominally voluntary this regulation had been carried a good deal further ; carried in some cases, it was alleged, to the point of actually impeding the system.

The area over which this further regulation operated was, however, a comparatively small one. There were at the beginning of 1914 about $10\frac{1}{2}$ million men and $3\frac{1}{4}$ million women employed in the industries and services of the country ; and of these, about 34 in the hundred men, and 11 in the hundred women, were enrolled in trade unions—using the expression in a wide sense to include practically all societies that dealt with the terms and conditions of employment of their members. In the narrower sense, the societies affiliated to the Trade Union Congress represented about one-fifth of the total employed population. The organised proportion of workpeople varied widely between the separate industries. In one or two—in coal-mining, in most of the textile, and some of the metal trades—it stood as high as 70 per cent. ; but in the majority there was an unorganised residue of at least one half ; while in the more scattered occupations, among the bulk of the " black-coated proletariat," in home and small-shop industry, in the distributive trades, in fishing and sea transport, in agriculture, and among the women generally, organisation had made little head-way. The facts that by the date of the Armistice the organised proportion of workpeople had grown to about 50 per cent., and that to-day the minority of 1914 is practically a two-thirds majority, indicate in themselves something like a social revolution.

Some of the implications of the change are note-worthy. It means not merely that the industrial area over which collective bargaining is possible has been extended. It means that a majority of the working people of the country have realised the manifold possibilities of group action. It means that the extent to which concerted action in pursuit of a common policy is possible among the various trade unions is now a matter of first-rate importance to the entire community. And so far as such action is even attempted it means that there is a bigger potential backing of interested people and financial resources behind it than at any time in the history of the country. But if we ask how far in fact such action was in 1914 and has since become possible we are faced with certain considerations in regard to organisation and to opinion, that modify the effect of the whole progress.

As regards organisation, the number of separate societies—somewhere about 1,200—has not varied very much for twenty years ; and counted as units, the vast majority still rest on a local craft basis. The number of national or general societies with effective centralised administration does not even now exceed, at an outside estimate, 150. On the other hand, " probably five-sixths of all the trade union membership, and practically all its effective force, are to be found among the hundred principal societies to which the Ministry of Labour has long confined its detailed statistics."* By 1914 the tendency to centralisation was in full swing ; and during the succeeding years it became a factor of importance second only to the actual growth in membership. The forms it has taken vary from complete fusions of regional or competing associations that covered practically the same classes of workers, to highly complex federations and affiliations among distinct groups in the great industries, with varying degrees of central control. And concurrently with this tendency there has emerged a difficulty in the

*Webb: *History of Trade Unionism.*

nature of the control itself; a difficulty which is really a particular case of the general truth that the industrial and the political centres of this country are anything from two to five hundred miles apart. In proportion as the administration has become centralised and the administrative unit expanded, both the actual and, so to speak, the psychological distance between Head Office and the district, the shop and the individual member have inevitably widened; until now the leaders of the larger associations have to adopt something like the same tactics in informing, educing, and interpreting the opinion of their vast constituencies as does the Government in regard to the country as a whole. And the difficulty is complicated by the fact that the process has roughly coincided with the supersession, actual in more cases than is apparent, of some of the older leaders and policies, by men of a different type, different training, and very different ideals. Here is at any rate one group of tendencies the war accelerated; one of the leading clues to the tangled history we are to unravel.

As regards opinion, no concise statement will cover all the facts, and no single policy will ever cover all the unions. Most of the principal societies were and are affiliated both to the Trade Union Congress and to the Labour party; but the former had its own left, right and centre, and the Labour party was a rather loose federation comprising, in addition to the Trade Unions, the I.L.P., the British Socialist Party, the Fabian Society, and one or two other non-vocational bodies that were very far indeed, once war broke out, from pulling together. The Trade Union Congress had its Parliamentary Committee, and the Labour party its National Executive, and both united with the General Federation of Trade Unions to form a Joint Board which dealt with a variety of concrete issues pretty much as they

b

arose. Then there were the local Trades and Labour
Councils, which the Labour party admitted to
affiliation and the Congress refused; there were
local branches of the I.L.P. and the various other
Socialist bodies; and there was the little group of
thirty-six Labour members, organising themselves
and their constituencies on orthodox Parliamentary
lines.

All this is perhaps somewhat confusing—and in
1914, in fact, the unions were finding it so, and
contemplating the general clear-up that is now in
progress; but it was as nothing compared with the
real confusion of opinions subsisting among the rank-
and-file. There one met not merely the official
programs of the recognised authorities, but all kinds
of doctrine promulgated by all kinds of organisation,
from semi-Capitalist to downright Communist, and
a maze of controversy upon almost every matter of
applied social or industrial policy. At the heart of
a good deal of it was the unsolved problem of the
nature of the ideal industrial unit—vocation or
industry, or a mixture of both. Beyond that,
generalisation is of little use, save to point out that
there was a wide dissatisfaction with the Capitalist
system so far as it was understood, a broad sentiment
in favour of some sort of collective control of some
industries, and a half-articulate demand for some
better representation of " working-class interests "
than anything in the prevailing system afforded.
From such a state of things it was easy to evoke a
common sentiment, difficult to frame a common
policy, almost impossible, except on rare occasions
and the narrowest issues, to evolve a common plan
of action.

But if large-scale organisation and general opinion
were thus inchoate, the actual workaday business of
the trade unions in regard to the " terms and conditions of employment " was to no small extent

stabilised. Parallel with, and in some measure consequent on, the expansion of the unions, there had been a steady progress in the organisation of the employers—not merely in the direction of what are usually called trade combinations, but towards concerted action in regard to labour. By the summer of 1914 over 1,500 national and local employers' associations were dealing collectively with labour matters, and the number was increasing at the rate of over two hundred a year—a good deal of the increase, of course, being due to the expansion of functions on the part of existing associations that originally dealt with trade and commercial questions only. And naturally, and, on the whole, beneficially, the relations between the corporate bodies on either side of industry tended to settle down. Says the Twelfth Report of the Ministry of Labour on Conciliation :

" The position in regard to the settlement of labour disputes in this country, prior to the war, was that the majority were settled by agreement between employers and workpeople without recourse to Government intervention. An outstanding feature of the industrial position in Great Britain had for many years been the permanent voluntary conciliation boards, established by agreement between employers and workpeople, unsupported by legal enactment, and depending for their success on the goodwill of the parties. During the course of half a century, voluntary conciliation boards or other suitable arrangements for the settlement of labour disputes had been established in all the well-organised industries, and this procedure was instrumental in settling large numbers of disputes "

—mainly before, that is, and sometimes after, direct action had been invoked by one side or other. Over

300 such boards were in existence at the beginning
of 1914, to say nothing of the joint district boards
for the miners set up under the Act of 1912, or the
joint boards on the railways set up after the Board of
Trade conference at the end of 1911.

In spite of this machinery, however, the three
years preceding the war were years of marked
" unrest " in industry.   The number of open disputes
originating in 1913 was nearly three times the average
of the years since 1900 ; while in respect of the number of workpeople affected, 1912 constituted an
even more startling maximum.   But it would be
misleading to base any general conclusion on these
facts alone.   These same years, it must be remembered, were fat years for commerce and industry ;
1913 is spoken of as having witnessed a " trade boom."
They were years, that is to say, of good employment ;
and the usual inverse correspondence between the
unemployment returns and the totals of industrial
disputes had persisted with remarkable accuracy
through the whole period since 1900.   Nothing in
fact illustrates more clearly the real nature of the
industrial system than the immediate increase in the
strike figures whenever the labour demand gave the
unions an opportunity.   The strike was in fact a
normal and necessary part of the system, recognised
as such, in at least a negative way, by the law.
The extent, therefore, to which the " unrest " of
1913 may be called abnormal is smaller than the
figures would suggest.   What is significant is that
in the analysis of the causes of those 1,500 disputes
of 1913, the two heads under which is revealed an
increase not only considerable in itself, but much
larger than the increase of the total in comparison
with previous years, are " the employment of
particular classes or persons " and " trade unionism " ;
wages as a cause of dispute shows an absolute decline
in importance.

Here we come upon a leading symptom of the complex social situation of the early century. The political labour movement was yet in its infancy, and there was behind it no such accepted school of political philosophy and tradition as informed the older political parties. For many years there had been a few trade union representatives in Parliament ; but it was not until 1900 that the new-formed Labour Representation Committee secured the return of the first two members on a definitely political " ticket " ; not until 1906 that the effort to stimulate a sense of political solidarity among working-men had any very marked effect on the election results. 29 political Labour candidates were then returned in addition to 23 trade union representatives ; the event being made the occasion of a speech* by Mr. Lloyd George in which the Radical program of succeeding years was put forward as an antidote to this " socialist mission among the workmen." Four more years were to pass before the trade unionists and the L.R.C. men were definitely united as a political unit ; and before the next appeal to the country was made, political Labour was handicapped by the Osborne judgment.

Apart, however, from that particular disability, the situation was one of intrinsic difficulty for the Labour movement, and the period tempts comparison with the age of Bismarck and Lasalle. The political creed of the new-born party was not so firmly established nor so widely recognised that it could easily maintain its integrity in face of an energetic Radical administration that was professedly trying to reach the heart of the working man with arrows taken from the Socialist quiver. Liberals as well as Labour men were proving themselves (on occasion) apt pupils of Quintus Fabius ; and though the presence of the Labour group may have done much to expedite

* Quoted in Beer : *History of British Socialism*, Vol. II.

the reformist measures of the period—national health
and unemployment insurance, minimum wage legislation, workmen's compensation, old age pensions
and the rest—it was the Liberals who earned (or
took) the credit. Further, the great constitutional
battles waged by the Liberal party left the Labour
group no choice but to sink its identity ; and " the
political necessity of supporting the Liberal party
bills relating to the Budget and the House of Lords,
and of not playing into the hands of a still more
reactionary front Opposition bench, were not readily
comprehended by the average workman." *   In the
country, the political forces of Labour were far from
consolidated. " Many   of   those   (wrote   W.   C.
Anderson at the close of 1911) who find its sinews
of war cannot when the crisis comes forget their old
faiths of Liberalism and Toryism. So miners at
Lanark are held at the moment of voting by their
old tradition, and nullify at the ballot-box the work
they themselves set going in the Trade Union
branches."†

The years following the elections of 1910 were in
fact years of disappointment, not merely with the
results of the political organisation of Labour, but
with the general policy of collectivist Socialism which
formed the mainstay of its program. While that
policy was apparently gaining support from the
Liberals, important sections of Labour were turning
towards Socialism of a more particularist, and in
some ways, incompatible, order. Syndicalism, which
relied on industrial coercion rather than the ballot-
box, was making rapid headway in Wales and on the
Clyde. Guild Socialism—one of the many important
contributions of the *New Age* to social history—was
moving towards its place as a recognised policy from
1908 onwards. At a critical moment the reaction

* Webb   *Op cit.*
† "*Daily News*" *Year Book*, 1912.

against Fabian collectivism was reinforced by Hilaire Belloc's brilliant attack on the " Servile State." And if, as has been stated,* the influence of Bergson strengthened the movement towards direct industrial action, that of Nietzsche confirmed the growing distrust of constitutional political democracy.

Thus, while Liberalism was approching its Philippi on the field of foreign policy, and political labour attempting with indifferent success to focus the heterogeneous mind of its constituency, the centre of action passed again to the industrial arena. The industrial organisation of the workers ran far ahead of their political evolution. The liaison between the militant forces of Labour and their political direction grew swiftly weaker. The principle that economic power precedes political power was drastically applied in the great upheavals of 1911 and 1912, which led in 1913 to the first proposals for a Triple Alliance. And while the militant arm was being trained on tangible issues with a view to its eventual use in a wider field, both means and ends of the political and constitutional movement were increasingly brought in question.

On all this suddenly broke the cataclasm of external war, of whose effects the story is now to be recounted · a story that must inevitably be concerned in the main with the difficulties, the differences, the struggles against the unforeseen obstacles and failures in circumstance and society of which history is made. We shall see the worker challenged by the national emergency to declare his relative loyalty to vocation, to class, and to the commonweal. We shall see the industrial Labour movement challenged to convert its offensive-defensive alliances of groups within a group to active agents of the national purpose, called on, and at last compelled to sacrifice securities of many years' earning to

---

* See Scott : *Syndicalism and Philosophic Realism.*

the common need. We shall see the political
Labour movement challenged to define exactly what
in national and international polity it stood for.
And remembering that not even the poorest worker
is wholly circumscribed by vocation, we shall watch
the whole nation ridden harder and harder by an
ordeal that was for nearly four years in doubt, spurred
by dire necessity to a pace at which its very relaxations savoured of violence, weakened from time to
time less by misfortune than by sheer weariness,
dazed by the endless monotone of the guns and
the machines, impaired in health physical and
spiritual by the strain of the one pitiless purpose
—emerging after all, swiftly and almost incredibly,
to a triumph too great for grasping. If at times we
dwell upon the darker side of the war period it is
in order that its sequel may be better comprehended.
History demands that human motives as well as
human actions be brought to light ; and to judge men
is at all times less profitable than to understand
them.

the common need. We shall see the political Labour movement challenged to define exactly what in national and international polity it stood for. And remembering that not even the poorest worker is wholly circumscribed by vocation, we shall watch the whole nation ridden harder and harder by an ordeal that was for nearly four years in doubt, spurred by dire necessity to a pace at which its very relaxations savoured of violence, weakened from time to time less by misfortune than by sheer weariness, dazed by the endless monotone of the guns and the machines, impaired in health physical and spiritual by the strain of the one pitiless purpose —emerging after all, swiftly and almost incredibly, to a triumph too great for grasping. If at times we dwell upon the darker side of the war period it is in order that its sequel may be better comprehended. History demands that human motives as well as human actions be brought to light ; and to judge men is at all times less profitable than to understand them.

the common need. We shall see the political Labour movement challenged to define exactly what in national and international polity it stood for. And remembering that not even the poorest worker is wholly circumscribed by vocation, we shall watch the whole nation ridden harder and harder by an ordeal that was for nearly four years in doubt, spurred by dire necessity to a pace at which its very relaxations savoured of violence, weakened from time to time less by misfortune than by sheer weariness, dazed by the endless monotone of the guns and the machines, impaired in health physical and spiritual by the strain of the one pitiless purpose—emerging after all, swiftly and almost incredibly, to a triumph too great for grasping. If at times we dwell upon the darker side of the war period it is in order that its sequel may be better comprehended. History demands that human motives as well as human actions be brought to light ; and to judge men is at all times less profitable than to understand them.

PART ONE.

From the Outbreak of War to the Munitions Act of July, 1915.

	1914.
War Emergency Workers' National Committee Formed	Aug. 6
National Industrial Truce Resolution ...	Aug. 24
Engineering and Shipbuilding Conferences on Labour Supply	Oct. to Jan.
	1915.
Committee on Production Appointed	Feb. 4
Clyde Strike of Engineers	Feb. 16
Shells and Fuzes Agreement	Mar. 5
D.O.R. Amendment No. 2 Act ...	Mar. 16
Treasury Conferences ... ... Mar.	17-19, 25
Command Paper on Bad Time-keeping	May 1
Enrolment open for N.E. Coast King's Squad	May 15
Ministry of Munitions Established ...	June 9
War Munitions Volunteer Enrolment Open	June 24
Munitions of War Act	July 2

(The dates given to Acts of Parliament are those of Royal Assent.)

CHAPTER I.

CATACLASM.

§ 1.

When on the morning of June 29th, 1914, **the** papers announced the assassination of an Austrian Archduke at Sarajevo, it was remarked that one more manifestation had occurred of the fit of minor violence that seemed to be possessing public affairs. Other topics on the morrow reoccupied the tops of the news columns, and Britain resumed its gaze at the domestic hearth oblivious of the fact that a corner of the house had taken fire. The militant suffrage movement continued its program of miniature explosions ; Marconi shares and Government finance drew more members to the House in mid-July than foreign policy ; Ulster gun-running provoked an occasional " sensation " and a few deaths ; and although Sir Edward Carson declared that he " saw no sign of peace " and warned the volunteers to be " ready to obey the call," it was not of a European War that he was understood to be thinking.

In short, despite a Government majority down to 38 at the end of June, it is to be presumed the country as a whole felt secure enough to allow itself the luxury of a little anarchy. Trade of course was not as good as it had been—but then 1913 had

witnessed a " boom," and in spite of the reaction
only the cotton industry, where from July 7th the
operatives were working 25 per cent. short time,
was seriously feeling the pinch. " The year 1914,"
says the *Labour Gazette* for the following January,
" opened with employment still good on the whole,
and very good in some industries, particularly coal-
mining, engineering and ship-building ; but with a
decided tendency to decline in the pig-iron, iron and
steel, tin-plate, and textile industries, which continued with little alteration during the first half of
the year. In July the decline in employment became
at once more marked and more general, and there was
every prospect of an approaching period of less
activity, especially in the pig-iron and the iron and
steel industries, and the cotton, woollen and lace
trades." None the less, the average amount of
unemployment up to the end of July—2·3 per cent.
—was barely more than half the average of the years
since 1900 ; only 1913 could show a better record.

And on the other side of the medal, as regards
what is quaintly called " industrial unrest," 1913
also held the record of the young century with a
total of 1,497 fresh disputes in the year—a figure
which, but for the supervention of " unrest " of
another and a wilder species, 1914 might easily
have beaten. Among the 836 separate trials of
strength that took place up to the end of July we
may notice one or two outstanding. In February
and March, 150,000 of the Yorkshire miners held out
for seven weeks to enforce a wage demand—more or
less successfully. In London a more fundamental
issue was ·at stake in the building industry.
Would the unionists undertake to work peaceably
with non-unionists ? Would they sign an undertaking to that effect—with penalties for non-observ-
ance ? They would neither sign nor do it : at the
Pearl Assurance Building in Holborn, at other jobs

where the same issue was raised, they struck work rather than do it; and conference, conciliation, arbitration, failed to make them. At length the London Master Builders declared a lock-out. The operatives endeavoured to close their ranks in a new industrial union, and undertook contracts on their own responsibility—even executed one, in Tavistock Square. Meanwhile, among the masters the question of a national stoppage was being considered; as a result, came an ultimatum to the effect that failing a settlement by August 15th the lock-out should be made national. Among the unions unity was by now threatening to break down; mournfully says the *Herald* on June 27th, " we would much have preferred to see the men go back beaten for the time being rather than go back as now, making sectional agreements and giving up the principle of the Federation." So matters stood in July, unsettled, inclining to defeat for the men. The aggregate duration of this dispute the *Labour Gazette* estimates at 2½ million working days; what might have been the equivalent of that in houses the *Labour Gazette* does not tell us. But this issue—this interference, if one likes to call it so, with the liberty of the master to employ whomsoever he pleased—was fundamental. It was part of the general closing of the ranks that had been so marked a feature of trade unionism since 1911—how important a part the stubbornness with which the London builders fought it may indicate. And yet at Woolwich, where a lightning strike on this same issue broke out on July 3rd, the men won their point in four days. Perhaps a certain cryptic phrase in a semi-official Austrian message of that same date had something to do with it.

Thus, with militant suffrage, Ulster gun-runnings, and an average of nearly four disputes a day in industry, did the corporate life of Britain run smoothly on : and "armed conflict is not impossible" whispered the Austrian telegram. Unbelievable, however, to the vast majority of Britons it remained for the first half of July, and even when the not impossible had become the all but actual it was merely "the Balkan cauldron on the boil" again for a certain Labour newspaper. After all, how should Labour—or, for that matter, honourable members of Parliament—know along what strands the blaze might run to Britain? In any case, for official Socialism, including the British National and Independent Labour Parties, the position had been defined in advance by the International Congress of 1907, with a resolution that under a threat of war (any war except the class war) the workers in every country must strive to prevent it

> "by all the means which seem to them most appropriate having regard to the sharpness of the class war and to the general political situation. Should war none the less break out their duty is to intervene to bring it promptly to an end, and with all their energies to use the political and economic crisis created by the war to rouse the populace from its slumbers and to hasten the fall of capitalist, domination."

For years past the British Labour party had been denouncing in general terms the "international competition in armaments," "the race for overseas markets," the entire policy of "imperialist expansion," in which it envisaged this country as taking part ; and when during the last days of July the stark certainty of European war emerged from the confusion of diplomatic issues, rendered the more repugnant by the prospect of a Russian alliance, such denunciation was echoed in resolution and manifesto by innumerable Labour organisations, and reinforced with all the traditional tenets of

International Socialism. There was no quarrel between the workers : the workers had no concern in the international struggle : the class war was the only war for them : Britain must not be " dragged in "—and so on, with the explicit approval (for what it was worth) of the International Socialist Bureau which " in assembly of July 29th " considered it " an obligation for the workers of all concerned nations not only to continue but even to strengthen their demonstrations against war in favour of peace "—though precisely how the demonstrations were to be strengthened the Bureau did not venture to indicate. The British Parliament-ary Labour Party was more explicit, calling upon all Labour organisations " to watch events vigilantly so as to oppose, if need be, in the most effective way, any action which may involve us in war " ; while the Labour Press was growing impatient : " We have had enough resolutions. It is the time for action " At least the Transport Workers might strike ! They could not mobilise without them. Still more urgent was the manifesto of the British section of the Socialist Bureau which, on August 1st, over the signatures of Keir Hardie and Arthur Henderson, summoned the " people of Britain " to

> " hold vast demonstrations against war in every industrial centre. Compel those of the govern-ing class and their Press who are eager to commit you to co-operate with Russian despotism to keep silence. . . . Proclaim that for you the days of plunder and butchery have gone by. Send messages of peace and fraternity to your fellows who have less liberty than you. Down with class rule ! Down with the rule of brute force ! Down with war ! Up with the peaceful rule of the people ! "

" Down with class rule ! " So far were we at this stage from the Dictatorship of the Proletariat !

On Sunday, August 2nd, the mass of protest culminated in a monster demonstration in Trafalgar Square, which by resolution denounced " secret alliances and understandings which in their origin were never sanctioned by the nations nor are even now communicated to them " ; protested against any, support of Russia ; more urgently than ever cried " Peace." " During the progress of the meeting," says a press report, " a Russian, a German, a Frenchman and a Swiss embraced each other, whilst Cunningham Grahame stepped forward, and they all stood with joined hands, the crowd cheering wildly. Thus was true international amity demonstrated." Not thus altogether. That same afternoon the naval reserves were called up. That same night throngs of excited Londoners swarmed down the Mall to Buckingham Palace, " rousing the populace from its slumbers " to some purpose with singing and cheering and other patriotic " demonstrating " continued into the small hours of the morning—albeit it is not recorded that they passed a resolution.

But while terms and methods might vary, official Labour was by no means the only camp throughout July opposed to war. " The whole spirit of Gladstonian Liberalism," says Colonel Repington, " hated war like the plague and most of all Continental war, which was positively anathema to the party in office. . . . Even the Cabinet was not united on the question of war until the violation of Belgian neutrality was an accomplished fact." In the popular estimate, bad enough as had been the Austrian attitude to Serbia, we could fairly wash our hands of it ; but the German attitude to Belgium— by that, stronger forces were let loose in Britain than resolution and manifesto could altogether cope with : class-consciousness was merged in a species of consciousness somewhat nearer the elemental ; and in whatever peril divided opinions on the European crisis might have placed the country in July, it was safely passed when Germany, over and above the confusion of diplomatic issues, gratuitously offered an absolutely clear and popular *casus belli*. Almost in a night—the night of August 2nd-3rd— the popular fear that Britain might be " dragged into " the war was changed to an apprehension lest by any betrayal of her honour she should be kept out of it ; and the Socialist contention that we should stand aside from the Belgian issue also became suddenly as the voice of one crying in a wilderness. On August 4th the German armies entered Belgium. At 11 o'clock that night Great Britain was at war. And what was Labour going to do about it ?

§ 2.

At this point we may usefully attempt some answer to the general question many a reader must have framed : what is the precise evidential value of such resolutions and manifestos and other printed or spoken utterances of Labour as we have just been quoting and shall doubtless have frequent occasion to quote in the sequel ? Well, as far as figures can throw light on it, here they are :

British Labour Party : estimated membership in 1914.

Trade Unions	101
Trades Councils and Local Labour Parties	179
Socialist Societies (including I.L.P) ...	2
Total affiliated membership	1,612,147

of which somewhere about one-thirtieth was then professedly and systematically Socialist ; but the entire membership, both collectively and through the principal constituent organisations, was represented on the International Socialist Bureau along with no less than 27 other countries. Here then was machinery for some two-fifths, let us say, of British Trade Unionism to become articulate on political issues. But if the question be pressed as to what degree of real sanction, on a given occasion, any such articulation possessed, it is evident that figures will not help much towards an answer. Clearly the expression of policy on specific issues must be the business of a representative body, or person ; and when it comes to guessing the actual degree of representation, other than statistical considerations become relevant, and the verdict will vary with the occasion.

Both in history and present fact, the basis of labour solidarity is the trade, the living ; as an industrial constituency therefore labour rests on a very tangible and definite foundation, from which it can and does exert a very real influence on the industrial field. But as a political constituency there is no such ready-made and tangible foundation ; there is no particular reason why any two trade unionists should be of like mind in other than industrial issues—*except in so far as they have become class-conscious and are imbued with similar ideals.* This is not to say that the political solidarity of labour is dependent upon the conversion of working men to revolutionaries. Heaven knows, class-consciousness is not necessarily revolutionary—it has been for centuries the basis of British constitutionalism. What does appear is that the political solidarity of Labour, unlike the industrial, has to be created—even if, in the end, as its would-be creators hope, the political should become exactly coterminous with the industrial constituency. In fact, a process of inculcation and permeation is going on, and much—perhaps most— of what purports to be Labour utterance is not so much Labour speaking as Labour being spoken to ; more exactly it is the conscious element addressing the semi-conscious or the unconscious. For that reason resolutions and manifestos of an alert minority are not to be valued altogether in accordance with their merely quantitative backing. In the absence of any equally coherent antagonistic centre of consciousness, there is a certain historic presumption that they represent more or less roughly the way the mass will go. Only when—as in the events of August 1914—the tacit *rapport* between the articulate nucleus and the rest of the constituency is broken by the irruption of normally dormant elements does the clue become less valuable—even then, by no means valueless.

§ 3.

Thus on Tuesday, August 4th, 1914, Great Britain went to war, as near united as on such an issue a modern nation can be : with an army, reservists and Territorials included, equal to about one-sixth of the subsequent enlistment in the British Isles alone : with an annual productive capacity of arms and munitions equal to rather less than a single week's output four years later. Mobilisation had begun on the Monday morning ; and as it were auto-matically, thousands of dockers, stevedores, seamen, firemen, engine drivers, signalmen, and general labourers were drawn to the docks, the railway sidings and the ports, and kept there on special pay-rates—some for a week, some for months—to move the armies : to whose services the Premier in Parliament made subsequent acknowledgment. Not only with the utmost speed, but with the utmost secrecy had the task to be carried through : and in proportion as news had to be withheld the atmosphere became heavy with gossip and rumour, oppressive with a vague sense of crisis and mystery, of colossal

forces moving unseen across England, of terrific
conflict in progress at her very gates. Troops passed
through the city streets almost in silence, and only
here and there, where perhaps some fool of a drum-
major played the reservists out of barracks to the
tune of "Dolly Gray," did the older women choke
with a poignant recollection of what it all might mean.
In such an atmosphere panic and suspicion were
inevitable : spy-hunt and German-baiting were
another expression of the temper that produced the
food panic of early August.

At the end of the first week of August, says the
Labour Gazette, food prices were advanced by 15 or
16 per cent.   But what the women knew was that
the loaf had risen ½d. ; sugar nearly double ; meat,
butter, cheese, bacon 1d. or 2d. on the pound—all
growing scarcer. Worse still were rumours, with only
too much truth in them, of rich people driving home
motor-cars crammed full of eatables—a process sum-
marily stopped by Royal Proclamation in September.   As for prices, the Board of Trade, on advice of
traders' committees, published reasonable maxima
from August 7th ; but took no power to enforce
them.   By September the panic rise had abated, but
the real war advance had set in—to continue apparently to the Greek kalends.

Thus from the poor people war lost no time in
exacting its price ; well for those whom it made in
money no poorer.   But the invisible foundations of
Labour were collapsing. Panic had overwhelmed
the Continental exchanges during that last week of
July ; by August 1st London and New York were
the only first-rank markets open, British Consols
were down six points, Bank Rate up to 10 per cent.
On the 2nd came the special, on the 6th the general
moratorium ;   and with locking-up of securities,
cancellation of contracts, curtailment of credit,
prohibitive freight insurances, and shortage of

money the unemployment Labour had dreaded became actual. The textile industries, already suffering badly, and the furniture trades, were first hit ; luxury trades and general export industry followed ; and by the end of the month there were some 18,000 additional men unemployed, notwithstanding enlistment, in the London area alone. " In September," to quote the summary given by G. D. H. Cole in " Labour in War-Time," " out of about 9,250,000 wage-earners in industrial occupations, including about 2,250,000 women, 98,000 men and 189,000 women were out of work, despite the fact that 616,000 such men had joined the forces." And in addition, about one in ten of the persons employed in July had been reduced to short time—and short money—by October.

§ 4.

With prices rising, unemployment apparently on the increase, autumn closing in, and a European war in progress, here was scope enough for whatever organisation Labour could put forward to migitate its own prospect—though " inevitably the Government got in first " grudgingly remarks our Labour historian, as if it were a sort of contest. The Government Committee on Distress was appointed the very day war was declared ; and on August 6th, following a peculiarly British tradition in such matters, it inaugurated the system of voluntary local distress committees which should " include representatives of the municipal, education and poor law authorities, distress committees (that is, the peace time unemployment relief committees, of which there were 16 at the end of July) trade unions, and philanthropic agencies," as well as women; by which bodies grants from the Prince of Wales'

Fund were to be administered, public works put in hand, and whatever possible done to maintain employment in their respective areas. Meanwhile Labour had " got in " on August 5th with an *ad hoc* conference of all the Socialist societies and Labour organisations ; from the conference a " War Emergency Workers' National Committee " was there and then appointed ; which committee met weekly during the rest of the year, and fortnightly for over twelve months after, proving always an alert, sometimes a constructive critic of official policy.

On some cardinal points, in fact, the Government policy proved so vulnerable that had distress materialised on anything like the scale apprehended, drastic alteration would have been imperative. There was, for example, the almost inevitable defect that relief could hardly be dissociated, on the distress committees, from the idea and the methods of organised charity ; necessary investigation proved too often inquisitorial, and the least deserving became the most accessible cases. Then there was a running competition between the claims of civil and military applications, in which Labour rightly alleged undue favour was extended to the latter. Worst of all was the absence until the end of October of any uniform principle or scale of relief ; with the result that equally well-meaning committees in neighbouring districts might be working on entirely divergent lines. Fulham and Willesden, for example, were allowing 12s. 6d. a week for a single adult, while Southwark was giving 3s. and Bethnal Green 4s. Many committees, moreover, attempted on official advice to give relief in kind only. " My own committee, for instance," wrote a contributor to the *Nation* on October 31st, " was forced to admit money relief on finding that various recipients of its tickets were sitting in the dark with parcels of dry tea and uncooked meat, because they had not a penny for coal or gas." On these and many other matters the Workers' Committee "made representations" to the Government Committee, frequently with effect, and when the latter took in hand the question of a standard relief scale, the Labour body fought hard for the " pound-a-week " family minimum. In that it did not succeed : the October scale gave 10s. to one adult, 20s. to the family with four children in London ; in the provinces 2s. less ; this being, however, a substantial advance on the original proposals.

As time went on the Workers' Committee widened its net. It investigated the conduct and costs of Government contracts, and published its findings ; it collected information and by reports or memoranda effectively informed public opinion on the increases in rents, food prices and coal prices ; it encouraged the provision of maternity schemes under the Enabling Act of 1915 ; of meals for school children under the 1914 Act ; and it appointed five members to the central committee on Women's Employment —a committee which, in addition to assisting the redistribution of women in industry, itself handled Government contracts for shirts, body belts and socks, and disbursed in eighteen months over £15,000 in wages through its own work rooms. All this was work that any Labour society, whether or no it supported the war, must admit to be necessary ; and the Workers' Committee owed much of its great influence to the fact that after August, 1914, it was the only platform on which all the heterogeneous societies could stand together. Its general policy, especially its insistent pressure on the Government in the direction of food purchase and control, was largely dictated by the Fabian Society —" or " (says Mr. Cole) " what is much the same, by Mr. Sidney Webb " ; and though this side of its work brought little direct result, through its effect on public opinion the Workers' Committee was to prove a decisive power in the political history of 1915.

§ 5.

While the Workers' Committee was thus concerning itself with the effect of the war-situation on the industrial population as a whole, the situation was threatening to throw completely out of gear the machinery by which that population was organised ; and on August 24th the executives of the Trades Union Congress, and the Labour Party, met to consider the matter. Briefly, the position was that the abnormal unemployment was causing an insupportable drain on the resources of the trade unions, at a time when their invested funds could only be realised at a grave disadvantage ; and it was urged that the unions were by now a sufficiently essential part of society to have a valid claim on the State for assistance. Some assistance they were of course entitled to under the National Insurance Act—to the extent, under certain conditions, of a refund of one-sixth of their expenditure on unemployment relief ; but far more was becoming necessary. They were hit by the withdrawal on military service of a large proportion of their subscribing members, while of the remainder more and more were being turned over every week from subscribers to claimants. It had been urged by the more zealous Socialist critics of the Government's relief policy that the unions should be made the administrative agencies for a State relief scheme ; but in fact the unions could hardly cope with the claims of their own members, and were practically compelled to desist from accepting any additional responsibilities. This was the case put before the Prime Minister on August

27th, with a request for State aid in realising trade union funds at short notice and for additional subsidies to palliate the emergency. The latter were granted in October with retrospective effect as from the outbreak of war; unions suffering abnormal unemployment were enabled, provided they made a special levy on their employed of 1d. or 2d. weekly, to obtain a maximum refund of one-sixth or one-third of their expenditure—that is, with the one-sixth already obtainable, one-third or one-half in all. Undoubtedly the scheme pressed hardest on the unions that most needed help; it would hardly have sufficed for a long-period drain, and the turn of events rather than the State subsidies saved the unions. As it was, after eight months of war, 182 unions had received in all some £76,756—a small enough total seeing that in some cases the unemployment expenditure exceeded £20,000 in the last quarter of 1914.

§ 6.

Yet despite widespread unemployment and distress among the rank-and-file of labour and the many practical difficulties with which its leaders had as best they could to contend, not these things but the universal tide of active patriotism will remain the dominant impression of this momentous autumn. Volunteers from all trades and classes were enlisting at the rate of nearly 100,000 a week: 174,901 during the first week of September; so that many a regiment would make a favour of it to put your name on a long waiting list, and many a depôt had to close its doors on a press of volunteers much as in peace time the dock gates used to close on a press of willing labourers. Outstanding industrial disputes were broken off, compromised, referred to

arbitration or waived altogether. Already in the
first fortnight of August, employers and trade
unionists on Clyde and Tyne had mutually agreed to
assist in every possible way the execution of all work
essential to the war—in the latter area, had even
recommended the removal of "all working restrictions." Other unions were taking up a similar
attitude , and the Labour Conference of August
25th, before it approached the Government for
assistance for the union funds, had embodied the
general opinion in a resolution " that an immediate
effort be made to terminate all existing disputes,
whether strikes or lock-outs, and whenever new
points of difficulty arise during the war-period, a
serious attempt should be made by all concerned
to reach an amicable settlement before resorting
to a strike or lock-out." From 72,000 men involved
in various disputes in mid-July the number fell to
" practically nil" by the following February: for
99 new disputes originating in July there were only
14 in August. This was the industrial truce, loyally
observed in spite of grave provocation during the
-first winter.

And lest it be thought that this was a small matter,
an obvious and unimportant concession, let it be
recalled that the three years preceding the war were
years of intense industrial struggle in which for the
unions principles as well as pence were at stake ;
and that, even as regards wages alone, the truce
involved the spontaneous surrender of the essential
factor in their bargaining power, in sheer reliance
on the goodwill of employers and the State. Whatever amelioration of the average working class
standard of living the next few years might have
brought was thus staked on the hazard ; and it was
a stake that the war-bonus principle of subsequent
wage advances did not in fact redeem.

To the political truce also, under which Parliamentary vacancies were to be refilled without contest, official Labour was a party; and when at the end of August a parliamentary recruiting campaign was inaugurated, the National Labour Party wholeheartedly supported it, recommending all its affiliated organisations to do the same, and placing its staff and its offices at the service of the campaign. The executive of the Trades Union Congress now stated its opinion that " upon the result of the struggle in which this country is now engaged rest the preservation and maintenance of free and unfettered democratic government "; and by the middle of October practically the whole official Labour movement had realised that " the victory of Germany would mean the death of democracy in Europe." Almost alone the Independent Labour Party continued to wave the standard of Socialist idealism: " Out of the darkness and the depth we hail our working-class comrades of every land. Across the roar of guns we send sympathy and greeting to the German socialists. . . . In tears of blood and bitterness the greater democracy will be born. With steadfast faith we greet the future; our cause is holy and imperishable, and the labour of our hands has not been in vain. Long live Freedom and Fraternity! Long live International Socialism! "

CHAPTER II.

GENERAL POST.

§ I.

From what men are thinking and saying to what
they are doing is in England generally a far cry.
It is apt to be farthest when, as in the time we have
now to record, they are acting under the immediate
pressure of unforeseen events, and being driven,
against their declared will, to strain their old systems
to breaking-point. These were days in which news
of the fighting came through only in carefully edited
reports, disseminated with a view not so much to
accurate information as to the manufacture of a
certain public opinion; and when no authentic
estimate of progress on the home front as regards
either men or munitions was allowed to appear at all.
They were the days of imaginary Russians in
England, of naval battles that were never fought,
and German landings that were never seen; days
when it was commonly said that war on such a scale
could hardly last twelve months, and Kitchener's
December hint of three years came as a shock to
recruits who had considered that a remote alternative to " the duration "; days, in short, when no
dimmest prevision of what England could and would
do in the way of simultaneous fighting and working

was possible to any man. Small wonder that the winter of 1914-15 presents something like a seething chaos to the historian.

For clue we shall follow at first the official totals and averages compiled mostly after the event ; but for any good that may come of the venture we must invoke the aid of the instructed imagination, in constant reminder that the truth of these things is only the generalised truth of the mathematician, and that we are dealing not with masses of abstract " labour " computable under a few score headings in round numbers or precise percentages, but with live men, women and children, parents, wives, brothers, sisters, friends of the men in France ; folk, most of them, to whose lives leisure, comfort, culture, as elsewhere understood, were largely foreign, to many of whom an eight-hour working day was a remote desideratum, among whom what skill at lathe or forge or loom a man had gained was his one precious possession, to be protected against exploitation as a richer man might guard his jewels against the thief ; folk from whom industry as well as war had already claimed its casualties by thousands, and to whom the industrial recovery was to mean breaking-up of homes, and journeyings to strange parts, and loss of old companions, and protracted hours of toil by day and night, and small thanks, and for four years no respite.

§ 2.

With the aid of the aforesaid abstractions, it is possible to make a rough general analysis of the intricate process of labour resettlement, which can be indicated most clearly in imaginary diagram form. Visualise, then, two parallel columns or tubes, open above, closed by stop-cocks below ; and let the one contain the total available supply of male labour, the other the total volume of employment as measured by jobs actually filled. It would be better if this second column could represent the total demand for labour, but there is no measuring the unsatisfied as well as the satisfied demand ; certain indications of it we shall adduce later. The custom had grown up of adjusting the level of the first column to that of the second, with the result that there was normally a labour surplus or margin. This surplus amounted at the outbreak of war to some 3.6 per cent. of the total volume in our first column ; but for the moment we will ignore it and assume, as the official statistics do, that the two columns start level ; and we will call the level 100. Then the taps are opened and the drain begins. Actually the collapse of credit and consequent decline in industry begin to tell on the second column a week or more before recruitment begins to drain the first. By August 5th the dual process is well started ; and what we may consider the first phase consists in the downward race of the two levels.

For three months the level of the second column falls below that of the first, creating an abnormal surplus of labour supply. At the end of August the labour level is down to about 97.7, while the second column has fallen to 95.1. During September both levels fall still faster, but the discrepancy decreases ; 91.2 and 89.8 are the readings. A month later the levels stand at 89.3 and 89.2 ; and by the end of November the two columns are practically level again, though still falling. In other words, abnormal male unemployment has disappeared.

After November the level of the first column tends to fall below that of the second, and the excess passes to the other side. The drain of enlistment continues at the rate of over 30,000 a week ; but a partial industrial recovery has diminished the drain on the volume of employment, while the special requirements of the war are all along being poured in increasing measure into the top of the second column, so that the net downward movement is now very small. In December the first column is down to 86.7, while the second stands at 89.1 ; with the result that fresh labour is now being poured into the first column to counteract the deficiency. " If we ask," says Mr. Cole, " whence this new male labour has come, the answer is that it has come partly from the absorption of those who were unemployed last July "—that is, the original surplus that we agreed to ignore in our comparison—" and partly by the entry of new labour into the industries concerned This has taken the form both of a return to work of men who had ceased to be so employed, and of a transference of labour from commercial and other occupations to industry."

Now it has been pointed out that the level of our second column, representing the volume of employment, gives us practically no indication of the total satisfied and unsatisfied demand for labour. Long before February it was evident that the level of the second column was tending to rise to a higher point than the first column could possibly attain by the process of simple replacement. The enhanced dependence of the greater part of the available labour on a small number of skilled trades was limiting the whole effective supply to the level they attained ; and as in them, under the existing system of production, the limits of replacement were approached, the problem of adjusting the labour supply here entered on its third and most exacting phase : the phase generally associated with the term " dilution."

§ 3.

The interpretation of this diagram (for it is no more, and barely adequate at that) in terms of particular reality has to reckon first with the fact that the two simple columns we have posited were actually composite and partly heterogeneous. The first column, representing labour supply, averages upwards of 500 separate trades and vocations, of which some two or three dozen (including the skilled engineering and shipbuilding trades, and coal-mining) were practically watertight, a large number of unskilled trades permeable in normal circumstances, and the rest permeable under varying degrees of pressure. Further, there was a certain causal dependence between the small number of " watertight " trades and the occupations usually associated with them : on 23 skilled mechanics, for example, in a particular factory in the spring of 1915 depended the employment of 900 juveniles ; and as women were increasingly brought in, the ratio rose even higher.

To trace the progress of the drain of recruitment in each case is not possible. The available data are classified under industries, and in any case, so far as the proportionate drain is concerned, we have no means of knowing the original proportions of fit men of military age each trade comprised. But it is clear in the first place that the drain bore no direct relation to the state of employment   it was not the dread, nor the passing reality, of unemployment that sent men into the Army, but a great positive response to the call for volunteers. There is little correspondence between the loss of men in the various industries and the respective unemployment figures for the end of July: The shipbuilding trades, for example, were then suffering nearly double the unemployment in the engineering group, but the latter sent a greater proportion of its men to the army ; the same paradox holds between the building trades and the coal miners, and the timber trades and the miscellaneous metal trades, and other pairs in which the fitness of the men would be approximately equal. " It is very far from being the fact," said the *Nation* in December, " that this reply (to the appeal for recruits) is a measure of falling trade. This might be said of one or two districts. But not of Manchester, where trade is reviving, and the men still pour into the new battalions. Nor of the Durham mining centres, where collieries have been closed down through the loss of soldier-workers. Not of the Welsh tin-plate industry, which is full of orders and where no rise of wages can stop the flowing away from works going at full pressure. It is not for lack of inducement that men are leaving : £7, £8, and even £10 a week have been offered and refused." Taking the country over, it was precisely the districts of densest industry that gave the highest proportion of men ; and the fact drives home the second point that the drain was proceeding irrespective also of the value to war-requirements of the trades in which the men were engaged. And therein lay the fundamental danger.

The situation arose that while in certain trades the first phase (of labour excess) persisted for months, in others the second phase (of deficiency) supervened within a few weeks, and in some the third phase (of dilution) was already becoming imminent. After six months of war the only trades remaining in the first phase, so far as regards men, were those concerned with building and building materials, furniture, and tin-plate ; while the second phase was pronounced in all trades engaged in ship-building, iron and steel, engineering, leather, woollen textiles, chemicals, saw-milling, food supply and coal-mining.

The effect was to raise the possibility of labour adjustment to the level of a first rank national problem, in which both the geographical and the inter-vocational mobility of labour were involved.

Although what we may assume to have been the most mobile section of labour was rapidly demonstrating its mobility by getting into khaki, redistribution up to a point went astonishingly well. The labour exchanges, the trade unions, even the newspapers acted as channels by which an excess here could be connected with a deficiency there. By the end of November war-unemployment had disappeared, and the surplus was only normal Succeeding months saw the amount steadily reduced still farther, until with the figure going below 1 per cent. in May there is an end of unemployment for the war-period—if the men only are considered, it was at an end by the new year. Before 1914 was out, workpeople were finding it difficult to get any sort of accommodation at such centres as Woolwich, Erith, Barrow and the Clyde.

The extent of the general movement may be inferred from the enormous intake of new labour in the principal industries. In six months the leather, chemical and explosive, and woollen textile industries had gained more labour than they had lost, and were employing more workpeople than in the previous July ; while in the ship-building, the iron and steel, and other trades the drain had been made up to a much larger extent than their original unemployed excess would account for, and what spare labour remained—as in the Lancashire cotton area—was either non-usable as yet, or non-mobile. But whereas the excess in the unskilled and the semi-skilled trades could be practically pooled for replacement where it was needed, for the all-important " water-tight " trades there was only the strictly relevant and limited surplus to draw on ; and as this was exhausted the search for fresh labour was pushed to unprecedented courses. Belgians were taken on, as temporary members of the trade unions earning the standard district rates : Board of Trade officers were sent to collect men—did collect and bring over a few hundreds—from Holland, even from Canada ; while at home, fresh supplies having dried up, armament firms were endeavouring to divert labour, and private firms endeavouring to retain it, by sheer competitive wage-offers. And all the while the drain was going on and the deficiency growing more and more perilous. Krupp's had solved the problem by the time it was seriously tackled in England. All their expert gun-makers had been promptly ordered out of the army, and by April 10,000 more men were said to be at work in Essen than when the war began. From the British Army some few men, at the instigation of the armament firms, were being asked, not ordered, to return in January ; and recruiting officers then received their first instructions to pass over certain trades. But the only need made public, and the only one recognised by the Secretary for War, was for soldiers and ever more soldiers. Recruiting officers might or might not observe the half-hearted instructions, but in any case there were the unofficial agencies, and the irresponsible women with their " king and country want you " and their white feathers and their myopia that could see no good in any male thing out of khaki. For one voice that might persuade a man to stay, there were dozens that would urge him to go. And if he so decided there was no authority could stop him, nor in the army either will or means to send him back again.

§ 4.

How all this was checked and complicated by the

incidence of the war-demand, a rough analysis of the second column of the diagram will show. Like the first, this column disintegrates—taking only the most general classification—into some seventy odd groups of industries, through which, as through the various trades, the drain of the war and the incidence of the war demands were very unevenly distributed, not only as between one industry and another, but as between different sections or areas of the same industry. See, for instance, how the catastrophe played havoc in that fairly compact business, coal-mining. The sudden cessation of export trade, due partly to the closing of the foreign markets and partly to the dearth of shipping to carry what could have been taken, made at once for reduction of employment. Then the warm weather and the general depression diminished the demand for domestic supplies, and the closing down of factories, particularly in the cotton trade, diminished the demand for industrial supplies ; many of the miners who remained, especially in the north of England, had to work short time. On the other hand, heavy Admiralty orders were coming in, and Welsh pits on naval supply were set going full pressure, while the demand for anthracite for the European market recovered after the first week or two ; with result that private shippers were short of best coal, and while some mining areas could not find enough labour, others were still unable to employ on full time what labour they had. Or take again the boot and shoe industry—one of the first to suffer by over-enlistment. Here, of course, army contracts held the field, and orders from the French Government were taken in September ; but the war demand, as in many other cases, differed from the peace demand, and while the men's trade was working overtime in Northampton, many of the women's firms were suffering at London and Leicester—until they could instal heavy machinery and get the army work to do ; while the box-makers—Government boots not wanting boxes—were left at a standstill. So also in the clothing trades : where firms could take, or could adapt their plant and instal fresh plant to take, the huge army contracts, overtime was being worked and shortage of labour complained of ; while in other branches of the industry where adaptation was less easy or contracts had not as yet begun to arrive, short time and unemployment were still on the increase, and large numbers of the women had recourse to the relief committees' workrooms. Among industries such as chemicals and glass manufacture, the shortage of foreign supplies hit the small firms at once, though the larger ones could manage to carry on at full pressure ; while the building and food trades were already responding in certain areas to the beginnings of the great army camps.

But it was mainly in regard to the armament and munitions supplies that the distribution of the war demand became crucial ; and in this matter the gradual straining of the old system to breaking point is even more clearly traceable than in regard to labour organisation. In 1914 the country depended for its war material on three principal Government factories and about 21 private armament firms, whose works were concentrated in a small number of areas—the banks of the Clyde, Thames, and Tyne, Birmingham, Sheffield, Coventry, Leeds, and one or two other towns ; and to these centres the huge increase in the demand was mainly directed. Sub-contracting of Government work was discountenanced by the War Office in peace time, but it had been sanctioned, on condition that entire responsibility was retained by the principal firm, as part of the Government plan for meeting unemployment in September, 1914. Under the pressure of necessity, and on official authority, the system was vastly

extended during the next six months—so widely,
in fact, that between 2,500 and 3,000 firms were
engaged wholly or in part on war supply. But
despite the extension,' sub-contracting remained
an unpopular system. It was unpopular with the
War Office, which distrusted the allocation of important work to firms it knew not, and considered
inexperienced ; it was unpopular with the armament
firms, whose private harvest after long, lean years of
peace was just beginning to be reaped, and who might
reasonably object, moreover, to sub-letting work for
which they had to retain responsibility, both as
regards delivery and quality ; and it was unpopular
with both masters and men in the sub-contracting
firms, who alleged that prices and profits were cut
ruinously fine, while the principal firms made fortunes. It was also liable to certain abuses in respect
both of finance and employment on which the
Workers' Committee kept a vigilant eye ; and as a
system it proved a definite failure.

Failure was in fact foreshadowed, as the Government afterwards admitted, in December, 1914, when
shortage of supplies and non-delivery of contracts
were already proving disastrous to the batteries in
France. None the less, the old system of centralisation was adhered to by the War Office, despite
increasing pressure from sub-contracting firms, from
the Army Command in France, and even from other
Government departments. To the difficulty arising
from the growing scarcity of skilled men was thus
added the difficulty of concentrating at the existing
centres what men were available. At the end of March
the efforts of armament firms to divert labour from
private work were reinforced by Government appeals
both to the trade unions and to the private employers.

Enquiry after enquiry was made into the amount
of fresh labour that could be drawn from private
sources, and as a last attempt to buttress the system

of concentration the Government took power, in the Defence of the Realm (Amendment) Act No. 2 (16th March) " to regulate or restrict the carrying on of work in any factory or workshop, or remove the plant therefrom, with a view to increasing the production of war materials in other factories or workshops." Private employers were given protection from any penalties that non-fulfilment of their contracts might entail ; and an Armaments Output Committee was appointed by Lord Kitchener (31st March) to supervise and facilitate the diversion of labour.

The task tackled on such lines proved impossible. Under the new Act the Government had power to take machinery out of a private works at Falmouth and set it up in a munitions factory at Aberdeen— but it could not compel the men who worked it to move into the next street. The competition for labour attained the pitch of fever. By poster, by press advertisement, even by personal appeal, the Admiralty and the armament firms ran up the auction price of skilled labour in all the chief industrial centres, while the War Office chose this very moment for a special effort to recruit all skilled men not actually on war work.

In the northern centres from a third to a half of the men thus drawn to munitions work proved disastrously mobile—until the frantic progress was stopped short by a regulation under the Defence of the Realm Act (29th April), which made canvassing labour already engaged on war work illegal.

Still the problem remained, and no merely negative effort could solve it. Enough harm had already resulted in regard to the level of wages and to the temper of the men ; more than enough in regard to the supply of munitions. Neither from the country nor the Cabinet could failure any longer remain concealed. For the old systems, both of labour supply and of production, breaking-point had arrived.

CHAPTER III.

GETTING DOWN TO IT.

§ 1.

The phrase " trade practices "—or as it is frequently put, " trade restrictions "—covers that mass of rules and customs by which, broadly speaking, the skilled trade unions safeguard their status in industry. Those rules have developed mainly by tradition and continuous adjustment to meet the changing circumstances of employment—in at least one case they can be traced back well over a century. They are part written, part understood, and frequently vary between different districts of the same trade, for which reason the local branch rather than the head office of a union tends to become their repository. In general they aim at defining an industrial field as the preserve of the skilled man, and at fixing a maximum proportion of apprentice or less skilled labour that shall be set to work in conjunction. They specify individual operations in a machine-shop, for example, that only skilled men shall perform (in some cases particular types of work are claimed by, and allotted to, the members of certain specified unions) ; they state the maximum number of machines that shall be " set up " or tended by one mechanic ; they define the conditions on which a man shall be entitled to recognition as "skilled"; they limit, in many cases, the number of shifts or the amount of overtime that certain classes may work; and in a host of minor directions they limit the power of the employer to dispose freely of his most highly trained labour. Behind them, more than behind any other aspect of trade unionism, lies the full force of organised skilled labour jealous of its "one precious possession"; and through them more immediately than in any other fashion does the reality of trade unionism come home to the average worker. To the frequent argument of the employers, valid within certain limits, that the rules tend to quantitative restriction of output, the unions reply that they provide a qualitative guarantee for both present and future.

Under war conditions, as we have seen, the quantitative restriction became speedily apparent. As early as October, 1914, employers on the Clyde were endeavouring without success to negotiate a relaxation of demarcation rules with the skilled unions. At successive conferences in both the shipbuilding and the engineering trades the same attempt was made with the same result. Not that the Labour leaders did not recognise the difficulty; an "unprecedented situation," they allowed, had arisen, and with it a "very difficult problem indeed," which there is reason to suppose they foresaw could be solved by nothing less than the ultimate sacrifice. But it was not their office to offer that out-of-hand; their *raison d'être* as executive bodies was to preserve these very safeguards. And even if they recommended the surrender, would the thousands of individual workers whose prospects were affected consent to make it? Or would they repudiate leaders who in their opinion had "sold the pass" too lightly? At all events, the leaders' immediate and obvious policy was to examine and put forward every possible alternative.

The Sheffield engineering conferences in December
and January will illustrate as well as any others
what was going on. The federated employers begin
by stating as a body that they can employ 12,500
more men at once and 15,000 before long, and propose
" that in consequence of the unions' inability to
supply the requisite amount of labour they agree to
remove certain trade restrictions without prejudice
during the continuance of the war." Counter-
proposals are put forward by the unions ; nothing is
agreed on. Then on January 2nd an official letter
requests both parties to give their " immediate
attention " to these matters. The employers, offering substantial guarantees as to restoration and
security, now advance a definite set of questions
which " shall not be pressed to an issue " during
war-time ; namely, the manning of machines, including the number to be tended by one man ; the
manning of hand operations ; the demarcation of
work between trades ; the employment of non-
union and female labour ; the limitation of overtime. To which the unions make counter-sugges-
tions : that firms not doing war-work should be
given contracts (notice how the deficiency of the
system was already observed by the men) ; that
firms working short time should transfer their men
to Government work ; that the Government should
offer subsistence allowances to induce men to move
(note again the defective incidence of the war-
demand) ; that skilled men should be brought over
from Canada and South Africa, even from Australia ;
that the skilled men already in the army should be
sent back.

Action along all these lines except the first was,
as we have seen, attempted during the winter ; but
without yielding any hope to either side that it would
be sufficient. Only in one case was any agreement
touching the essential problem reached as yet ;

Messrs. Vickers at Crayford obtained in November
the sanction of the Amalgamated Society of Engineers
to the employment of women—not in place of skilled
labour—but on " purely automatic machines used
for the production of repetition work." Elsewhere,
on Clyde and Tyne, and even in London, where
union leaders had been in negotiation with Government officials, was nothing but deadlock. In the
men's view, any sacrifice they might make would
certainly result in enhanced profit for the firms in
which they made it ; and no guarantee as to restoration coming from the very people who stood to gain
by the concession was acceptable. Further, it may
be argued that just as private employers were bound
to resist a diversion of labour that involved the
setting aside of their obligations to their shareholders,
so the trade union leaders were bound to resist the
grant of concessions that involved the setting aside
of their obligations to their constituents. It is true
that only in the former case had the obligations a
legal sanction ; but they were if anything the more
binding for the absence of it in the latter. And as in
the one case the ultimate responsibility had to be
shouldered by the State itself, so, and rightly so, it
had eventually to be accepted in the other. It
was both logical and necessary that the Government
should be associated with the abrogation of the trade
practices and with the pledge to restore them.

§ 2.

The Government, however, was far from eager
to venture in a region than which, in its own view,
" it would be difficult to name a more perilous field
for even the slightest advance of Government interference." " I can only say," adds Lord Askwith,
" that it had to be attempted " ; and accordingly

on February 4th, 1915, the Treasury " Committee
on Production," consisting of Lord (then Sir George)
Askwith, Sir Francis Hopwood for the Admiralty,
and Sir George Gibb for the Army Council, was
instructed to enquire and report

> " after consultation with the representatives of
> employers and workmen, upon the best steps to
> be taken to ensure that the productive powers of
> the employees in the engineering and ship-
> building establishments working for Government
> purposes shall be made fully available."

Pretty much as we have stated it already, each
side argued its case at length before the Committee ;
and the latter, doing what it could at once, produced
first a recommendation (which shortly became the
basis of an agreement) as to the making up of broken
squads of rivetters in the shipyards, and next a series
of proposals in regard to the production of shells
and fuzes. These proposals, which got nearer the
essential problem, were briefly that the employers
concerned should give an undertaking to the committee as representing the Government (not, observe,
merely to the unions) that the enhanced earnings of
the men on piece work should not be taken as subsequent ground for cutting the rates—it being hoped
that the removal of this apprehension would induce
the men to higher output ; and that female labour
should be more widely used. The Committee also
recommended that each contracting firm should give
an undertaking to the Government " to be held on
behalf of the Unions " that any departure from trade
practice made during the war should not be allowed
to prejudice the position of the workers or their.
societies in regard to the subsequent restoration of
the *status quo ;* and that no dispute arising on
Government work should be allowed to go the length
of strike or lock-out, but failing other settlement
should be referred to a Government arbitration

tribunal — which tribunal the Committee itself became.

Early in March, 1915, the Engineering Employers' Federation and the Trade Unions concerned concluded on these lines the " Shells and Fuzes Agreement " (confirmed by ballot of the men on April 8th). For the first time the unions now agreed that skilled men setting up machines or making tools and gauges might be supplemented by other " competent " workmen ; and that in suitable cases semi-skilled or female labour might be employed on what had been " skilled " work. Among the safeguards prescribed was the stipulation that any employer making use of the agreement should notify his acceptance of all its provisions to the local offices of the unions concerned ; and it is noteworthy that the employers also agreed " to take all possible steps to ensure distribution of Government work throughout the kingdom."

The next step taken by the Committee went still farther in recommending (8th March) a broad waiving of demarcation rules between trades on Government work, and a wider use of unskilled or semi-skilled labour. And a fourth report, which, according to Lord Askwith, the Government declined to publish in spite of strong pressure from the Committee, got to the root of the matter with proposals for Government control of the armament and shipbuilding firms and the limitation of profits.

Meanwhile the somewhat protracted negotiations suffered a startling interruption.

§ 3.

Scotsmen were wont to boast that the Glasgow tram was the cheapest conveyance in the kingdom. Certainly there was no vehicle that could reveal such

leagues of Gehenna for a penny. Nowhere has the
tyranny of the machine come so near completion as
in these drab and dreary vistas under the everlasting
smoke-drifts, where the very earth is hideous, and
over mile on mile of foundry, factory, shipyard, the
passage of day and night, summer and winter, year
in, year out, is measured by whistle and siren in
monotonous lengths of labour. Even in normal times
this material uniformity of circumstance tends to
instil in the workers in this region a certain psychological homogeneity, a mental solidarity in which
local issues speedily gather the momentum of mass-
impulse, and opinions that in a more varied community might be merely sectional spread by an
almost unchecked contagion through a vast population. Under war conditions, when extra labour of all
sorts was being crowded into an already congested
area, and work was being pressed with an ever-
increasing intensity, this regional characteristic was
inevitably accentuated.   It is this psychological
homogeneity that has always rendered the Clyde—
and some of the South Wales mining areas—difficult
to manage even by the Labour leaders ; and although
in these areas, as in all others, the patriotic stimulus
was felt and responded to, the circumstances of
the war added much to the difficulty of control.
Here were thousands of people who were affected by
the lack of housing accommodation, the extension
in working hours, and the rise in prices, all in very
much the same way. The propaganda of the
Workers' War Emergency Committee was having its
effect. The wage question was becoming an urgent
matter in a number of different trades at once ;
dilution was already a dangerous topic ; and there
was the vague suspicion that the employers or the
Government might take advantage of the war still
further to worsen their conditions ; that, in fact,
the latter had actually begun to do so by attempts

to " buy off " their leaders, who in any case were
pledged to the industrial truce, the political truce and
the recruiting campaign.   But by far the most potent
factor of all was the question of the profits made by
the armament firms : the suspicion—to quote an
official report*—" that while they (the workers) were
called upon to be patriotic and refrain from using
the strong economic position they occupied, employers, merchants and traders were being allowed
perfect freedom to exploit to the fullest the nation's
needs."

Such were some of the causes that raised the
monthly total of fresh wage disputes from 11 in
January to 47 in February, 1915.   But on the Clyde,
which saw the gravest of them, the immediate cause
was the refusal of the engineering employers to
concede a wage increase which the Glasgow district
committee of the Amalgamated Society of Engineers
had decided to apply for before the war began.
Trouble on this question had been brewing since
the beginning of December.   At the end of January
the men in some 15 shops refused to work overtime
as a protest against the inadequacy of the employers'
offer.   The trade union officials failed to secure a
change in their attitude, and the subsequent strike
was led by a " Central Withdrawal of Labour Committee " composed largely of the local shop stewards.
Between 8,000 and 10,000 of the engineers came out
on February 16th, and stayed out for a fortnight,
in defiance of the trade union executives and the
Government, who were bringing all possible pressure
to bear on them.   The dispute was settled early in
March by the Committee on Production, whose
decision the men had agreed in advance to accept.
The awards given, stated the Committee, were " to
be regarded as war wages, and recognised as due to
and dependent on the existence of the abnormal

* See Askwith : Industrial Disputes.

conditions now prevailing "—a qualification which left the standard of living unaffected, save in so far as the earnings on overtime might temporarily raise it.

This same month saw serious trouble among the London dockers, Edinburgh navvies, Dundee jute-workers and other trades. It marked the end, in fact, of the truce in industry, and started in certain sections of the " popular " press an undiscriminating campaign against Labour. In some quarters industrial conscription was urged on the Government, and the cry was " put 'em in khaki." The effect was doubly unfortunate. The Clyde workers were already distrustful enough of their official leaders, of their employers, of the Government ; they had had to fight their own battle for the recent wage increase—which, but for the fight, it looked as though they would never have got ; and when the demagogic press rained pitiless abuse upon them, with the implication that they alone, and not their masters, were to blame for the stoppage, little wonder if the more ardent spirits came to the conclusion that for the rest of the war it was likely to be the worker *contra mundum.* For the subsequent intensification of " class-consciousness " the blame cannot be confined to one side only.

Such was the atmosphere in which the final negotiations for dilution had to be carried through—not, as it turned out, by the Committee on Production, but by the Government *in propria persona.*

§ 4.

The Cabinet decision to take the final negotiations for dilution out of the hands of the Committee on Production was arrived at, according to Lord Askwith, on March 11th. It appears that in view of the state of Labour opinion, of the urgency of the matter, and of the unlikelihood of anything save the very strongest of appeals availing to move the rank and file, the Government had decided that a direct Ministerial approach to the leaders was necessary. If nothing else were gained, one result of any agreement so reached would be to deprive further labour " unrest " of the official support of the trade union executives, on at least the questions dealt with. Further, the Government may not unreasonably have hoped to strengthen the hands of the executives in the difficult task that they alone could carry through by an absolutely unqualified recognition of their importance. But more immediately relevant was the fact that in proportion as the Committee on Production approached the general question of dilution it would find itself increasingly " up against " fundamental matters of policy as to which it could not negotiate. Particularly was this the case in regard to the question of war-profits—a question which the Board of Trade had been considering in detail for some time past. And the fact that the Board was already engaged on intricate negotiations with the armament firms would at this stage have rendered abortive any attempt to discuss the general problem in the presence of both sides. It may be pointed out, however, that the delay in applying the principle of the limitation of war profits was probably the fundamental cause of the industrial unrest of 1915. The fact that action, when it came, was retrospective, did not diminish the labour difficulties that arose in the meantime.

On March 17th Mr. Lloyd George, Mr. Runciman, and other representatives of the Government and the Opposition met the delegates of the Trade Union Congress, the General Federation of Trade Unions, and thirty-three other societies concerned in engineering, shipbuilding, metal, wood, leather and textile trades, transport and general labour ; and after three days' debate the workmen's representatives (with the important exceptions of the Amalgamated Society of Engineers and the Miners' Federation) " agreed to recommend to their members " proposals for the reference, without stoppage of work, of all disputes affecting war-supplies to arbitration—failing settlement by other means—by the Board of Trade or the Committee on Production ; for the appointment by the Government of an advisory committee representing the organised workers ; also, provided the Government made certain safeguards applicable to all its contracts, for the " relaxation of the present trade practices," which the representatives at the conference declared to be " imperative " and recommended their unions to " take into favourable consideration." Thus— on paper—the ultimate sacrifice was agreed on. But the miners withdrew altogether from an undertaking that appeared to involve compulsory arbitration ; while the engineers were only brought in at a second conference a week later when the Government representatives gave a definite undertaking as to the limitation of profits " with a view to securing that benefits resulting from the relaxation of trade restrictions or practices shall accrue to the State." It is noteworthy that Lord Kitchener, speaking in the House of Lords on March 15th, had made what was generally interpreted as a promise to the workmen of a share in the abnormal profits, and that the workers' representatives at the first Treasury conference had intimated that profit-sharing schemes were not what they wanted.

The Labour Advisory Committee indicated in the agreement was promptly set up, with Mr. Arthur Henderson, M.P., who had presided over the workers' side of the Conference, as its chairman. For some months that body was the only tangible result of the proceedings. Little was done—in some cases less than nothing—to facilitate dilution ; and neither side appeared to be in any particular hurry to carry out the bargain. The agreement of the engineers was not confirmed by ballot of the men until June 16th ; the Government pledge to limit profits was not put into effect until July 2nd. In the meantime, as British gunners will not forget, Ypres and Neuve Chapelle and Festubert had made their caustic comment on the whole procedure.

CHAPTER IV.

Push and Go.

§ 1.

"The psychology of the public," remarked the Under Secretary for War on June 10th, 1915, "is a peculiar and recondite study." Coming from that quarter, the remark had a plaintive tone. An under-informed public opinion and an over-censored press had taken, in the second week of May, their sudden and spectacular revenge; and it is an ominous symptom of the condition of British government at the time that effective criticism of the conduct of vital affairs should have been made by none of the official custodians of the national safety, but by way of a newspaper "exposure." Yet it was no news to some members of the public and of the Government that "the want of an adequate supply of high explosive shells was a fatal bar to our success"; though the fact that less than 16 per cent. of the shell contracts entered into by the business men of the country were being fulfilled to time in May was not then public property.

With regard to the relative importance as factors in the munitions failure, of the sub-contracting system of supply on the one hand and the trade

union restrictions on the other, it is now possible
to speak with some certainty. During the period
May to December, 1915, the proportion of shell
contracts punctually fulfilled rose from 16 to 80 per
cent. ; the output of machine-guns increased in the
ratio of 1 to 5 ; while engineering firms not previously on munitions work produced in the third
week of December three times as many high explosive
shell bodies as was turned out by all the arsenals and
works in the United Kingdom in the month of May.
Much of the increase under the first two items was,
of course, due to the completion of arrangements
inaugurated under the old system. The effect of
the new material organisation was not pronounced
until the autumn. But during this same period the
number of cases of substitution of female and
unskilled for skilled labour in existing establishments
(apart from the national factories) was nearly 20
per cent. lower than in the lowest of the three succeeding half-years. The maximum periods of " dilution "
were the second quarters of 1916 and 1917, when it
took place in direct response to the withdrawal of
men from the workshops to the fighting forces.
During the later months of 1915, when the national
organisation of supply was being built up, the amount
of actual " dilution " was comparatively negligible.
As late as December 20th, 1915, Mr. Lloyd George
was complaining that in spite of negotiations and
agreements, the substitution of unskilled for skilled
labour had made practically no progress. In other
words, the first great increase in munitions output
was obtained mainly under the existing rules of trade
unionism ; and though it was undoubtedly true that
a still greater increase might have resulted from an
earlier relaxation of the trade practices, for the
initial deficiency not the labour custom but the
system of production was primarily responsible.
The realisation of this fact by the men concerned

tended not a little to weaken the subsequent position of the Government as a critic of Labour.

§ 2.

The principal stages in the readjustment of the labour supply during the spring of 1915 have already been indicated ; it remains now to show in brief outline the process by which the system of production was reorganised.

In the Defence of the Realm Amendment (No. 2) Act (March 16th, 1915) the Government had extended the power it possessed under the Act of 1914 to cover firms that were not actually on war-work ; its immediate motive would seem to have been the enforcement of the centralised system of production by the restriction of private work, and the consequent indirect compulsion of labour to munitions supply. Mr. Lloyd George had assured the House of Commons that the Act would not be administered without the co-operation of the manufacturers ; and " we are on the look-out," said he, " for a good, strong business man with some go in him, who will be able to push the thing through." The War Office Armaments Output Committee had accordingly been set up under Mr. G. M. Booth ; and what Mr. Booth was originally intended to " push " was undoubtedly labour.

The limits to which labour could be " pushed," however, were already ominously apparent ; and it became evident that if the old system of contracts was dependent on the further mobility of labour either it or the war would have to be abandoned. Even Parliament was beginning to realise the position. On April 21st, for example, the House of Commons had debated a resolution :

"That this House, while welcoming well-considered steps for increasing the mobility and efficiency of labour, is of opinion that it is urgently necessary that the resources of all firms capable of producing or of co-operating in producing munitions of war should be enlisted under a unified administration in direct touch with such firms."

Mr. Hewins, in moving the resolution, stated bluntly that "the Government had got hold of the wrong end of the stick in trying to deal with the transfer of great masses of labour from one works to another or from one district to another." Apart from the workmen's point of view, firms would often go on paying trade union rates for years at a loss rather than disperse the labour forces they had got together; and, in short, the needful next step was not the concentration of labour, but the distribution of work. Mr. Lloyd George expressed his general agreement with the motion; it may safely be assumed that his agreement actually extended to the obvious inference. The necessity of some modification would appear to have led to the appointment, on April 8th, of the Treasury Committee on Munitions, under Mr. Lloyd George himself. This Committee was, in fact, a policy committee with wide and independent powers, while the War Office Committee became in practice its executive organ. The failure of the sub-contracting system was candidly described by Mr. Lloyd George in the House of Commons on April 21st; and under the direction of the Treasury Committee the problem was at last changed from centralising the labour supply to re-distributing the work.

It is not necessary to trace the various steps by which the final plan of re-distribution was arrived at. Both the labour problem and the problem of supervision made it evident that some geographical basis of classification would be necessary. At first a scheme of A and B areas was contemplated—the A area to consist of a twenty-mile radius from any of the principal armament factories, the B area to comprise the smaller firms who might be encouraged to produce by co-operation what none of them could produce independently. But it appeared that the scheme could work well only while the B areas—in which lay the firms new to war-work—were undeveloped ; in proportion as their capacity expanded the system of division was likely to create more trouble than harmony. Some grouping, however, was essential if the productive capacity of the smaller establishments was to be utilised ; and after various tentative classifications, a total of twelve areas was decided upon (two each in Scotland and Ireland), in each of which a small panel of employers was to act as a board of management, consulting the Government authorities in regard to production, and the local Labour committees, set up under the National Labour Advisory Committee, on matters affecting employment.

But the key to the system was meanwhile being forged at Leeds. It took the shape of a scheme for a National Shell Factory. And it was accepted by the Government on May 13th—the day before Colonel Repington's famous message appeared in *The Times*.

§ 3.

Meanwhile, the labour problem had entered on a phase of serious difficulty. The Clyde strike had been followed by a series of wage demands which were pressed with considerable resolution, in several cases to the length of a dispute. Neuve Chapelle had roused the public to a vague sense of danger ;

and in the absence of complete information as to the munitions situation, attention was focussed almost exclusively on labour troubles. At the same time, Labour opinion was aggravated by a series of unfortunate events.

First, there was Mr. Asquith's speech in the food prices debate of February 11th, expressing a *non possumus* attitude in face of the Labour request for control. There was, said the Prime Minister, no evidence of a serious shortage of meat ; there was no likelihood of a serious shortage of wheat—" after next June " ; sugar was more likely to fall than to rise any farther ; and, in short, there was nothing the Government could do except recommend the country " to make the sacrifices which patriotism and public spirit demand." This was the official reply to the campaign of the Workers' War Emergency Committee ; it came at a moment when the rise in prices was being sharply felt, when wage demands were being generally resisted, when nothing whatever had been done in regard to the limitation of profits, and when the labour supply problem was severely testing the temper of the workers. The exasperation it aroused was directed against the Labour party as well as the Government.

A second step that met with the disapproval of organised labour was the issue on March 16th by the Board of Trade of a circular inviting women who were " prepared, if needed, to accept paid work of any kind—industrial, agricultural, clerical, etc.—to enter themselves upon the register of women for war-service at the Labour Exchanges." 40,000 women and girls were still registered as unemployed, and the labour opposition was based on the fear that by the tapping of new sources of female labour the general standard of living would be lowered. The immediate result was an energetic campaign to organise the women, in which the men's societies gave material assistance. One or two societies, of which the most important was the N.U.R., themselves admitted the women to membership. Others followed the lead of the A.S.E. in referring the women to the National Federation of Women Workers or to the organisations of unskilled labour. In some cases, as among the dockers at Liverpool, the London compositors and other crafts, the men opposed the introduction of women's labour with success; but in the vastly expanding field of munitions the practice of employing women on repetition work in the engineering shops secured a wide tacit approval before the principle of dilution was at all generally conceded; though the proportion of women placed from the special register, despite the enrolment of 33,000 in the first fortnight, was not above 10 per cent.

From the Labour point of view a more sinister omen now arose at Liverpool, where a section of the dockers had been refusing to work overtime. Lord Kitchener, through their trade union leader, appealed to the men to revise their decision in view of the congestion at the port, and added · " If this appeal has no effect I shall have to consider the steps that will have to be taken to ensure what is required at Liverpool being done." The appeal had no effect, despite its endorsement by Mr. Sexton; and in April Lord Derby hit upon the idea of enrolling a military battalion to carry on the Government work, from the ranks of the Dockers' Union. The battalion was inaugurated on April 12th, with 350 volunteers who were guaranteed both civil and military pay. The strike ended. The fear of " industrial conscription " remained. And as often happens in such cases, the events at Liverpool, though involving only a very small section of the workers, contributed to the embitterment of general opinion on both sides.

But by far the most important development on

the psychological side was the drink agitation. The effect of excessive drinking on time-keeping in the armament factories and the shipyards had been discussed at the first Treasury Conference. It was revived on a much wider scale when the question of munitions output began to attract press attention in March. On the 29th a deputation of the leading shipbuilding employers pressed the matter on the attention of the Government. The next day a letter from the King to Mr. Lloyd George expressed His Majesty's " deepest concern " at the " grave situation now existing in Our armament factories," and made an offer of total renunciation on the part of the Royal Household. The campaign was followed up with undiscriminating vigour and less tact by the majority of the Press and many public speakers ; the general anxiety about munitions found a palliative in sweeping accusations of " slacking " and drunkenness among the workers. The case against Labour was formally presented to Parliament and the country in a Command Paper, published on May 1st, wherein the evidence of the employers and many Government officers was set forth.

The natural and evident result was to enrage Labour : to such an extent, in fact, that even before the notorious White Paper appeared both Mr. Asquith and Mr. Lloyd George were at pains to narrow down the scope of the accusation. From the Labour side it was pointed out that the official report contained the statements of one side only ; that even these were far from justifying the campaign of abuse. In any case, so sweeping a writ of accusation would not run ; and, as regards the truth of the matter, it must be recalled that though much time had undoubtedly been lost, it was not proven that the prohibition of drinking facilities would have saved it all, or even a major part of it. Large numbers of the fittest men had been withdrawn from industry; the remainder were working at unprecedented pressure, earning much extra money on overtime, and secure of employment; the canteen system was undeveloped, and the systematic study of welfare and industrial fatigue hardly begun. The quality of food had deteriorated, facilities for getting it were curtailed, and the hours of labour both excessive and ill-adjusted The drink question was undoubtedly a real one, and at a later stage was successfully dealt with; but it does not appear that the Press contributed very materially to the final solution. The proposals for liquor taxation introduced as a sequel to the Command Paper proved distinctly unacceptable to the House of Commons and to general opinion; and the sole net result of the episode was to embitter the workers. Seeing that dilution had yet to be carried into effect, to which end the co-operation of the workers was admittedly essential, the affair constituted a first-class psychological blunder.

§ 4.

A more hopeful development was now in progress on the Tyne. During April local committees were set up in Newcastle and Glasgow to deal with the general question of munitions production, and on the 21st of that month the Newcastle Committee (on which the Government, the employers and the workmen were equally represented) launched its campaign of enrolment for a " King's Squad " of munition workers. Skilled men not on war work were invited to offer their labour wherever it was wanted on telegraphic instruction from the committee; were guaranteed their district rate of wages as a minimum, and also that long-desired and long-withheld inducement, a subsistence allowance. The

scheme proved a distinct success, both as regards
quantity and quality of the men enrolled ; and an
application of the same idea on a national scale
seemed to promise a solution of the labour difficulties
which the new production programme appeared
likely to intensify.

Meanwhile, among the minor consequences of the
policy of " push and go," the political crisis had
supervened. On May 13th Mr. Asquith had denied
that a Coalition Government was contemplated, and
" I am not aware," he added, " that it would meet
with general assent." Within a week he announced
its formation ; and when on June 3rd a somewhat
exasperated House of Commons reassembled after
the Whitsun recess, its immediate sanction was
requested for a *fait accompli*. Already it was known
that among the changes proposed was the elevation
of the chairman of the Munitions Committee to
Ministerial rank ; and on June 9th Mr. Lloyd George
duly became Minister of Munitions. Fourteen days
later he introduced the Bill by which voluntarism
in munitions supply was to reach its overdue end.
General industrial compulsion had in fact been freely
talked of, in some quarters strongly urged ; and it
was as a final effort to avert it that the War Munitions
Volunteer scheme was given a trial. Mr. Lloyd
George was candid on the subject :

" We had a very frank discussion between the
leaders of the Trade Unions and myself, and I
was bound to point out that if there were an
inadequate supply of labour . . . compulsion
would be inevitable. They put forward as an
alternative that the Government should give
them the chance of supplying that number of
men. They said, ' Give us seven days, and if
in seven days we cannot get the men we will
admit that our case is considerably weakened.'
. . . We have arranged terms upon which the

men are to be enlisted, and to-morrow the seven days begin. Advertisements will appear in all the papers. An office has been organised, and the trade union representatives are sitting there in council directing the recruiting operations. . . . We have 180 town halls in different parts of the country placed entirely at our disposal as recruiting offices. . . . If there are any honourable friends of mine who are opposed to compulsion, the most effective service they can render to voluntarism is to make this army a success."

The " army " was a success—on paper. 46,000 volunteers had enrolled for the six months' contract of service during the first week. By the end of July the number had reached 100,000. But on examination of the returns it appeared that four-fifths of the men were already engaged on Government work of one sort and another ; and of the remaining one-fifth, when employers' protests and the men's qualifications and other limiting factors had been considered, only a few thousands were available to increase the munitions supply.

Before this result had emerged, however, the whole field of munitions industry had passed under a drastic, though loosely defined measure of State control. On July 2nd the Royal Assent was given to " an Act to make provision for furthering the efficient manufacture, transport, and supply of munitions for the present war ; and for purposes incidental thereto."

§ 5.

The Munitions Act of 1915 has been described as the most decisive step in State control of industry taken during the war. It has also been described as the " Slavery Act," and as a " highly dangerous measure, none the less because Mr. Lloyd George succeeded in persuading many of the trade union leaders to accept it."* Its labour provisions were cordially and increasingly disliked on the Clyde and in other large centres ; yet it and the succeeding Acts " were accepted by overwhelming majorities at successive trade union and Labour party con- ferences."† By the greater part of moderate opinion it was heartily welcomed ; and justly, since it recognised the logical consequences of the position the Government had already taken up in industry. It gave an admittedly dictatorial control to the Minister of Munitions over a very large field ; but it was an admittedly necessary control such as no other office, and least of all Parliament itself, could have exercised. And in its main purpose, if in politics that dangerous plea may ever be admitted, the end attained amply justified the means.

As regards labour, the Munitions Act provided that any dispute between employers and employed, or between different sections of workpeople, affecting wages or conditions of employment in munitions work, might be referred to the Board of Trade, failing other settlement ; that no strike or lock-out should take place within three weeks of such reference ; and that the Board of Trade's award should be binding on all parties. The provision might also be applied by Royal Proclamation to disputes in other industries directly or indirectly affecting the muni- tions supply. As regards capital, the Minister of Munitions received power to " control " munitions establishments by order ; and the application of control entailed the surrender to the State of four- fifths of the profit made in excess of the average of the last two normal years. It also entailed the

* Cole : *Labour in Wartime.*
† Webb : *History of Trade Unionism.*

suspension of "any rule practice or custom not having the force of law which tends to restrict production or employment," and the punishment of any person who induced others to continue the suspended practice. It entailed the acceptance by the employer of a schedule of conditions providing for the record of war-time changes in practice, consultation with the workmen concerned in regard to proposed changes, and the eventual restoration of pre-war conditions. And it necessitated the approval by the Minister of Munitions of changes of wage-rates in controlled establishments.

Further, no-one might employ a workman who within the previous six weeks had been employed on munitions work, unless the man held a certificate granting the consent of his previous employer to his departure, or the certificate of a munitions tribunal stating that the consent had been unreasonably withheld; provision being made for the appointment by the Minister of Munitions of tribunals to which the workman, or his trade union representative, might appeal. The six months' contract entered into by the War Munitions Volunteers now became legally enforcible, and the authorisation of badges for war-work was sanctioned. Lastly, the power taken in the Defence of the Realm (Amendment) Act of April, 1915, as regards the regulation or restriction of work in engineering establishments, was now extended to cover the employment of labour; power was also taken "to regulate and control the supply of metals and material that may be required for any articles for use in war." The Act was to have effect only so long as the office of Minister of Munitions and the Ministry existed; except that the provisions relating to disputes were to continue in force for "twelve months after the conclusion of the present war," so far as the restoration of trade practices was concerned.

Such were the main provisions of the measure by which the production of munitions was at last, in some degree, made a national concern. As regards the labour engaged therein (mining and textile industries not being included) control was imposed by means of the pressure put on the employer. Compulsory arbitration was indeed established in munition trades; with the effect of rendering all subsequent strikes nominally " unofficial " and therefore not entitled to assistance from the funds of the unions—this effect being confirmed in advance by the consent of the union leaders to the Act. Industrial conscription was not as yet applied. The workman outside the munitions industries was still free to enlist, to continue at his work, to dispose of his labour as he pleased. The workman on munitions work was indeed made liable to a penalty of six weeks' unemployment if he left it without his employer's consent; but in the absence of military conscription, he could, if he chose and could afford it, simply wait the time out. As regards the suspension of trade practices, the Act clinched the Treasury agreement—on paper; but no legislation could enforce the suspension, or probihit " ca'canny," or compel the introduction of dilutees in practice. As regards the actual effort put forward by the workers, therefore, the problem was, as it had always been, fundamentally psychological; and on this aspect of it a brief comment may be made in conclusion.

We have seen how in August, 1914, the national sense rose suddenly predominant over practically all other forms of " group consciousness." The psychological problem of succeeding months was to maintain that predominance; and as the strain of the war-effort in industry began to tell, and the pressure of new circumstances tended to stimulate sectional modes of feeling, an increasingly effective presentment of the war was necessary. Instead, the problem was interpreted simply as a matter of maintaining and inflating public optimism. That interpretation was too shallow. It was based on a gross under-estimate of the national will to victory. The memory of what Majuba˙ meant in the Boer wars might have suggested that misfortune had in Britain its tonic value. The suppression of bad news, including much that neutrals and even the enemy were allowed to know, defeated even the inadequate policy it was meant to serve, for bad news coming late and vague is far more depressing, far more alarming, than the prompt frank statement. And nothing could so much have reawakened the predominant national sense as a more general awareness of imminent danger.

In this connection it must be pointed out that the Government was obliged to make its most exacting appeals to precisely that part of the population in which the national sense was most liable to be submerged. The vantage-ground from which the appeal was made had been undermined by the long delay over price and profit-regulation ; indiscriminate popular criticism and abuse of the class appealed to, directly invited failure of the national sense. It is a valid criticism of Lord Askwith's that the presentment of the situation by which Mr. Lloyd George secured the assent of the Labour leaders to dilution never reached the rank-and-file ; and that time should have been allowed—as in the end it had to be—for that realisation to deepen and broaden.

Not that Labour, and especially Labour leaders, had not made mistakes, though theirs was originally a more generous error. It would perhaps have been better for all parties had Labour leaders clearly realised that their first national duty, to which all other considerations should have come second, was to maintain the closest possible touch with their constituents. The participation of the Labour party in the Coalition

Government was for this reason of doubtful expediency. Whether it was necessary at so early a stage for the War Emergency Committee to proceed so largely by way of agitation is a matter of opinion ; the propaganda did not achieve so much as to put quieter and more conservative methods out of court. At least both Ministers and Labour leaders would have done well to remember that in proportion as the latter were used to govern, rather than to represent their peculiar constituencies, the way was being prepared for trouble of an exceptionally difficult nature.

None the less, despite the impression created by Press and Government utterances at the time, and by the necessary attention history must devote to difficulties, the nation had on the whole done well. Strikes and disputes had interrupted only the smallest proportion of the industrial effort. Greater exertion was yet to be called for, and ultimately secured ; but for the major effort the nation was at last prepared to set its house in order.

PART TWO.

FROM THE MUNITIONS ACT TO THE LABOUR WAR-AIMS CONFERENCE IN LONDON, DECEMBER 28TH, 1917.

	1915.
Leaving Certificate in force	July 14
South Wales Miners' Strike	July 15
Fairfield Shipwrights' Strike	Aug. 26
Central Labour Supply Committee ...	Sept. 20
Balfour-Macassey Report published ...	Dec. 14
	1916.
Munitions Amendment Act	Jan. 27
Military Service Act	Jan. 27
Parkhead Strike	Mar. 17
Trade Union Congress	June 30
Conferences on Dilution...	Oct.–Nov.
German Peace Overtures	Dec. 13
	1917.
First Russian Revolution	Mar. 15
Tyne Engineers' Strike	Mar. 20–23
Barrow Engineers' Strike ...	Mar. 21–Apl. 4
Albert Hall Pro-Russian Demonstration	Mar. 31
Schedule of Protected Occupations ...	Apl. 21
Unofficial Strikes in Munition Industries	May

1917.

Shop Stewards' Conference at Birming-
ham ... ...   June 9–10
Commission on Industrial Unrest
appointed ... ...   June 12
First Whitley Report ... ...   June 29
Labour Party Conference on Stockholm   Aug. 10
Munitions Act ... ...⎫
Corn Production Act ... ...⎭   Aug. 21
First Inter-Allied Socialist Conference   Aug. 28
The 12½ per cent. Bonus awarded ...   Oct. 13
Leaving Certificate abolished ... ...   Oct. 15
Soviet Revolution in Russia ... ...   Nov. 7
Coventry Strike of Shop Stewards ...   Nov. 26
Shop Stewards' Agreement with Engi-
neering Employers ... ...   Dec. 17
London War-Aims Conference ... ...   Dec. 28

CHAPTER I.

THE VALLEY OF THE SHADOW.

All things considered, the summer of 1915 was for Britain the most dangerous period of the war. In the west the first phase was over, and the prospect of an early decision was receding before the infinity of effort and sacrifice involved in the ghastly process of "attrition." German spirits were sustained by the successes of the eastern frontier, where Hindenburg and Mackensen were shattering, blow on blow, that "Russian steam-roller" on which so many wanton British hopes were riding. But British policy in the near East, ill-devised and ill-supported, had to withstand successively the defection of Greece, the hostility of Bulgaria, the annihilation of the Serbs, and the tragedy of Gallipoli.

§ 1.

At home the party truce seemed merely to have paved the way for bitter personal and departmental feuds that were hardly concealed from Press or Parliament, while remaining unchecked by free responsible criticism. Folk were already doubtful whether constitutional representative government must not be included in the casualty list, and, in

fact, the issues of the war were debated in a clearer
atmosphere, with more sincerity, and to better
purpose by the Trade Union Congress at Bristol
than by the House of Commons at Westminster.
In the country at large a recruiting system that was
neither voluntary nor conscriptive was securing the
minimum of result with the maximum of irritation—
at the cost indeed of more irritation than conscription
itself would have produced, since the constant
flagellation of the national spirit tended at last to
impair its essential soundness. The procedure may
perhaps have been designed so to sicken the nation
of voluntarism as to make conscription when it came
the less unwelcome. If so, it was a timorous and
foolish plan. It is well known how a man engaging
himself upon an exhaustive task of endurance will
lash his resolution to the mast of some artificial
constraint, foreseeing that there may come times
when that alone will prevent a temporary failure
of the will betraying his primal purpose. So armies
emerge with victory from the insupportable ordeal
of war, and so nations themselves are best enabled
to sustain their hour of crisis. The discipline is
the effective expression of a general purpose, and to
the private individual, though he may not know it,
mitigates and renders tolerable the strain. It was
in this respect the misfortune of the workers that no
such accepted discipline was possible throughout
industry, the instrument of its execution not having
been evolved.

Coercion had indeed been charged with more
than it could possibly accomplish, and its inadequacy
left no safeguard against the failure of the contingent
will. But to argue from that occasional failure a
desertion of the common purpose; to indulge, as did
certain journalists, in frothy rant about German gold
and British traitors, was to render very traitorous
disservice to the common weal, and to insult the

vast majority of working-men.   Antagonism to the
general purpose there was, though little as yet, and
less at any time than there appeared to be ; but
it could not safely be inferred from every industrial
dispute, and the inference, as we shall see, was
indignantly and passionately repudiated even by
the strikers of the Clyde.

By June, 1915, circumstances were already putting
the " contingent will " in industry to a severe strain.
The limitation of employers' profits to 20 per cent.
above what was made " during the greatest boom in
British engineering " had not commended itself to
all the workers as an adequate *quid pro quo* for the
sacrifice of their normal peace-time traditions.   It
might of course be argued that the sacrifice should
have been made out of hand ; and so it would have
been had human beings been other than human—
save that in that case there would have been no war.
But apart from dilution, food prices were advanced
by over 30 per cent. in July, 1915 ; and while there
was as yet neither control nor promise of control,
there was plenty of evidence of profiteering.   Spectacular cases, like that of the firm of millers who in
May, 1915, paid additional dividends of 17½ per
cent. on their ordinary shares and still carried forward
a balance equivalent to 54 per cent., or such cases of
coal and shipping profits as the Workers' Committee
published, increased the anxiety of the workers.
Wage advances had hitherto been sporadic, and what
Lord Askwith calls the first cycle had hardly begun.
Piece-workers were in many cases doing well, and
better than the time-workers, among whom were the
most highly skilled trades—whence further discontent ; but in very few cases were the rates advanced
proportionally to the cost of living, and the extra
money was at least as hardly earned as that extra
20 per cent. of the employers.   Behind all this lay
a change in the general point of view : the transition,

namely, from the hope of an early issue to the war, when the normal conditions could be resumed without much difficulty, to the realisation that the abnormal circumstances might last for years, and pre-war status never perhaps be reattainable. This meant a painful readjustment in the standpoint of almost every individual, and its effect among the workers was to sharpen the intensity with which new developments were scrutinised and to put a stricter insistence into wage or other demands.

At this happy conjuncture of circumstances came the manifesto of the German Social Democrats, explaining in apologetic fashion their attitude towards the German war-credits, and calling upon their government " in the name of culture and humanity," to " show their readiness to enter upon peace negotiations." The document was aimed expressly at the British Socialists. It was widely quoted both in the general and in the Labour press, and to more damaging effect than would have followed the release of the much demanded despatches from Gallipoli. No concerted reply from the British Labour Party proved possible—to the disappointment of its left wing. The majority was as keen on winning the war as the House of Commons. But war-weariness was reinforcing the theoretical objections of the minority. " No-conscription Fellowships," " Stop-the-war Committees," " Leagues against war," " Fellowships of Reconciliation " were springing up. Certain I.L.P. branches were reinforcing the Union of Democratic Control in opposition first to conscription and second to war itself ; and the old heresy of the " workers having no quarrel " lifted its head again. There were those, of course, who sincerely believed in that fallacy. There were others who knew enough of the psychology and philosophy of politics to recognise it for the specious nonsense it was, and who yet used it as propaganda to the end of their wished-for revolution. To such propagandists the long delay of the Government in facing what everyone knew to be inevitable gave exactly the right atmosphere and the golden opportunity.

Yet under this ill-favoured crust of circumstance the means of ultimate victory were forming—rather were being formed by a miracle of human improvisation. The subsidised extensions of existing armament works inaugurated under War Office régime were now nearing completion, and the proportion of fulfilled contracts was improving. The district Boards of Management were now being assembled under the Ministry of Munitions, capacities of individual firms more closely ascertained, contracts more widely distributed, and supervision decentralised. By the beginning of September, 16 new national factories had been organised ; the majority being existing establishments, or parts of establishments, taken over as going concerns by the Ministry of Munitions, and extended or altered in accordance with the other production of their districts. By December the number had risen to 33. In such of these as were devoted principally to shell-making the employment of women on repetition work was now increasing. In addition, over 2,000 firms, comprising $1\frac{1}{4}$ million workers, had been brought under control by the end of 1915, the operation entailing, by the Munitions Act, limitation of profits and the suspension of trade practices. But in the latter respect there was as yet little that was hopeful to report : in fact, the latter half of 1915 may be envisaged as a period of not too encouraging experiments in the possibilities of the control of labour by means of the Munitions Act.

§ 2.

The first of these experiments—in which, according to Lord Askwith, the effect of the Munitions Act was discounted at the very outset by the action of the Minister of Munitions—took place in the South Wales coalfields during and immediately after the passage of the Act.

In February, 1915, the railwaymen had secured a national war-bonus of 2s. per week to men earning over 30s., 3s. to those earning less. Other wage applications followed, including those of the Transport Workers' Federation; and at the end of the month the Miners' Federation of Great Britain requested a general advance of 20 per cent. of earnings, to be awarded on a national basis. This latter provision was an attempt to supersede the Coal Mines Minimum Wage Act, by which wages were settled by local negotiation. On this latter procedure the Prime Minister insisted, and arbitration in the various areas resulted during March in awards of from 15 per cent. on the standard rates to $17\frac{1}{2}$ in South Wales. South Wales, however, had a proposition of its own—namely, that the existing district wage agreement should be replaced altogether; and notice was given to terminate it on June 30th. Under the old arrangement wages advanced above a certain minimum, in accordance with the selling price of coal, to a certain maximum which had already been reached in 1913; so that the abnormal prices of the war-period had no further effect on wages. The $17\frac{1}{2}$ per cent. awarded had actually brought wages past this maximum, the old agreement being thus virtually set aside; but the South Wales Miners' Federation wanted a new agreement with an enhanced minimum (approximately the pre-war level) and no maximum at all. On this basis the owners declined to negotiate, offering instead to submit the claim to the arbitration of the Committee on Production. This the miners refused.

Now the miners (along with the textile workers) had been exempted from the Treasury Agreements and from the Munitions Act on the ostensible ground that wage-regulating machinery for their industries was already in existence. They were now called upon by the Board of Trade to use it, or alternatively —since the choice was foregone—to let the Government Committee arbitrate. The miners were so far persuaded as to lay their case before Sir George Askwith, who framed proposals for a settlement. Messrs Henderson, Brace and Roberts on July 1st, by a narrow majority, secured the assent of the Miners' Council to Sir George's principles ; and Mr. Runciman secured a still more reluctant assent from the mine-owners. Then the trouble fairly began. The acceptance of the Miners' Council was at once qualified by demands for further concessions, backed by a strike threat ; and Mr. Runciman's " no " was backed by the promise of the Minister of Munitions on July 8th that " he would not hesitate to advise a Royal Proclamation bringing the difference under the Munitions of War Act "—and thereby making a stoppage of work illegal. A frank defiance followed. On July 12th, the conference of miners' delegates threw over a further attempt of its executive council to continue the negotiations and the working of the mines, and resolved that " we do not accept anything less than our original proposals, and that we stop the collieries on Thursday next unless these terms are conceded." On the 13th, to the hearty satisfaction of the general public, the South Wales Mining Industry was proclaimed under the Munitions Act. On the 15th, 200,000 men stopped work.

Whether the proclamation was merely a *grand geste* arising from a misinterpretation of the men's temper ; or whether the Government did not actually desire the trial of strength to be carried through— four days of the stoppage sufficed to secure a settlement which has been described in one account as a tribute to the persuasive abilities of Mr. Lloyd George. Seeing that, according to Mr. G. D. H. Cole (*Labour in Wartime*) the men " not only got most of their demands" (including the new minimum, the abolition of the maximum, and the bonus turn as requested) " but also succeeded in practically smashing the Act on the first occasion on which it was used," the Minister's persuasiveness took a somewhat appealing form. " No penalties were exacted (continues Mr. Cole) and no attempt was made to apply it (the Act) to any individual." Thus ended the first lesson under the Munitions Act.

" A further disappointment," remarks the Labour Year-Book for 1916, " was caused a month later by Mr. Runciman interpreting a point in the agreement in a sense other than the apparent meaning of the words. . . . A strike immediately threatened. This was averted by Mr. Runciman revising his decision." Apparently both the miners and the President of the Board of Trade had got the lesson by heart.

§ 3.

A second experiment arose out of a circular sent out by the Ministry of Munitions early in August, recommending an extension of the employment of women on machine-work, including non-repetition lathe work and operations in tool-making. Lang's of Johnstone (Clydeside), among other firms, informed their employees of their intention to make the change ; and were informed in reply that the

Executive Council of the Society of Engineers were prepared strenuously to oppose it, and further that the local committee would allow no woman to work a lathe, and that if the attempt were made "the men would know how to protect their rights." This constituted something like a test-case for both sides ; and the fact that the Ministry refrained from forcing the issue and withdrew the circular—probably for adequate tactical reasons—none the less tended to encourage the men, and discourage the employers, in the battle that was now joined over dilution.

A third case must be singled out for notice on account of its sequel. At Fairfield on the Clyde there was a brief strike in July over a demarcation quarrel between coppersmiths and plumbers, for which the leaders were fined under the Munitions Act 2s. 6d. each. A further strike broke out on August 26th arising from the dismissal of two shipwrights for alleged loitering. It was alleged by the subsequent Commission of Enquiry that the firm had maintained a right to enter upon the clearance certificates a statement of the reasons for dismissal ; this, at any rate, was the ostensible ground on which the shipwrights struck work. Whether or no it was correct, the strike prior to arbitration was clearly illegal ; and by way of trying sterner measures, 17 men were fined £10 each by a general munitions tribunal. Fourteen paid : three refused and went to prison.

Now the actual imprisonment of trade unionists for withholding labour, clearly enough as it had been foreshadowed in the Munitions Act, brought home the reality of the situation in sudden force to the Clyde workers, and the interned men were regarded as martyrs. " They were not victims," said Mr. Pringle afterwards in the House of Commons ; " they were presented with £8 apiece and with diamond bracelets for their wives, and had gold watches offered to them." The immediate result was the threat of a complete stoppage on the Clyde unless the men were released : a difficult and dangerous situation.   Lord Balfour of Burleigh and Mr. (now Sir) Lynden Macassey were sent down to investigate the cause of the dispute ; but as their Commission had no power to release the men, a pistol-point demand was made to the Minister of Munitions, and the unions refused to take further part in the enquiry. The demand was resisted by the Government, and the men were got out of prison by the unions paying the remaining proportion of their fines.   The danger point thus turned, the Commissioners resumed their enquiry with a wider scope, thus affording the workers a safer means of stating grievances.   The investigation continued for the rest of the year, with an increasing amount of labour trouble to engage its attention ; and a number of the principal recommendations of the report on Clyde Munition Workers (Cd 8136, 1915) were subsequently dealt with by legislation.

§ 4.

The foregoing were very far from being the only cases in which opposition to the Munitions Act took an acute form.   Dilution was resisted from point to point, every step upward contested, every alteration in working rules jealously scrutinised. Apart, in fact, from the employment of women on repetition work in the national factories, progress was negligible.   Employers were not in a position to force their new prerogative too far, since now that the limits of coercion had been practically explored, it appeared that the result of so doing might be worse than their present condition in respect of labour.   The principal unions were becoming more concerned to secure certain changes in the law as affecting munition workers than to facilitate further concessions, and even the personal influence of the Minister of Munitions appeared to have reached a temporary limitation.

The appointment of the Central Labour Supply Committee in September, 1915, to deal with the dilution question gave the unions their chance. The Committee drew up and circulated a comprehensive scheme for dilution based on the principle "that no skilled man shall be employed on work which can be done by semi-skilled or unskilled labour." The scheme suggested the foundation of local labour advisory boards, and made detailed recommendations as to procedure and the employment of women. At the same time the Labour Supply Committee put forward standard rates of pay for women employed on work customarily done by men, and for male semi-skilled or unskilled "dilutees." These rates also were circulated to employers during October—but it may be noted that as they could not yet, under the Munitions Act, be applied compulsorily, the effect on wages was small. That they should be so applied was an additional demand of the trade unions ; and the unions seized their opportunity in a fashion which the following resolution of the engineers sufficiently indicates :

> "That we as an executive council are not prepared to take any part in any conference which has for its object the dilution of skilled labour until the Ministry of Munitions takes steps to render legal and mandatory the rates of pay and conditions of labour to those semi-skilled and unskilled men who may take the places of our members transferred to more highly skilled work."

The engineers also backed the Federation of Women Workers in a similar demand. This was not philanthropy on the part of the skilled men towards the women and the unskilled : it was to ensure that dilution should not result in a lowering of the rates " customarily paid for the job."

§ 5.

Meanwhile at a series of trade union conferences the criticisms of Labour respecting the working of the Munitions Act were being formulated as amendments.   The faults in the present situation, partly as thus defined, partly as indicated in the Balfour-Macassey report, may be summarised as follows :

(1) Many cases had occurred in which the administration of the Munitions Act had been unnecessarily harsh and provocative.   Changes in working rules had been made without sufficient, sometimes without the statutory minimum of consultation with the employees; and it was at least suspected by the workmen that there were cases in which the employers had attempted to avail themselves of the dilution provisions for the purpose of private work.

(2) The action of the leaving certificate was the most unpopular feature of all.   The power of the employer to delay or withhold its issue had been used in many cases to penalise the workers.   The refusal of certificates had been made the means, for example, of retaining workpeople at rates far less than they could otherwise have obtained, sometimes less than the district rates ; it had been used also to prevent workers transferring their labour to their home districts when opportunity arose, or changing their occupation on the ground of health or suitability ; it had also enabled employers to " stand-off " their workers two or three days a week at will, reducing their earnings while keeping them tied to the particular establish-

ment. In such cases the onus of appeal against
refusal pressed unduly hard on the employees, and
involved the almost certain loss of several days'
pay even when the Munitions Tribunal awarded a
certificate.

(3) The awards of the Tribunals were open to
criticism for lack of uniformity; and it was urged
that some form of appeal should be provided,
powers obtained to compensate a workman wrong-
fully dismissed, and imprisonment under the Munitions Act abolished.

(4) Arbitration procedure also had been too slow
in operation, and delay had accrued from confusion
as to the right quarter in which cases should be dealt
with. Some provision for a preliminary local investigation of disputes by the Government, the employers
and the workmen might, it was thought, have
averted a good deal of trouble.

An indication of the extent to which these
criticisms were met in the Munitions Amendment
Act of January, 1916, may bring this somewhat
depressing chapter to a close. The Act, which
became law on January 27th, 1916, after a decidedly
rough passage through Parliament, enlarged both
the scope of " munitions work " and the power of
the Government still further to extend it, by establishing " control " over Government establishments;
building and shipbuilding concerned in the prosecution of the war were now included, and provision
was made for the inclusion, in certain cases, of
public utility services. As regards the leaving
certificate, the concessions did not go very far to
meet the Labour criticism. Leaving certificates
were to be made uniform in style, and free of any
endorsement; they were to be promptly issued in
all cases of dismissal or more than two days' suspension, save where deliberate misconduct had been
used in order to obtain dismissal; grounds of

justifiable dismissal were indicated, and the tribunals were empowered to levy compensation on an employer for a workman unfairly dismissed or refused a certificate. Arrangement was made for appeal tribunals; reference to arbitration was made compulsory for all bona-fide differences within 21 days of reporting, and imprisonment for offences under the Munitions Acts was abolished. As regards the wage-question, the Minister of Munitions received authority to give enforcible " directions " as to the rates for female and for unskilled and semi-skilled labour in controlled establishments; which he forthwith did, establishing a minimum rate of £1 per week for women of 18 and over employed on work " customarily done by men," save that women employed in place of " fully skilled tradesmen " were to get the time-rates of the men they replaced. As regards other than time-rates, " the principle upon which the directions proceed is that of systems of payment by results ; equal payment shall be made to women as to the men for an equal amount of work done." The principle on which male " dilutees " were to be paid was that the rates, whether time or piece, were to be " the same as customarily obtain for the operations when performed by skilled labour." For both the women and the male dilutees special arbitration tribunals were established, the former of which soon had plenty to do.

Thus was the position of the worker further safe-guarded—in several thousand cases materially improved. The new provisions, while not altogether satisfying the trade union executives, went far to meet their main requirements, and secured from those bodies a general assent. Unfortunately that assent no longer implied quite as much as in the earlier days of 1915. New centres of consciousness were developing in the body politic, and trouble of an exceptionally difficult nature was toward.

CHAPTER II.

CRISIS.

The spring of 1917 was marked by the first manifestation on a national scale of certain developments in organisation and opinion from which a distinct phase in British social history took its rise—a phase of which the climax was not to be reached until after the close of the European war. The origin of these developments lies farther back than the date at which this history commences ; but their growth was infinitely accelerated by the industrial incidence of war and revolution, and it is therefore necessary to examine two aspects of that incidence in some detail.

§ 1.

Whether it was the fault of the House of Commons, the Cabinet, or the war in general and nobody in particular, the fact remains that in the debate on compulsory service, as in that on the munitions supply, Parliament was a very poor second to the Press. When at length the Military Service Bill was introduced in January, 1916, discussion was fervent and impassioned ; but for giving any sort of lead to public opinion it was at least three months too late. " We are not governed," exclaimed one of the nation's representatives on that occasion, " by the Northcliffe press " ; but he did not develop his thesis ; and the fact that the most clamant and persistent advocacy of conscription came from quarters so far inimical to Labour ideals as to have harboured the hope of industrial as well as military compulsion, was to labour eyes a somewhat sinister omen.

At this distance the general case for conscription needs no rehearsing ; but in the Labour world opposition was bound to be tenacious. Not merely was the whole tradition of the British Labour movement antagonistic to the principle ; circumstances gave additional point to the abstract objection. From the start, Labour had been apprehensive of industrial compulsion, especially since the speech at Manchester, in which Mr. Lloyd George had hinted at its desirability. The dockers' battalion at Liverpool looked like an omen. The Derby scheme of attesting munition workers and sending them back to work with a khaki armlet roused further apprehension. The operation of the leaving certificate clause of the Munitions Act savoured of the reality ; and so intensely was it resented on the Clyde that the Minister of Munitions on December 30th, 1915, could hardly secure an audience from the workers. Then the particular quarter from which the advocacy of conscription chiefly came suggested to its Labour opponents that the nation was in fact being urged to " compulsion for compulsion's sake." " We emphatically protest," resolved the Trade Union Congress in September, 1915, " against the sinister efforts of a section of the reactionary press in formulating newspaper policies for party purposes and attempting to foist on this country conscription which always proves a burden to the workers and will divide the nation at a time when absolute unanimity is essential." Sufficient men, the Congress averred, could and would be secured by voluntary means; and the Labour movement, by way of making good its contention, gave its full support to what Lord Derby called "the last effort on behalf of voluntary service."

The results of Lord Derby's attestation scheme, which was put in operation on October 21st, were published on January 4th, 1916. Out of 5,011,411 men of military age (as indicated by the National Register compiled on August 15th), 215,431 had enlisted, and over two million had attested for service under the group system; of these latter Lord Derby estimated that 831,062 would be actually available. But by the register figures over a million single men had not offered themselves, of whom 651,160 held no badge or other claim to special exemption.

Mr. Asquith on November 2nd had stated that "the obligation of the married man to serve ought not to be enforced or held to be binding upon him unless and until . . . the unmarried men are dealt with"; and that if, after other means had been tried, "there should still be found a substantial number of men of military age not required for other purposes who without excuse hold back from the service of their country," then the case for compulsion would be established. Lord Derby's figures, subject to conjectural modification as they might be, were taken as indicating that contingency; and on January 5th, 1916, the Premier reluctantly introduced the Military Service Bill in direct fulfilment of his pledge.

In the new situation created by Lord Derby's report, Labour opinion in the House of Commons was divided; outside it, the Trade Union Congress and the Labour party reaffirmed their opposition. But with the passage into law of the Military Service

Act, the immediate concern of labour was the position of munition workers, whether actually employed or no. Nominal immunity from recruitment had hitherto been provided for by the issue of badges by private employers, with or without official authorisation, and by Government departments, to employees who were considered indispensable. The supervision of " badging " operations had been transferred in July, 1915, to the Ministry of Munitions in accordance with the Munitions Act ; and an attempt at a uniform issue was made, on the basis of lists of trades and of contracting firms previously drawn up, as well as of controlled establishments. This basis had been supplemented by the starring of men on the National Register according to occupation ; and the War Service badge and the starred occupation were equally valid—in theory —against Lord Derby's canvassers. The issue of badges to individual men in other than Government establishments was still at the discretion of the employer ; and the trade unions had regarded the arrangement as at least capable of abuse. When under the National Service Act the badges—more strictly speaking, the certificates that went with them—were made equivalent to exemption certificates, the conditions under which they were issued and retained became much more important. Was the man, whose employment on munition work was temporarily suspended, to become immediately liable to conscription ? Was the operation of the Act, asked Mr. Dillon in Parliament, to say in effect to the munition worker : " You must obey your master, and do everything he orders, or you go to the trenches ? "

These and a wide range of other considerations bearing on indirect industrial compulsion were debated in the House of Commons during January ; and amendments were introduced to meet them, of which the most important were—that no exemption certificate should bind a man to any specified employer or establishment; that a man's habitual occupation, if he were not at the moment engaged in it but was seeking to return to it, might be considered; and that two months' grace should be given to a man whose occupation was gone in consequence of his relinquishing munition work— six weeks, that is, during which, if he had no leaving certificate, employers were debarred by the Munitions Act from engaging him, and another fortnight in which to find fresh work.

These exemptions, necessary as they were, met with small popular approval; partly on account of their extent, more because, as Lord Derby put it to the House of Lords, " grocers, pawnbrokers' assistants, all classes of men," had gone into munitions work to secure exemption, and people wanted them fetched out again. The period of grace, moreover, was used in many cases simply to dodge the recruiting officer. It must be added that the labour criticism rested too much upon the assumption that munitions work was positively preferable to military service—a totally irrelevant consideration—and too little on the broad ground of national efficiency. In any case the result of the first Military Service Act was disappointing; and in May, 1916, a second Act was passed, relating to married men of military age not previously attested. In the debate on this measure the Government had to resist strong pressure in both Houses to allow the local tribunals the right of scrutinising Departmental exemption certificates ; and its critics were hardly contented with the information that a special committee was reviewing such exemptions.

The Somme offensive of 1916 had other effects on the labour situation than that with which we are presently concerned, and to some of them we shall have occasion to return shortly ; but it brought to something like crisis the competition between the army and the workshops for the reserve man-power of the country. Not merely were over 30,000 badges withdrawn in six months ; the occupation lists by which local Tribunals were guided had to be repeatedly revised, and the age limits, below which no exemption could be granted, were fixed in various trades. In September, 1916, a " Man-power Distribution Board " was established—the nucleus of the Ministry of National Service—" to determine all questions arising between Government departments relating to the allocation or economic utilisation of man-power " ; and one of its first decisions was in effect that no further exemption certificates should be granted by Government departments over the heads of Appeal Tribunals. Then in November, 1916, came that curious arrangement known as the " Trade Card Scheme " : a scheme both begun and withdrawn to an accompaniment of Labour protest, and productive of no little friction among the trade unions themselves. The unions had objected to the prerogative of the employer in regard to exemption ; they were now to exercise it on their own account. By agreement, first with the engineers, subsequently with a majority of the skilled unions, the Government empowered the societies to issue cards of exemption to their own fully qualified members engaged in munitions production, on the understanding that men ceasing to be so engaged would at once enrol as War Munitions Volunteers.

This was perhaps the first definite enlistment of the trade unions in the direct administrative service of the State. It was met, of course, with the hostile criticism of the opponents of trade unionism in general ; but also with the opposition of the unskilled unions, who cordially resented the advantage given

to their fellows. In particular, the craft unions
represented in the railway shops were accused of
seducing members from the National (Industrial)
Union of Railwaymen by the promise of the trade
card ; and the situation thus created within the
Labour world had an important bearing upon
subsequent events.

"The railway engineers (wrote the *New Statesman* in May, 1917) found themselves exempt
if they belonged to one union and conscripted
if they belonged to another, and great was the
internal scandal. Meanwhile, the War Office
insisted on getting an additional 500,000 soldiers,
and the Ministry of Munitions (which to this
day still tells the engineering workmen that no
more skilled engineers can be spared from industry) publicly announced the withdrawal of the
Trade Card Scheme and the substitution of an
extremely complicated series of crafts and
processes, avowedly as being for the purpose
of supplying for the Army, from the establishments of the Ministry, as many men as
possible ! "

The exemption scheme based on the schedules of
protected occupations was, in fact, more logical in
principle, more effective in administration, and more
equitable in its incidence ; but at its inauguration it
appeared to an embarrassed Government and an
exasperated public that one source of friction in the
Labour world had only been removed by the substitution of a worse.

§ 2.

Apart altogether from the military requirements
of man-power, the enormous increase in munitions of
war demanded by the unprecedented scale of opera-

tions in 1916 would alone have rendered the question of dilution increasingly important. But when first the Derby scheme, and then the Military Service Acts began to take their quota from the man-power still remaining in the country, the question became crucial.

Dilution, said Mr. Kellaway (Deputy Minister of Munitions) in the House of Commons (April 27th, 1917), was an unfortunate and much-abused term.

"What is implied by the term is this, that skilled men are kept exclusively at work which skilled men alone can do, that women are utilised for all processes which they are capable of performing or can be trained to perform, that semi-skilled and unskilled men are either up-graded and gradually given more skilled work, or are utilised for a class of work at which skilled men would be wasted and which women in the nature of things are not capable of performing."

To that definition the trade union executives agreed, and as such they had lent their countenance to the system. What progress had been made there are no precise statistics to show: as regards women, however, it is recorded that in controlled firms the proportion employed had increased from 7.1 per cent. before the war to 21.2 per cent. at the end of December, 1916; while for the engineering industry as such the figures were 2.8 and 21.5 respectively.

On the whole, however, the extension of dilution had been fitly described by Mr. Lloyd George in September, 1915, as "a great rearguard action." There was even in September, 1915, ample evidence to show that the last word on the question rested with neither the Government nor the trade union executives, but with the workshops; and the shops had a point of view of their own. There, of course, the conservatism of the skilled crafts and the reluc-

F 2

tance of the men to train in war-time newcomers
who might prove their competitors in peace were at
a maximum ; the pressure of the leaving certificate,
the onus of appeal to the tribunals were most keenly
resented, while the conduct of individual employers
and what was known of the profits of individual
firms were most jealously scrutinised. But there was
more than this, as the Minister of Munitions found by
his personal experiences in the Glasgow area in
December, 1915, when he met the shop stewards.
" I can assure him," said David Kirkwood, by way
of introducing Mr. Lloyd George to the workers at
Parkhead Forge, " that every word he says will be
carefully weighed. We regard him with suspicion
because every act with which his name is associated
has the taint of slavery about it." After which
it is hardly necessary to relate that the proceedings
were stormy, and that Arthur Henderson, as one of
the trade union leaders assenting to the Munitions
Act, was repudiated to his face. Not merely were
the complaints of the rank-and-file and their deep-
rooted suspicions of the Government and of their
own official leaders emphatically vented on this
occasion, but a new demand emerged in unmistakeable language—the demand that dilution must
be carried through under the direct control of the
workers. Dilution, said a representative of the
Clyde Workers' Committee, was in essence no new
thing ; every new sub-division of labour and every
standardisation of parts had made for its effectual
extension. But its present proposed acceleration
would be accepted in the workshops only on conditions , namely, that the benefits should accrue, not
to a class, but to the entire community ; that it must
not tend to the detriment of any grade of labour, and
that organised Labour must have a share in its
control.

" These conditions (he went on) can only be

fulfilled by the Government's compliance with the demands of the Clyde Workers' Committee, that all industries and national resources must be taken over by the Government—not merely 'controlled,' but taken over completely—and that organised Labour should be vested with the right to take part directly and equally with the present managers in the management and administration in every department of industry. I have used the word 'demand' advisedly, as this is no propagandist statement. It is our fixed determination to force the matter to an issue."

This demand was to some extent admitted in the appointment during January, 1916, of special "Dilution Commissions" for the Clyde and Tyne areas, under whose supervision detailed dilution schemes for individual establishments were drawn up in full and frank consultation with the shop stewards and the local trade union officials. In all such schemes it was provided that a shop committee should be formed to discuss with the management difficulties arising in the operation of the scheme ; and the prescribed safeguards were reaffirmed, in some cases strengthened. This procedure resulted in a substantial increase of dilution during 1916.

As the year wore on, however, further difficulties arose. In the first place, it was suspected—not, as subsequently appeared, without reason—that dilution was being used not only for the agreed purpose of increasing the munitions supply, but for the very far from agreed purpose of releasing fit men for the army. On the face of it, there was no inequity in such a proceeding ; and the fact that it was disputed reflects in significant measure the growing exasperation of the skilled men, their diminishing consciousness of the claims of the nation, and their deepening distrust of Government control generally. The difficulties with which the Government had to contend were, Heaven knows, grave enough ; and if they resulted, during the autumn of 1916 and the spring of 1917, in some rather ill-fated enterprises, there was considerable excuse. It was particularly unfortunate, however, that the proposal to enrol volunteers of both sexes and of all descriptions for whatever " national service " might be deemed necessary was allowed to appear as a preliminary to general industrial compulsion ; for other causes were by that time reinforcing the alarm invariably raised by the mention of any such project.

Among them was the old question of profits, which had reappeared in connection with the Excess Profits Tax. The question whether the tax should be levied on the excess profits allowed by the Munitions Act to armament firms was somewhat fully debated by the House of Commons in July, 1916 ; and the prominence into which the matter was thus brought had a direct bearing upon the difficult question of *dilution on private work*.

That any such proposal was necessary, the Government explained, was due to the unforeseen duration of the war and the continued demand of the military authorities for men. It involved a direct breach of the pledge originally given as to the conditions under which dilution should be carried out ; and it appeared to run counter to the only condition under which dilution could be made acceptable to the men—that of direct service to the nation. Even in 1915 trouble had arisen from the suspicion that some employers were using the dilution agreement to facilitate the execution of private contracts ; and when towards the close of 1916 the unions were asked, on the plea of national necessity, to countenance such procedure, they were not careless to enquire as to the corresponding sacrifice to be made by the private employer. They were assured by the Chancellor of the Exchequer (Mr. McKenna) that " all the provisions of the Munitions Acts relative to the limitation of profits " should be applied ; but what was actually applied was the existing Excess Profits Tax, in which the Munitions Levy was subsequently merged—the distinction being that while the Munitions Act impounded, broadly speaking, all profit made in excess of a fixed amount plus 20 per cent., the Tax allowed the employer to retain 20 per cent. of as much excess over the average as he could manage to make. More important, however, was the apprehension of the unions that while much of the war equipment would automatically lapse in munitions industry, in private industry the alterations in plant, extensions of repetition work, introduction of automatic lathes and other fool-proof machinery would certainly survive the war ; and what then would be the position of skilled labour as against cheaper-working " dilutees " ?

Under the stress of necessity, however, the Government, hoping for the eventual consent of the trade unions with which it had been in negotiation, introduced in April, 1917, a new Munitions Bill, under which the Minister of Munitions was to receive power to apply the provisions of the principal Act to any class of work which he declared by Order to be of national importance. In a House of Commons that mustered on a division 110 members, and dropped in debate as low as 7 actually present, Liberals and Labour men voiced an ineffectual opposition. But in the country—at last—occurred the inevitable explosion.

CHAPTER III.

___

UNOFFICIAL.

The years 1916-1918 were marked by such a
series of apparently spontaneous and heterogeneous
movements as almost invariably heralds a period
of revolutionary change in organised society. For
any adequate account of these movements the data
are scattered and fragmentary; and in attempting
to connect them in a general survey the reader must
be forewarned against imputing an importance to
single phenomena greater than that which in fact
they possessed. In many cases the same individuals,
or similar groups, appear in different connexions
that have to be examined separately; and the
difficulty of framing an historical perspective is
enhanced by the necessity of distinguishing in the
general situation activities arising, almost inevitably,
out of the constitutional effects of the war from
those which rested on a more abiding foundation.
The extent to ,which in the present chapter we are
dealing, despite appearances, with an essential unity
will best be indicated by its sequel.

§ 1.

Contrary to much popular belief, the shop steward
was not one of the infernal devices occasioned by the

war. More especially in the areas of large scale
enterprise, it had long been necessary for the trade
unionists in individual shops or departments, or for
their local " lodges," to appoint some leading hand
in the establishment to collect the union subscriptions,
inspect the cards of new-comers, whip-up for special
meetings or special levies, and in general represent
the organisation on the spot ; and in many cases it
became the practice for the steward to represent
his own group of workers in informal negotiations
with the foremen or the management on points of
workshop practice. If, therefore, circumstances arose
by which the national executives of the trade unions,
and along with them the district branches, were
placed in a position disapproved of by the rank-and-
file ; if at the same time a vast increase occurred in
the number of matters requiring detailed negotiation
and settlement in the workshop, the shop steward
would inevitably become the rallying point of the
men concerned, and might become, if things went
far enough, a centre of opposition to the official
leadership.   That, in brief, is the history of the shop
stewards movement.

It is well known that in the dilution agreements
of 1915 the trade union executives, broadly speaking,
failed to carry either the mass of their members
or a majority of their local branches with them ; and
among other results there followed a decline in the
position of the average district committee. On the
one hand, it could do little, against the resistance of
its members, to enforce the official policy—the less,
in fact, as all details of dilution procedure had
necessarily to be settled in the individual establishment ; on the other hand, it was precluded from
leading or organising any protest movement even
if it wished, since it could neither call nor finance a
strike, being under at least negative control from
headquarters. Branch secretaries of the unions

were in fact to be found leading the unofficial movement ; but no official definitely associated therewith
could be recognised or accredited by the unions,
and shop stewards—whether already functioning as
such or newly appointed by the workers—were thus
forced into opposition. This was the position on the
Clyde in 1915 in a number of different trades at
once ; and naturally the shop stewards of the
different trades drew together, cohering at last as
the Central Withdrawal of Labour Committee in
the engineering strike of February, 1915. On this
occasion the Clyde District Committee of the A.S.E.
and the unofficial strike committee came into open
variance ; and when the action of the latter was
followed by a better settlement than. the men had
been advised to accept by the former, the lesson
seemed obvious. The Withdrawal of Labour Committee became the Clyde Workers' Committee, and
subordinate local or shop committees were organised
throughout the area, the Munitions Act of 1915
acting as an effective spur to their formation.

At this stage there is no need to impute disaffection
on national issues to the shop stewards. " I am as
much a patriot," said one of them before the Macassey
Commission, " as anyone in this room. We have
been looked upon as unpatriotic in this matter.
I have seven relatives fighting in the trenches and
on the sea. No man dare tell me that I am sacrificing
their lives by remaining out. I am standing out for
the Trade Union cause, a perfectly legitimate proceeding." Nor is there much ground for the
accusation of " agitating." The shop stewards in
leading the 1915 strikes were undoubtedly acting
under an overwhelming pressure from the mass, and
their journal maintained with some justice at a
later date : " Shop stewards do not ' bring ' men
out on strike ; the shop stewards' functions do not
include ' leadership.' As a matter of fact, the whole

movement is a repudiation of leadership. It is a means of organised expression on the part of the mass ; it reverses the methods of the past ; instead of dragging men out by platform oratory, it provides the means for the rank-and-file to receive information direct through the shop stewards and to decide for themselves what course of action they shall adopt. By a thorough organisation of every workshop and the co-ordination of workshop committees the shop stewards movement provides the means of real democratic expression."

None the less, a workshop policy of a more than merely negative kind was emerging even in 1915— a policy which, all things considered, does appear to have been a "real democratic expression." The Clyde Workers' Committee, Mr. Lloyd George was informed on his visit to Glasgow, decided "to have nothing to do with dilution of labour unless the Government is prepared to nationalise the munitions industry, and give the workers a share in the management and control of labour." This latter demand was subsequently reiterated in many, including official, quarters ; but what the shop stewards meant by it was not merely nor mainly the association of the trade union executives with the Government, but the association of the workers in the shops with the immediate management.

This demand, as we have seen, was in fact recognised in the procedure of the Clyde and Tyne Dilution Commissions, and its recognition alone made success in their difficult task attainable ; but the temper in which it was coming to be conceived by the more aggressive leaders was made patent to the whole country in the Clyde strikes of March, 1916. Kirkwood, convener of shop stewards, claimed at Beardmore's shipyard the right to enter, without permission asked or granted, any department of the works to examine the conditions under which dilution was being carried out ; and following a refusal, the men in shop after shop struck work—principally the engineers engaged on guns and gun-mountings—until about 10,000 were affected. Behind the dispute, as usual, was more than the ostensible cause ; the refusal of a recent wage application, resentment at the provisions and the administration of the Munitions Acts, dissatisfaction with the details of dilution in various establishments, and more generally a spirit of aggressive defiance both of the trade unions and of the Government of the country—all found a vent in the stoppage. Considering the nature of the work affected the episode was certainly suggestive of a sinister design, and in deporting six of the leading shop-stewards under the Defence of the Realm Act the Government had both material and legal justification. From this episode may perhaps be dated the emergence of a revolutionary tendency among a minority of the " left wing." The accumulating resentment of the Clyde workers of the conditions imposed upon them by the Munitions Act, the prominence into which the whole question of the profits of private industry had been brought ; the nervous tension resulting from long and unremittent overtime ; and an increased sense of power with which the sense of responsibility to the community had not kept pace—now lent a new cogency to the abstract denunciations of the capitalist system with which the men had long been only too familiar. Further, to many of them it appeared as if the Government were in alliance with their employers and *ipso facto* committed to the active support of the capitalist regime : their official leaders were " bound hand and foot " and by many of them repudiated as reactionary. " The support given to the Munitions Act by the officials," stated a leaflet issued by the Clyde Workers' Committee, " was an act of treachery to the working classes." More than ever it looked like the worker *contra mundum*. Two results of some importance followed : nationalisation, that hardy annual of the Labour movement, was now seen to be less than useless unless it were inseparably associated with control by the workers, from top to bottom ; and in the existing circumstances, the industrial issue inevitably took on a political complexion. Here in fact was the nucleus of a genuine revolutionary movement, in which by no means all the shop stewards committees, even on the Clyde, were ready to join ; but at this point the evolution of the extreme left was reinforced by the resurgence of an older unofficial movement in the new connexion. An expression of the views of the Clyde Workers' Committee in April, 1916, aptly illustrates the development of opinion. "Our purpose must not be misconstrued ; we are out for unity and closer organisation of all trades, one union being the ultimate aim. We will support the officials just so long as they rightly represent the workers, but we will act independently when they misrepresent them. Being composed of delegates from every shop and untrammelled by obsolete rule or law, we claim to represent the true feeling of the workers."

§ 2.

Arising from an earlier nationalising movement, there had been formed in 1912 an unofficial " Metal, Engineering and Shipbuilding Amalgamation Committee " of which the object was to promote amalgamation on an industrial basis between the various unions in, more particularly, the trades enumerated. The method adopted—the only one possible in the circumstances—was that of propaganda in the workshops and the trade union branches with a view to

bringing pressure to bear from below on the national
executives   Up to the outbreak of war the policy
had produced little direct and tangible result , but
with the weakening in the authority of the trade
union executives that resulted from the dilution
negotiations, an atmosphere favourable to the industrial movement was, created, and in 1916 active
steps towards its prime object were taken by the
Amalgamation Committee.   Conferences of the adherents of the movement—Socialist societies, trade
union branches, shop committees and other unofficial
organisations—were held at Sheffield and Leeds in
the latter half of 1916 ; and by the November
meeting a sort of ultimatum was delivered to the
executive of the Amalgamated Society of Engineers
demanding that a definite approach to other unions
with a view to amalgamation be made within three
months.   The only result of the meeting was
apparently the issue of a statement by the Society
of Engineers, setting forth efforts already made
towards industrial amalgamation and the difficulties
encountered.   But the unofficial committee was not
going to let it rest at that.   If the A.S.E. executive
would take no action, someone else must clearly
be called on ; and at a conference in Birmingham
held on March 3rd and 4th, 1917 (the date is
significant) the various Trades Councils, Union
branches, and other bodies instructed the National
Amalgamation Committee itself to convene a preliminary conference of the trade unions concerned
in engineering.

This decision appeared to give great satisfaction
to all concerned in it—especially the committee.
Here was a definite snub to those retrograde national
leaders, in that an unofficial body had been charged
by the workers to convene a conference of the officials
themselves.   The workers, it was maintained, were
ripe for amalgamation with the ultimate ideal of one

big union " out to foster the class spirit as against the craft prejudice." The distinction between craft and unskilled unions was an anachronism—although the engineers' society and many of the engineering shop stewards did not quite see it in that light. The emancipation of the worker could only be achieved by action on a broad class basis, and solidarity was all in all.

Little response seems to have been made by the trade unions to the invitation of the Amalgamation Committee ; but in the immediate sequel the leaders of the movement seem to have got in touch with the American " Industrial Workers of the World " which stood for the same principle ; and on Sunday, June 10th, 1917, a demonstration in Trafalgar Square was organised in support of the I.W.W. and the " one big union " idea. Having attained the plinth of the Nelson Column, the aspirations of the movement seem to have somewhat declined ; and though further conferences were held during 1917 their virility—on at least the original issue—seems to have been somewhat to seek.

The movement, it must be noted, had the support of none of the official Labour organisations behind it. Its attitude on the craft question rendered it unpopular among many of the unions, and its policy was too avowedly Syndicalist to have the support of the Labour Party or the I.L.P. But apart from its main policy of industrial unionism, another tendency had been gaining strength in the movement in virtue of the adherence of the " left wing " shop stewards.

The Leeds Conference of 1916, along with its demand of the A.S.E., had decided that " the control of policy and action should be vested in the workshop." This, as we saw, was very much what the shop stewards on the Clyde were demanding of the Minister of Munitions in 1915. During 1916 this demand gained force among the rank-and-file through-

out the country, until it became the strongest plank
in the unofficial movement. Many of the shop
committees now established became propagandist
centres of a coherent policy, the active effects of
which were soon to appear. " Remember," wrote
J. T. Murphy to the local Amalgamation Committees,
in March, 1917, " it is not only the amalgamation of
unions you require, but the amalgamation of the
workers in the workshop. Let your propaganda
take concrete form by transforming the Amalgamation Committees into Workers Committees. Make
the amalgamation of unions incidental, the amalgamation of the workers fundamental." They were
in fact already doing so : Murphy was directing
the tributary towards the main stream. That was
immediately before the news of the first Russian
revolution.

§ 3.

At this point it is necessary to recall certain general
aspects of the social situation in those winter months
of 1916-1917 when events seemed to conspire for
crisis.

The failure of the Somme offensive to bring a
positive decision in the war appreciably nearer was
followed by an increase in the activity of the various
groups opposed to its continuance. Apart from the
expressly pacifist organisations at which we have
glanced already, the Independent Labour Party
was taking up a more definitely pacifist attitude, and
. being driven by the unmistakeable " will to win "
manifest in other sections of the Labour movement
to a somewhat extreme position. The second anni-
versary of the commencement of hostilities, for
example, had set the *Labour Leader* wondering how
much longer the " slaughter " was to continue ; " if

the war is to end before August comes again it must
be because the people will to have it so. To the
Governments we shall look in vain. They express
no thought of reconciliation; the word 'peace' is
treason in their ears."

In the second week of December came the German
peace overtures—tentative proposals on the basis of
the *status quo*, for which not even the Radical press
had a good word to say. There was no question of
their acceptance, and the episode served merely to
define the resolution of the allied Powers to win the
war. But the mere suggestion of negotiations raised
the hopes of the pacifist element, and on the argument
of the *Labour Leader* it was to "the peoples" that
opponents of the war tended to turn. Now to no
small extent opposition to the war was becoming
characteristic of the unofficial movement; not
merely because the unorthodox by nature are
generally unorthodox in more respects than one,
but because, in the view of the more uncompromising
leaders, the war was anyway a "capitalist war,"
and the only war worth fighting was the class-war
for the workers. But also in December, 1916, Mr.
Lloyd George, newly become Prime Minister, offered
six posts in his Ministry to the official Labour leaders;
which posts, in conformity with the general attitude
of official Labour, and with the confirmation, by a
6 to 1 majority vote, of the official Labour Party,
were accepted. Not only the left wing had mis-
givings on the move; the decision, said the *New
Statesman*, with an emphasis not as it turned out
altogether misplaced, "may possibly have destroyed
all chance of an independent and influential Parliamentary Party of Labour for another generation."
The immediate result, of course, was a hardening of
both official and unofficial opposition on the left.

Profound, however, as may have been the
influence of these developments in the long run,

they were of too general a nature to provoke any immediate crisis. For that material and immediate causes were requisite ; and, as luck and bad management would have it, material and immediate causes at this critical juncture were forthcoming.

The Trade Card scheme, as we saw, had not been unprovocative of trouble at its inception. Twenty-five of the most important skilled unions, however, were interested in its maintenance ; and when in April, 1917, its withdrawal was decided upon by the Government, the union executives were immediately faced with the prospect of more trouble in the workshops throughout the kingdom than they could cope with. What authority they yet retained had been further undermined by their negotiations with the Government as to dilution on private work ; and it was no longer to the national leaders that the discontented trade unionists were looking. Here at last was the immediate occasion of an explosion to which all the forces behind the unofficial movement were converging. Mass meetings, led by the shop stewards, were held in munitions and shipyard centres from the English Channel to the Firth of Forth. Unofficial strikes had already broken out in April : in the first fortnight of May, Manchester, Liverpool, Birkenhead, Barrow, Coventry, Sheffield, Derby, Bristol, London, Southampton, and parts of the Tyne and Clyde went up in mutiny ; and in London a three-cornered tragi-comedy reached its *dénouement*.

As to where the control of the rank-and-file rested at the moment there could be no manner of doubt. " I will be no party," said the Minister of Munitions (Dr. Addison), " to allowing the Ministry of Munitions to be used as an instrument for defeating the trade union movement." But there were the shop stewards, now joined in conference in London, knocking peremptorily at the door of the Ministry of Munitions; and much as the officials of 50 unions concerned might " reaffirm their conviction that in war-time trade disputes should be dealt with in a constitutional manner, and deeply deplore the existing unauthorised strike," the knocking had to be answered. Ten warrants were issued, eight of the leaders arrested; but that proved no answer. " Joint Engineering Shop Stewards Committee repudiate any interference by the Official Executives," said the Committee in pointed, unpolite reply to the trade unions. Here was a new Fourth Estate—the rank-and-file to wit—come to town, to the acute discomfiture of Fleet Street as well as Whitehall; and how was an unfortunate Minister to greet it?

There appears to be no record of the conference at which it was arranged that the executive of the Engineers' Society should introduce the recalcitrants. Thus, at any rate, was the " unofficial strike committee," ushered in at the door in Whitehall Gardens, enabled to state its case, to be assured of no more police proceedings for the present, and withdraw. But neither the question of dilution on private work nor that of the status of the shop steward was settled. The former, after months of further negotiation, was dropped by Mr. Churchill and the Munitions Bill re-introduced in August without it. The latter was settled, after a further strike at Coventry, by agreement between the Engineering Employers' Federation and thirteen trade unions (of which the A.S.E. was not one) in December, 1917. The parties agreed to recognise the right of the workers to elect shop stewards for negotiation with the management of individual works within the limits of trade union practice and agreements; the recognition being accorded " in order that a further safeguard may be provided against disputes arising between employers and their workpeople."

The industrial issue was thus to some extent

disposed of.   Other aspects of the unofficial movement remained ; but the " unrest " of May, 1917,
was, in fact, despite its mode of expression, mainly
concerned with immediate industrial questions, and
less with revolution than the majority of the newspapers affected to believe.   Perhaps it was in Printing House Square that some irresponsible parodist
first sang—

> " The people's flag is palest pink,
> It's not so red as you might think. . . ."

But meanwhile, in the quarter of the northern
sunrise, the authentic colour had made its appearance ; and England was to have at least the
reflection.

CHAPTER IV.

" OUT OF THE DARKNESS . . . "

§ 1.

For the Socialists of Western Europe perhaps the
most significant aspect of the Russian revolution
really lay in the relations it exhibited between the
" intelligentsia " and the " proletariat." In this
connexion, the subsequent careers of Kerensky,
Miliukoff, Tcheidze, and others are peculiarly instructive ; but even from the day to day events of
March, April, and May, 1917, most profitable lessons
were to be drawn by those who had eyes to read
them. Such lessons, however, have little relevance
to the history of affairs and men of action. It is
upon sentiment and impulse, not upon reason and
statesmanship, that world events immediately react ;
and the guidance these latter elements might give
to the energies of the former is hardly ever available
until eager hopes and passionate aspirations have
been seared and tired and broken in their blind flight
upwards.

There were few men in England to whom the end
of Russian Tsardom did not bring some sense of
relief in that third week of March, 1917—though
there were some among them who would regret
it later. To the working classes the news came at a

fateful moment, when the fundamental cleavage of
Labour opinion was already becoming manifest.
The Trade Union movement was splitting upon
causes which were not solely industrial ; the Labour
members of Parliament were divided in the lobbies
of the House , the Independent Labour Party was
at open variance with the National Labour Party
of which it was nominally a part as to the whole
conduct and purpose of the war ; within the Trade
Unions themselves left and right sections were
beginning to cohere ; the British Socialist Party
had definitely divided into " National " and " pacifist " groups ; other propagandist organisations and
counter-organisations were vigorously canvassing
war-aims and the rival schools of peace ; and throughout the whole population a broad dualism was
becoming more and more definite as to a range of
fundamental questions on which compromise was
essentially—was at last to become patently—impossible.   Under such circumstances the revolution in
Russia assumed for the minority two outstanding
aspects : it seemed a terrific vindication of the
rights and the power of the mass of workers ; and it
seemed an authoritative endorsement of the ideas
that had been put forward as to a " people's peace."
What was supposed to be the most oppressed " proletariat " in Europe had suddenly demonstrated the
essential instability of the rule of force, the essential
solidarity of the people—even the military arm
had turned out to be theirs at a crisis.   As for the
war, had not the Socialists said there was no quarrel
between the workers, and were not the Russian
soldiers proving the contention by fraternising with
the Germans across the trenches ? The new fraternity
was perhaps a little one-sided—but no matter ; there
was no very precise parallel between the precedent
conditions of workers and soldiers in Russia and in
England—but no matter ; in cold blood no quite

obvious analogy was traceable between what at least began as a political revolution in Russia, and the hypothetical industrial revolution in England that would begin, if at all, in the workshops—but no matter. The "people's flag" had been raised, and Tsardom had fallen; and to many leaders of English Labour opinion the news brought a sense of almost personal triumph.

> "This meeting (resolved the great Albert Hall demonstration of Labour on March 31st) sends joyful congratulations to the democrats of Russia, and calls upon the Governments of Great Britain and of every country, neutral and belligerent alike, to follow the Russian example by establishing Industrial Freedom, Freedom of Speech and the Press, the Abolition of Social, Religious and National distinctions, an immediate amnesty for Political and Religious offences, and Universal Suffrage."

—from which considered opinion the impression made by the news from Russia may sufficiently be inferred. It was significant that few features of the Revolution evoked more enthusiasm on this occasion than the fact that the Russian soldiery had refused to fire on the mob. The manifesto of the Provisional Government to the effect that "the time has come for the people to take into their own hands the decision of questions of war and peace" was also much applauded. It is to be noted, however, that the famous phrase "No annexations and no indemnities" was the motto not of the Provisional Government, but of the Petrograd Soviet, and marked in fact the beginning of that more drastic conflict in Russian politics of which the issue was "Bolshevism."

Second thoughts on the progress of affairs in Russia led to some reserve of judgment, not to say misgiving, in many sections of British opinion; but in the case of the Socialist Left, far from misgiving, to the most spectacular piece of utter folly for which that section, during the whole war-period, was responsible—which is saying not a little. The Independent Labour Party, and the British Socialist Party—that is, the pacifist rump of Hyndman's old society—acting as the " United Socialist Council " convened a conference of Left Wing organisations at Leeds on June 9th. The conveners had some little difficulty in getting the use of a hall, and the delegates in finding hotel accommodation ; but the meeting was held, and the Soviet formula subscribed to, among others. The *tour de force*, however, was the passage of a resolution calling on constituent bodies " at once to establish in every town, urban district, and rural district, Councils of Workmen's and Soldiers' delegates for initiating and co-ordinating working class activity in support of the policy set out in the foregoing resolutions and to work strenuously for a peace made by the peoples of the various countries and for the complete political and economic emancipation of international labour." The conveners of the conference—Jowett, Snowden, Lansbury, Macdonald, Smillie, Williams and others —were appointed there and then a provisional committee to supervise the formation of the local " Soviets " ; and communications were to be addressed to the Secretary, " Workers' and Soldiers' Council."

One Toole of the Clerks' Union ventured to point out towards the close of the meeting that the participation of the soldiers, in view of the King's Regulations and other small difficulties, was likely to be problematic ; but the delegates, having struck a blow at the political organisation of Labour from which for at least four years it was not to recover, · departed well satisfied with the day's proceedings ; and the trouble began.

Its first-fruits fell accurately on the heads of two leaders of the conference. The Russians had invited the Independent Labour Party, along with the British majority, to send representatives to Petrograd, and the Government after some hesitation issued passports to Jowett and Macdonald. But the Seamen's and Firemen's Union, whose " Captain " Tupper alleged he had been refused a hearing by the Leeds Conference, withdrew its members from the vessel that was to take them ; and, encouraged by the demagogue press, obstreperously proclaimed through the mouth of " Captain " Tupper that it would see no pacifist delegates set sail. The unsavoury business had two results of some importance : first, in that it actually prevented the visit, to which the British Government had consented, of the whole Labour delegation to Russia at a critical period of that country's affairs ; and, second, in that it provided the Labour movement with a conspicuous proof of the efficacy of direct action— a proof at which the constitutional parties had, since it suited their purpose, openly connived.

Meanwhile, the Leeds Committee set to work to arrange inaugural conferences for the establishment of " Councils of Workers' and Soldiers' Delegates " in thirteen specified areas—to the accompaniment of incitements from the demagogue press to its readers to break up the meetings. Meetings were attempted, in London, Newcastle, Swansea and elsewhere, and duly dispersed with considerable rioting ; the end of the matter being the prohibition of the Workmen's and Soldiers' Councils under the Defence of the Realm Act. And if broken heads and wrecked assembly halls were the net result, oblivion might suitably have swallowed up the whole episode ; but in fact by its partisans and opponents alike the Soviet movement in Britain was so well advertised as to leave a lasting impression on the electorate, and what little prospect remained to Labour of obtaining any measure of political unity or recognition was considerably postponed. Whether by way of compensation the seeds of revolution had been scattered a little wider time was to show ; at least the bitter soil in which they ripen had been well turned.

§ 2.

The summer of 1917 thus found the evolution of Labour opinion in a highly complex condition, the main tendencies of which it will be convenient before going farther to review.

In the first place the strictly industrial questions of the leaving certificate and the extension of dilution to private work were still unsettled ; and the latter had the effect of keeping prominent the general controversy as to profit-making in industry. Hitherto this matter had been mainly discussed in connexion with munitions manufacture ; but 1917 extended the field of controversy and brought into it a new demand enunciated by a new organisation.

The Triple Alliance of the Miners' Federation, the National Union of Railwaymen, and the Transport Workers' Federation, took its rise from an approach made by the miners to the other organisations in 1913. The formulation of a definite scheme of mutual support began in the following April, and was temporarily interrupted by the outbreak of war ; but there were cogent reasons why the interruptions should not be allowed to last. "It is clear," wrote Robert Smillie in 1915, " that capital is now organised for the purpose of attacking trade unionism, and for defence against trade union advance. . . . It will be wise, indeed essential, to have the working agreement ready for the days of peace after the war. It is then that we may expect an attack on Labour by the employers ; it is now, in the midst of war, that we must prepare for the industrial conflicts that the military peace will bring." The Alliance was therefore completed and finally ratified by the executives of the three component bodies in December, 1915 ; and a potential combination of over one and a quarter million workers entered the field. " The predominant idea of the Alliance," wrote Smillie, " is that each of these great fighting organisations, before embarking upon any big movement, either defensive or aggressive, should formulate its programme and submit it to the others, and that upon joint proposals, joint action should be taken." The executive consisted of a committee of two members of each of the allied societies, with whom rested the power to call a full conference of the three executives ; and any decision as to action rested with the conference so called, but could be taken only after the issue " has been before the members of the three organisations and decided by such methods as the constitution of each organisation provides." The Alliance was thus essentially a militant organisation, in sharp contrast with the Trade Union Congress which had no executive authority ; its basis was industrial, not craft, unionism, so that instead of action being confined to specified trades, while the rest had to suffer, all the workers in an industry, or if necessary in all three industries, should act at once and in concert. Although, therefore, the Alliance might, and did, deliberate and deputise the Government on matters of general industrial policy, its existence was justified solely by its ability to command united direct action in the last resort. Not illogically the more aggressive elements among the workers came to regard its executive as their advance guard in the war on " capitalism " ; and when in June, 1917, a full delegate conference of the Alliance demanded " the conscription of wealth and property in order to achieve a real equality of sacrifice " it seemed to many as if the advance guard were moving.

It is probable, however, that the emergence of the Triple Alliance as a definite and accredited organisation actually stabilised the situation in industry. It stood—as any fighting organisation must stand— for discipline within the ranks of its members, and its leaders had been careful to avoid any such position as might impair the strict integrity of their allegiance. With the demonstration of May, 1917, the aggressive impetus of the shop steward movement was temporarily spent ; and the more revolutionary elements were bound to recognise that in the Alliance was a weapon of far greater promise than lay in sporadic movements of the rank-and-file. The policy of industrial unionism found as it were a definite working model at which to aim, while the very magnitude of the new organisation made it apparent that any weakening of trade union solidarity would diminish the chances of its effective employment. The Alliance leaders were professedly taking a long view ; and the mere thought of what might follow on the first blow struck with their united forces seems to have rendered them cautious almost to the point of conservatism.

§ 3.

But in fact the industrial issues of this year of crisis were altogether overshadowed by the international controversy on war-aims , and one effect of this latter was a virtual reintegration of the unofficial movement. It was by no means the case that the rank-and-file revolt in the engineering unions was entirely permeated with opposition to the war ; and the crystallisation of opinion about the war-issue—in which the Russian question was now involved—gradually superseded the industrial formation.

This broad question of war-aims was brought into prominence, as we saw, at the close of 1916 jointly by the German peace offer and by President Wilson's appeal to the belligerents to state their terms. But from the start there had been two clear lines of thought in England : namely, that represented by the Independent Labour Party with its campaign against secret diplomacy, and in favour of a negotiated peace ; and that represented by the popular press and subscribed to by the majority of trade union and general opinion, in favour of the " knock-out blow " and peace by dictation. The former policy was reinforced by many smaller organisations than the I.L.P., including some local labour councils and shop stewards committees, but notably by the Union of Democratic Control. This was an independent society of the " intellectuals " formed in September, 1914, to advocate four principles of peace :

1. No province shall be transferred from one Government to another without the consent by plebiscite or otherwise of the population of such province.

2. No treaty, arrangement, or undertaking shall be entered upon in the name of Great Britain without the sanction of Parliament. Adequate machinery for ensuring democratic control of foreign policy shall be created.

3. The foreign policy of Great Britain shall not be aimed at creating alliances for the purpose of maintaining the balance of power, but shall be directed to concerted action between the Powers, and the setting up of an International Council, whose deliberations and decisions shall be public, with such machinery for securing international agreement as shall be the guarantee of an abiding peace.

4. Great Britain shall propose, as part of the peace settlement, a plan for the drastic reduction, by consent, of the armaments of all the belligerent Powers, and to facilitate

that policy shall attempt to secure the general nationalisation of the manufacture of armaments and the control of
the export of armaments by one country to another.

This was the official program of the society that
sustained the most vigorous of all the attacks of the
demagogue press—a fact largely due to the
advanced Socialist opinions of many of its members.
In such attacks there was evident, of course, the
typical British fear—not the fear of the enemy,
but the fear of the minority ; the impulse that
drives the average citizen to join the biggest crowd,
and that renders too ardent a zeal for progress " bad
form " in the Universities and other centres of
polite society.   It was, in fact, largely because the
Union was suspected of penetrating such preserves
that it was so much more seriously attacked than
its program or personnel would appear to warrant ;
but despite vilification it had secured the adherence
of 117 local organisations, of which 49 were trades
councils and local Labour parties, by January, 1916—
an individual membership of over 300,000 ; and it
continued to expand.

Now both these opposing schools of opinion were
during 1917 reinforced by circumstances.   In
January President Wilson had arrived at the
philosophic conclusion " that it must be a peace
without victory. . . . Victory would mean peace
forced upon the loser, a victor's terms imposed
upon the vanquished.   It would be accepted in
humiliation, under duress, at intolerable sacrifice,
and would leave a sting, a resentment, a bitter
memory upon which terms of peace would rest,
not permanently, but only upon quicksand."   A
durable peace must entail the limitation of naval and
military armaments and a recognition of the principle
" that no right anywhere exists to hand peoples
about from potentate to potentate as if they were
property."   German submarine tactics speedily

changed American opinion; but even when on
April 6th the United States entered the war, it was
as a friend, not an ally, of the Entente; as a foe,
not of the German people, but of Prussian militarism;
as an avenging force by which the world " must be
made safe for democracy." In pursuance of which
noble aim some hundreds of American citizens were
speedily clapped in gaol for the indiscreet expression
of their opinions.

In Britain also the progress of the war hardened
the public temper, and journalists became unable
to discern any intermediate shades between black
and white. Advocates of peace by negotiation,
advanced Socialists, I.L.P. and U.D.C. speakers,
conscientious objectors, sundry poets, artists, musi-
cians, vegetarians, and other persons of doubtful
vocation, critics of the Government or the Army
Council, folk who wore their hair long and lived at
Golders Green, persons who affected to believe in a
possible regeneration of the "Hun," undergraduates
who erred in tone or affected the wrong kind of
neckwear, any who doubted that all the rest were
in receipt of German gold—were liable to be dubbed
"pacifists"; and the Pope was either suspect or
pro-German. But now it was these pestilential
Russians—under-equipped, disorganised, beaten after
titanic struggle, in the agony of famine, civil war
and revolution—who were talking of a negotiated
peace, and urging the working-classes of all countries
to join them. At which International Socialism, in
England and elsewhere, lifted its head again. Pity
the poor patriot!

§ 4.

The International Socialist Bureau, which we left
in Chapter I urging the workers to " continue their

demonstrations against war," had in fact been attempting throughout 1915 and 1916 to secure a common program among neutral, enemy, and allied Socialists on which the International could be re-erected ; but it had elicited little more than general expressions of opinion in favour of the democratic control of foreign policy, the rights of nations, and the limitation of armaments. After the first Russian revolution international headquarters were shifted to Stockholm, a Dutch-Scandinavian Committee constituted, and negotiations started with a view to a full international congress. The movement was supported by the Petrograd Soviet—and by Arthur Henderson, whose advocacy of it in August, 1917, cost him his seat in the British Cabinet. Labour opinion in England was then strongly favourable to the project, despite Government opposition to any meeting with the enemy Socialists. In view, however, of the hesitancy of the Majority Socialists in allied countries, of the Miners' Federation and much other Labour opinion in Britain, and of the lack of any clear platform on which a general Socialist congress could stand, enthusiasm for it gradually declined. After the Bolshevik revolution in Russia (November, 1917), Lenin promptly severed the Russian connexion with inter-allied Socialism ; and with the opening of Russo-German peace negotiations at Brest, it finally became clear that the first task of International Socialism was to achieve, if possible, a common inter-allied program. This task was taken in hand by a Committee of the British Labour movement in the autumn of 1917.

The result was the famous Memorandum on War Aims adopted by the British Labour movement at London on December 28th, 1917, and by a conference of inter-allied Labour and Socialist parties in the following February. In this document the fundamental principles of the old International, the points of agreement already reached among allied Labour parties, the doctrines enunciated by President Wilson, and the ideals of the " left-wing " Liberal and Labour opinion in England were embodied. The war was envisaged as a war of liberation to abolish further war and the fear of war, and establish the League of Free Nations ; and the proposed territorial resettlement was to follow the principle of self-determination of all populations, ignoring " imperialist designs " for the acquisition, by military force, of new territories or new economic advantages. The memorandum insisted on the principle of the " open door " in international economic intercourse ; on the necessity, throughout the post-war period of scarcity, for State control and international allocation of supplies ; and on the provision in every country of public works for the avoidance of unemployment " which, if it is now in any country allowed to occur, is as much the result of Government neglect as is any epidemic disease." In conclusion, the document submitted that " the working-classes, having made such sacrifices during the war, are entitled to take part in securing a democratic world peace," and that therefore each Government should include at least one representative of Labour and Socialism in its peace delegation.

The importance of this document, and of the complex history that led up to it, was not merely intrinsic. It was the immediate product of British Labour and Fabian Socialism ; but its principles were not exclusively Labour nor Socialist, and in defining them the Socialist intellectuals were doing what they had done since 1889—paving a road for Liberalism. The Memorandum on War Aims marks in fact the emergence of official Labour as the spokesman of a body of opinion that was never confined to the trade unions, the Socialist parties and the

H

" proletariat " ; wherein lay the possibility—and it was recognised—of a new constitutional party in British and European politics. Much was therefore to depend upon its organisation and such leadership as Heaven vouchsafed to send it ; much also upon the counteracting forces that controlled public opinion and the working of the constitutional machine Should the new party win through to adequate representation, Labour might find itself called on to accept a position in the State of wider power and greater responsibility. Should it fail— the trade unions knew of other weapons that might be used to subserve their narrower ends ; but what might happen to the rest of the embryo party, and the embryo policy, and the rest of the nation, a merciful Providence hesitated as yet to reveal.

CHAPTER V.

GETTING ON WITH THE WAR.

§ 1.

The gradual mobilisation of Labour opinion during 1917 on the wide ground of national policy did not in itself dispose of the difficulties that had arisen in the industrial field. To some extent no doubt the unofficial demonstration in May had relieved the situation ; but the fundamental causes remained to be dealt with, and the first necessity (assuming one did not know already) was to find out what they were. On June 12th, therefore, the Prime Minister appointed a "Commission of Inquiry into Industrial Unrest," which was to examine the condition of eight specified areas and report to the Government at the earliest possible moment. Within a month the reports were to hand ; and notwithstanding the record of celerity thus established for Government Commissions, a very interesting collection of statements resulted.

"The great majority of the causes of industrial unrest specified in the reports (wrote Mr. G. N. Barnes in his summary) have their root in certain psychological conditions. Want of confidence is a fundamental cause, of which many of the causes given are merely manifestations.

It shows itself in the feeling that there has been
inequality of sacrifice, that the Government has
broken solemn pledges, that the Trade Union
officials are no longer to be relied upon, and
that there is a woeful uncertainty as to the
industrial future."

Of specific causes the most generally emphasized
were three : the rise in the cost of living, with which
wages had failed to advance proportionally ; the
restriction on personal freedom imposed more
especially by the leaving certificate ; and a general
lack of confidence in the Government. Of minor
causes there were many : skilled men on time-rates
were earning less than lower grades on piece-work ;
housing conditions were becoming intolerable in
Scotland, Wales, the North-East Coast and some other
areas; while the administration of the Military Service
and Munitions Acts and the delay in arbitration
procedure were reinforcing a number of local
troubles that ·varied from area to area. In general
there was a strong feeling of patriotism on all sides
throughout the country, and revolutionary feeling
was not extensive ; but the food question, the man-
power question, and some others required immediate
and careful handling.

The district reports on which this summary was
based merit some attention in the light of subsequent
events ; particularly that respecting Wales, which
contained an instructive survey of the peculiar
social and geographical conditions that so largely
determine the formation of opinion in this area.

Here as elsewhere the workers as a whole were
"strongly loyal and patriotic," and there was no
foundation whatever for the (Fleet Street) allegation
of German influence. But at the same time

"the conviction that Capital and Labour are
necessarily hostile, a conviction engendered by
conflict on industrial matters, has been accen-

tuated by the fact that the social conditions of the working classes are of an unsatisfactory character. . . . By the propaganda of a small but earnest group of men whose teachings are rapidly permeating the entire trade union movement . . . hostility to Capitalism has now become part of the political creed of the majority of Trade Unionists in the mining if not in other industries, and unless the employers are prepared to meet the men part of the way, disaster must overtake the mining industry in the South Wales coalfield. Nearly all movements initiated by the South Wales Miners' Federation during recent years, consciously or unconsciously, are directed towards the overthrow of the present capitalist system, and the establishment of a new industrial order under which the workers will have a greater measure of control over their industry and a larger measure of the produce of their labour. Opinions are as yet divided as to whether such overthrow is to be accomplished by political or industrial action, or by both. Until recently the political method was most popular, but industrial action is now in the ascendant."

§ 2.

During the following months Government action of varying kinds was taken to relieve several of the more serious disabilities of labour. In regard to the control of food prices very little had hitherto been done; the attention of the Government had been concentrated on the question of securing supplies, more especially of sugar, grain, and meat. The public scarcely realised the magnitude of the problem that was involved in interference at the retail end of distribution; but the occasion for it, whatever the difficulties, had unmistakeably arrived. According to official statistics (which, valid or no, were certainly good enough argument against the Government) average retail food prices had advanced by December, 1914, 16 per cent. on the July figure. Twelve months later the total advance was given as 44 per cent., and by the end of 1916 the formidable increase of 84 per cent. was reached. No general price control had as yet been imposed; and when it is remembered that the real burden of any given percentage increase becomes more onerous as the price level advances, the urgency of the problem may be realised. In no case had wage rates risen in proportion (the wages of skilled engineers were stated to have risen by less than 20 per cent.), while cases of rampant profiteering were openly admitted   Retail prices had as yet only been fixed for milk, potatoes, and certain cereals; the first step of cardinal importance was the institution of the subsidized ninepenny loaf, in July, 1917—by which time the average price increase was 104 per cent. During the rest of the year control was extended and the rationing system developed, first on a voluntary, finally on a compulsory basis, under the administration of Lord Rhondda; but the food queue remained an unavoidable feature of the winter of 1917, and the suspicion—in many cases the reality—of "profiteering" survived the Armistice. None the less, the Government succeeded in arresting for four months at the close of 1917 the upward movement of food prices, and during the first quarter of 1918 in actually reversing it. In view of the intricate problems involved in respect not only of distribution, but of supply, profit-regulation, transport by land and sea, and administration, this achievement deserved much fuller recognition than the circumstances allowed it to obtain. It is impossible to omit the obvious remark that had the attempt been made earlier, no small part of the wage-problem might have been forestalled.

§ 3.

In other matters negative action was principally required. Whether or no the 28 engineering unions had been fully convinced of the necessity for dilution on private work, there appeared little prospect of its successful application ; and after a most troublesome controversy of several months' duration the proposal was dropped by the new Minister of Munitions (Mr. Churchill). "Even in the area of war munitions," the Minister informed the House of Commons (August 15th, 1917), " even in the controlled establishments, we have not been able to carry out dilution, although it is agreed, further than we can carry the local agreements of the parties concerned. Therefore this clause, which I now propose to omit, is valueless without agreement, and unnecessary should agreement be reached." It was dropped by the Government with regret ; but the opposition of the engineers had triumphed.

The Government also came to the conclusion, guided doubtless by the recommendations of the recent Commission, that the abolition of the leaving certificate was desirable ; but this was not quite so simple a matter. The classes most adversely affected by the leaving certificate had been the most highly skilled grades whose wages were upon a time-basis ; who, being unable by transfer of their labour to other places or occupations to obtain competitive wages or piece-work rates, were actually earning in many cases less than the unskilled piece-workers whom they themselves had trained. Although, therefore, power to abolish the leaving certificate was obtained in the new Munitions Act of 1917, some adjustment in the earnings of skilled men was a necessary preliminary, if the latter were to be retained in their present occupations. That adjustment was made by the award of a 12½ per cent. bonus on earnings to skilled engineering time-workers, which came into force on October 14th, 1917—the day before the abolition of the leaving certificate.

The complete history of the famous " twelve-and-a-half per cent." is recorded in a spirited account by Lord Askwith, with liberal citation of official papers. The principal criticisms made by the Chairman of the Committee on Production—than whom no-one can be better qualified to speak on the subject—are :

First, the award constituted a fatal example of that " lack of co-ordination between Departments " with which Lord Askwith so vigorously charges the Government.

Second, it contravened the principle, which the Committee on Production and the Minister of Labour had been endeavouring to pursue, of correlating all wage advances in general accordance with the cost of living, and avoiding sectional awards from which individual groups of workers might gain undue advantage. The 12½ per cent. operating as a flat rate advance would give a greater proportional increase in some cases than in others, and in view of the multiplicity of varying circumstances, and of adjustments that had already been made, the matter was one that could only be dealt with case by case.

Third, the scope of the award was so loosely defined that it would be impossible to set any clear and just limits to its application.

This contention was most amply justified by the immediate sequel. Claims arose, and were vigorously

pressed, by analogous trades both in and out of
munitions work, through so wide an area that at
last it became necessary to abrogate the entire basis
of the original award by a compensating grant to
piece-workers. In an official account quoted by
Lord Askwith it is stated :

> "The agitation for the 12½ per cent. bonus spread to all
> trades, and by January it had been secured by workmen
> employed on munitions work, and paid as plain time-
> workers in engineering shops, boiler shops, foundries, ship-
> building and ship-repairing establishments, iron and steel
> trades, electricity-generating stations and electrical con-
> tracting trades, nut and bolt trades, brass foundries and
> brass-works, bridge-building and constructional engineering,
> hollow-ware trade, spring-making works, hot stamping
> works, tube works, and wagon-building trades. In January,
> by which time considerable unrest had arisen among
> piece-workers, who were not eligible for the bonus, the War
> Cabinet decided, after obtaining the advice of the Com-
> mittee on Production, to grant a bonus of 7½ per cent. to
> piece-workers and other men on systems of payment by
> results. Before many months, practically every trade had
> secured either the bonus or an equivalent. The bonus,
> intended originally as a compensation to certain skilled
> men on munitions work, failed entirely in its original
> purpose, and merely became an advance of wages which all
> trades claimed and many secured. Designed in the first
> place to allay unrest, this disturbance of comparative rates
> was a principal cause of much labour unrest."

"My view is," adds Lord Askwith, with characteristic diffidence, "that in Labour matters the Government had no policy, never gave signs of having a
policy, and could not be induced to have a policy."
In view of which verdict it is of interest to turn to
the efforts of the Government to find one.

§ 4.

1916 witnessed the establishment by the Government of an unprecedented number of Committees

in connexion with questions of demobilisation, domestic policy and post-war reconstruction. Of these Committees, one at least—that dealing with " Relations between Employers and Employed " was to become famous. The Whitley Committee was appointed by the Cabinet Committee on Reconstruction in October, 1916, and the subsequent change of Government and the formation of new Ministries passed over its head without affecting the continuity of its deliberations. Its terms of reference were :

> (1) to make and consider suggestions for securing a permanent improvement in the relations between employers and workmen ;
>
> (2) to recommend means for securing that industrial conditions affecting the relations between employers and workmen shall be systematically reviewed by those concerned, with a view to improving conditions in the future.

The Committee included prominent employers and representative Trade Unionists over whom the Right Hon. J. H. Whitley, M.P., presided ; on the Labour side were men of such divergent outlook as Mr. J. R. Clynes, Mr. Robert Smillie, Mr. F. S. Button and Mr. J. J. Mallon. The first report, however, which was published in July, 1917, was unanimous.

As the basis of any permanent improvement in the relations between Employers and Employed the Committee decided that the " cash nexus " was no longer sufficient and that the workpeople " should have a greater opportunity of participating in the discussion about and adjustment of those parts of industry by which they are most affected." To this end the Committee recommended

> " the establishment for each industry of an organisation representative of employers and workpeople to have as its object the regular

consideration of matters affecting the progress and well-being of the trade from the point of view of all those engaged in it, so far as this is consistent with the general interest of the community."

The Joint Industrial Councils thus proposed were to consist of representatives of associations of employers and workpeople in the well-organised industries ; they were to consider not only wages and allied questions, but such matters as Education, Industrial Research and Statistics, Welfare and Scientific Management. The Councils were to rest on an entirely voluntary basis, and the validity of their proceedings was thus made dependent upon the adequacy of organisation on either side. They were, however, to receive the recognition of the Government as the representative bodies for their respective industries.

Certain principles implicit in this scheme require emphasis. First, it presupposed the existence of a common interest between employers and workpeople. It was therefore not to be expected that the more Marxian elements in the Trade Unions would embrace it. Second, its adoption by the War Cabinet implied the fullest recognition of the principle of Trade Unionism that had yet been received from the Government. Third, that recognition was granted on a *de facto* basis of industry, not vocation ; but the approval that this basis might have received from the advocates of industrial unionism was largely forestalled by the presupposition of a common interest between the two sides. Fourth, it suggested that the management of industry was the concern of those strictly engaged within it, and thus implied a departure from the principles of bureaucratic State Socialism.

The reception of the scheme by the press and public opinion was such as might have been expected

in view of the foregoing considerations. By the
vast majority of moderate and conservative opinion
it was welcomed ; partly as affording a prospect of
greater " industrial harmony " in future and partly,
though less generally, as affording a constitutional
means by which the desire of Labour for a share in
control might be realised. The only pronounced
opposition came from the " left wing," and was clearly
voiced by the National Guilds League, whose object
was " the abolition of the wage-system and
the establishment of self-government in industry
through a system of National Guilds working in
conjunction with the State." In the view of this
body

> " this demand the Report entirely, and scarcely by accident,
> ignores , it concerns itself throughout with the operation of
> joint bodies of employers and workers. We want, therefore,
> to point out and to emphasise the fact that no scheme of
> so-called ' joint control ' can meet the demand of the
> workers , and that no such scheme can give, in any way,
> or under any circumstances, any real control. Labour
> cannot secure the control of industrial affairs through the
> agency of a composite body."

This attitude was officially taken up by one or two
trade unions ; but the abstract opposition to the
principle did not, in the long run, entirely prevail
against the tangible advantages that could be
secured by means of regular joint consultation.

Subsequent reports of the Committee dealt with
the decentralisation of the scheme, with the less
organised industries and with conciliation and
arbitration ; and certain of the recommendations
were met in later legislation. The immediate result,
however, was the adoption of the scheme as part of
the policy of the Government and an active
endeavour made by the Ministry of Labour to bring
it into being. The first Joint Industrial Council—
that for the Pottery Industry—was established in
January, 1918.

§ 5.

Taken as a whole, the year 1917 is characterised
by the emergence of a whole series of problems—
administrative, political, social, industrial, and international—whose solution was not to be discovered
during the period of the war, nor for long after.

Some aspects of the change in society are well
described in the War Cabinet Report for the year :

" On the one hand, not only have enormous numbers of
men, and latterly of women also, been mobilised for military
and naval purposes, but the vast majority of the people
are now working directly or indirectly on public service.
If they are not in the Army, the Navy, the Civil Service,
they are growing food, or making munitions, or engaged
in the work of organising, transporting or distributing the
national supplies.   On the other hand, the State has taken
control for the period of the war over certain national
industries, such as the railways, shipping, coal and iron
mines, and the great majority of engineering businesses.
It has also made itself responsible for the securing of
adequate quantities of certain staple commodities and
services, such as food, coal, timber and other raw materials,
railroad and sea transportation, and for distributing the
available supplies justly as between individual and individual in the national interest.

Thus the war, and especially the year 1917, has brought
about a transformation of the social and administrative
structure of the State, much of which is bound to be
permanent.

Taking the year as a whole the Administration has been
brought into far closer contact with every aspect of the life
of the people, the provinces and the metropolis have been
linked more closely together, and the whole community
has received an education in the problems of practical
democracy such as it never had before."

For labour, when all has been said of disputes
and difficulties encountered, the year placed to the
permanent credit of the workers a stupendous
achievement.   The rate of output of heavy guns and

filled shell had doubled in the twelve months, to say nothing of other arms and supplies, shipbuilding, repair work, replacement, and all the contributory processes to the colossal production ; this in spite of the constant diminution of the man-power available, and of the accumulating strain of continual overtime and absence of holidays. Within the limits set by legislation and national agreements the actual adjustments by which this result was secured were determined district by district and factory by factory between the workers and the managements concerned. No small part of this co-operation was made possible solely by the fact of the national emergency ; by the sense, however vague, that the effort was directly for the nation ; it did not follow that the lines of industrial development on which the war production was secured could be carried forward for post-war production under the pre-war system of private ownership. The year ended on a note of comparative and superficial calm both in the munitions centres and the battlefields ; and the great German offensive of the following spring was met in the workshops by a loyal disregard of old and new grievances alike. None the less, the events of 1917 had called spirits from the vasty deep of social consciousness which no merely military victory would be altogether sufficient to lay again.

PART THREE.

FROM DECEMBER, 1917, TO THE GENERAL ELECTION OF DECEMBER, 1918.

1918.

Franchise Act	Feb. 6
Coal Mines Control Agreement (Confirmation) Act	
Second Inter-Allied Socialist Conference	Feb. 20
Peace of Brest-Litovsk	Mar. 2
Embargo Strike at Coventry	July 23
Fisher Education Act	Aug. 8
Trade Boards Act	
London Socialist Conference	Sept. 17
Armistice	Nov. 11
Wages (Temporary Regulation) Act ...	Nov. 21
General Election	Dec. 14

CHAPTER I.

ANGEL UNWINDING DESTINIES.

Among the esoteric symbols applicable to the year 1918 is that of the " Angel unwinding Destinies." It is associate with the elements of " attraction and repulsion, life, terrors, and all kinds of strife, of separation, disruption, destruction, promise and menace "—a connexion in which that climactic " eleventh hour of the eleventh day of the eleventh month " has a strange and peculiar significance. The interpretation of such phantasms we leave to the curious and absent-minded—the more willingly perhaps when for six years or so it refuses to be cheerful ; but the record of 1918 is in fact of such a nature as to excuse the invocation of sun and stars and any other powers black magic wots of. It was indeed—to quote the War Cabinet Report (whose blue covers were surely innocent of any trace of spellbinding) " one of the most remarkable years in the world's history " ; in which " the magnitude and intensity of the operations, the swift reversal of the fortunes of war, and the political upheavals following the military disaster among the Central Powers mark the year of climax." For a year which began with the imposition of a German peace on Russia, the Ukraine, and Rumania, followed by an enemy " break through " in the north of France to within 42 miles of Paris—and ended a few months later in the social and military collapse of the Central Empires, the epithet " remarkable " is a mild one.

§ 1.

Military events had a drastic and immediate reaction upon the labour situation. Before 1917 was out the defection of Russia had made necessary a complete re-examination of the position as to man-power ; and during December and January con-ferences were in progress between the Minister of National Service (Sir Auckland Geddes) and the groups of trade unions with a view to an agreed revision of the schedules of protected occupations. Between 420,000 and 450,000 additional men were wanted for military service ; and, broadly speaking, the Government proposed to take them largely from the munition shops by cancelling the exemption certificates of the men under 24. The age limits of military service were not as yet extended, but there was to be a thorough comb-out of the workshops ; and since the leaving certificate had now been abolished, the two months' immunity allowed to the man ceasing work on munitions was cancelled.

It is significant that the submission of the national requirements to the trade unions was accompanied by a statement from the Prime Minister on War Aims—necessarily in general rather than in specific terms, but calculated to disarm labour suspicions as to the probable nature of the peace. On the whole, and in the face of considerable reluctance on the part of the trade unions, the Government succeeded in proving the case for the new proposals ; but the Amalgamated Society of Engineers voted heavily against the scheme and stood out from the collective negotiations, claiming separate consideration.

The situation of this Society was peculiar. Its independent attitude rendered it distinctly unpopular with other engineering unions ; while at the same time, for quite other reasons, its national executive was opposed by many of its own members in the districts. The unofficial movement was now again active, and its opposition was increasingly directed towards the general, not merely the industrial policy of the Government. Delegates of Shop Stewards and Workers' Committees meeting at Manchester on December 30th, 1917, declared themselves in favour of an early peace on the Russian model, and decided to oppose further demands of the Government for soldiers. Through the early months of the following year this attitude was repeatedly expressed, and in March an unofficial conference at Sheffield decided in favour of a general strike. Participation of several A.S.E. members and local branches brought upon them a sharp rebuke from the Society :

"In the interest of the Society and organised Labour generally it is necessary for the Executive Council to repudiate emphatically the continuance of the method of certain sections of the membership of the society in arrogating to themselves the right to call unofficial meetings with a view to forcing their policy upon the membership without regard to the constitution of the society or to the constitutional methods provided both locally and centrally for the adjustment of grievances.

, " Such action cannot but have a detrimental effect upon the credit of the society, and, in the opinion of the E.C., it is seriously weakening the prestige of the society in the minds of the public. It must be remembered that the cause for which our comrades are fighting overseas is one which the nation believes to be just, and any action taken by a section of the community which would tend to weaken the nation would be disastrous to the future of the working class movement.

" The war has inevitably had the effect of impeding the freedom of action of the constitutional machinery of Trade Unionism, but it has to be borne in mind that our part, and the part of Labour as a whole, with other sections of the community, has been to make sacrifices. Those sacrifices have been too often ill requited by the Government and the ruling classes ; but, however much Labour has been abused, and its just claims ignored and misrepresented, we are conscious of our duty to the community and to the soldiers, most of whom are men of our class and status."

It will be recalled that the A.S.E. had refused to become a party to the agreement of December, 1917, by which the Engineering Employers recognised the status of the Shop Stewards ; and it must be added that the policy of the Minister of Munitions in facilitating such recognition was severely criticised by certain leaders of trade union as well as of general opinion.

§ 2.

Up to the time of the German offensive there was grave apprehension in many quarters—and indeed fair prospect—of very serious industrial trouble. The sudden threat to the nation in March, 1918, once more restored common sense and a better temper. The response of the workshops in both men and munitions was not least among the determining causes of the final victory.

To appreciate that response it must be premised that between the institution of the schedule of protected occupations in May, 1917, and the end of that year the munition centres had given up nearly 68,000 men for military service. In the three months following the first Military Service Act of 1918, they gave 32,000 more ; following the German offensive, they released 40,000 in five weeks ; and from the second Military Service Act (which extended the age limits to 19 and 50) to the end of June (when the military situation had been saved and the Americans were coming into action), the workshops gave another 32,000 of their youngest and fittest

men : a total of 172,000 in twelve months. Yet
thanks to the continued efforts of labour, including,
be it remembered, the women and girls as well as the
men, the various managements and the Ministry of
Munitions itself, output had continually increased ;
and in reply to the German attack unprecedented
speed and quantity were obtained. Mr. G. A. B.
Dewar, in his graphic review of " The Great Munition
Feat," writes :

> " If we take the production of heavy guns at the figure
> 100 before the German thrust, it stands at 172 in the five
> weeks following March 21st ; very heavy howitzers at 218 ;
> heavy ammunition at 213 ; machine guns at 132 ; small
> arms ammunition at 142 ; hand grenades at 166. So we
> made good. The situation was saved. It was not to the
> credit of labour alone, but labour subjected to the strain of
> three-and-a-half years of monotonous work must be allowed
> a good share of the thanks. Moreover, as to that one-
> fourth of 1 per cent. of time which had been flung away on
> disputes and strikes, it must be remembered that the men
> and women in between fifteen and sixteen hundred firms,
> wherever required and requested, gave up the Easter
> holiday and worked hard instead on munitions. . . . There
> were selfish and passionate outbreaks from time to time.
> There was heavy drinking in 1915. There were sullen
> periods and patches, not only on Clydeside but through the
> industrial districts during later parts of the war. There
> was a revolutionary cult in 1917 and 1918. . . . When
> however, we have resurveyed all these disaffections, and
> gone even into the thousands of tribunal prosecutions
> against individuals under the Munitions of War Acts, the
> broad fact emerges that labour's effort in the war was
> impressive and magnificent. There has been nothing
> resembling it in the history of England. The goods were
> delivered."

CHAPTER II.

————

THE STRANDS ARE PARTED.

§ 1.

At the close of a previous chapter we left the British Labour movement—or its official thinking machinery—making a definite bid for a national and international party of progress and enlightenment. By the books the bid would appear to have succeeded. The War Aims programme had already been approved by the industrial and the political organisations of labour in Britain; in February, 1918, its principles were accepted by delegates from central Labour and Socialist parties of 10 other nations. The United States, Germany, Austria, and Russia, were not associated with the declaration; and it is to be noticed that in the case of the last-named, Lenin indicated thus early that he had no use for such constitutional and moderate Labour parties as were meeting in London, and refused to allow delegates from other sections of Russian Socialism to attend.

Now the official brains of the British Labour party were not unaware that in pursuing this line of national and international policy they were leading the movement towards a wider field than any in which it had yet functioned. If the National

Labour Party were to become a fact as well as a
name, the limitations of the trade union basis and
the trade union outlook would have to be exceeded.
There was much sympathy outside the " working "
class for the programme the Labour men were
putting forward ; and a deliberate attempt was made
to organise the general body of opinion. To this
end a new constitution for the Labour party was
drawn up during the latter part of 1917, and approved
by a special conference on February 26th, 1918.

By the new constitution, in the first place, the
party now became a definitely Socialist organisation,
with this among its aims :

> To secure for the producers by hand or by
> brain the full fruits of their industry, and the
> most equitable distribution thereof that may be
> possible, upon the basis of common ownership
> of the means of production and the best obtain-
> able system of popular administration and
> control of each industry or service.

As regards particulars, that aspiration was modest
and non-committal to a degree ; but it was definitely
Socialist.   In the second place, individual membership of the party was now formally recognised and
provided for, by means of the local branches.   The
representation on the party executive of the various
corporate bodies was retained, but that of the local
branches and of the women was strengthened ; to
the first were allotted 13 places on the executive
committee, to the local branches 5, and to the women
4.   This meant, in effect, that the representatives
of trade unions as such would not have a majority
on the executive ; and it was hoped that the
possibility of over half the members being selected
on other than vocational grounds, would broaden
the character of the party policy and extend its
basis of support in the country.

Concealed in this reorganisation of the party was

an important and final decision. Not merely was political emphasis transferred from vocation to the broad fact of citizenship ; but a definite choice was made as to the means by which the aims of the party were to be realised. The activity of the trade unions, as such, and of the Triple Alliance in the sphere of politics, had ultimate reference to the possibility of direct industrial action. That method was not absolutely discarded by the constitution of the Labour party, but it was decidedly shelved. Industrial action for political ends could only be sanctioned by the party as a whole when the occasion was of so desperate a nature as to convince the general "consumer" and the non-manual worker of its necessity; and occasions of so unmistakeably desperate a character were presumably unlikely to arise. In any such case, the necessity of convincing non-union members of the party would probably postpone the use of force until the general sense of the community had been affected. A party thus constituted was obviously unsuited to achieve a "dictatorship of the proletariat," or any other sort of revolution. But not all of its members nor all of its leaders were as yet alive to the fact. The sharpest pair of eyes was in Moscow.

§ 2.

Having dealt, so far successfully, with the broad issues of the war, the Labour leaders turned their attention to the more domestic issues of the peace ; and a specification of the "New Social Order" was drawn up and adopted by a conference of the party in June, 1918. "The four pillars of the house that we propose to erect," said the Labour party—or (as Mr. Cole puts it) what is much the same, Mr. Sidney Webb—"resting upon the common foundation of the democratic control of society in all its activities, may be termed respectively

    (a) the universal enforcement of the national
        minimum ;

    (b) the democratic control of industry ;

    (c) the revolution in national finance ;

    (d) the surplus wealth for the common good."

On which " four pillars " were to rest, among other items, State prevention, as well as relief, of unemployment ; immediate nationalisation of the cardinal productive and distributive services ; a capital levy to pay off war-debt ; and an extended program of positive social legislation. The abolition of " the individualist system of capitalist production, based on the private ownership and competitive administration of land and capital," and of " the political system and ideas in which it naturally found expression," were frankly desired ; and the party disclaimed " belief in any of the problems of the world being solved by goodwill alone." What it stood for, however, was not force but science, and most especially that typically Fabian hybrid, " social science." But the organisation of the " New Social Order " in industry or politics, and the means by which it was to be attained, were scarcely indicated ; and to some critics it appeared as if the " house that we propose to erect " would stand not upon any firm foundation, common or otherwise, but upon a bridge of which the main piers were somewhat far apart and the middle attenuated.

§ 3.

The changes in the constitution of the Labour party, state Mr. and Mrs. Webb, " led to a considerable accession of membership, largely from the professional and middle classes, which was steadily

increased as the unsatisfactory character of the
Treaty of Peace, the continued militarism of the
Government, and the aggression of a Protectionist
capitalism, became manifest." In the result, the
party secured a considerable infusion of middle-
class brains, especially at headquarters, and tended
increasingly to become a party of the intellectuals.
And it had to encounter some of the difficulties that
such parties have almost invariably encountered
elsewhere, and not seldom been floored by—particularly in Russia. For example: The conservative
"right wing" of the trade union movement has
always been the less vocal, and is therefore, in these
very vocal times, seldom distinctly audible. None
the less, men like Barnes, Roberts, Wardle, Parker,
who declined to relinquish their Ministerial duties
when Labour decided to end the political truce,
represented a mode of thought that persisted, and
persists, among many of the older craft unionists.
The adoption by the party of an extensive nationalising programme was not altogether to the liking
of the conservative elements in its own ranks, and
in face of the advanced social legislation proposed
by the Government a certain amount of defection
probably took place. Then the explicit pacificism
of the Independent Labour party had been virtually
repudiated by the Trade Union Congress, and the
breach with that important body over the war issues
was not to be healed within a few weeks—or even a
few years—of the Armistice. On the extreme left
of the Labour party was the British Socialist party,
with its organ, *The Call*, hoping for a world revolution
to follow the war, " in which the hitherto exploited
and oppressed classes in all countries would seize
the reins of power, overthrow the rule of the capitalist
and landlord classes, establish the direct rule of the
workers and peasants by means of Soviets, and wind
up the capitalist order of society." Such aspirations

became common to many of the unofficial committees
in the latter half of 1918, and their increased pre-
valence was due to a curious concatenation of
events.

In the earlier part of the year the amount of
definite adherence to Bolshevik principles in Britain
was not great, for the dissolution of the Russian
Constituent Assembly, and the terror in Petrograd,
had given pause to many who sympathised with the
first Russian revolution. But the invasion of
Russian territory by the forces of the British and
French Governments on and after August 2nd, 1918,
tended to precipitate British opinion. The Bolsheviks
were now formally alluded to as " the enemy " in
War Office announcements; and although it had
not been possible to declare war upon the *de facto*
government—since that would have implied a
recognition—operations were in fact conducted by
the Allies on every accessible frontier of the former
Empire. The reasons for this policy being of a
purely military nature—part in fact of the general
strategy of the war—neither Parliament nor the
country was required to express an opinion on it;
but the Labour party saw fit to express and reiterate
its most emphatic opinion, and to conduct a vigorous
agitation against the Government. The effect on
the Government policy was absolutely nil—save
perhaps in so far as there was an increase in the
activity of official and unofficial propaganda and of
those various modes which lie so delicately in between.
But the effect on Labour was profound; and it was
one of fate's cruellest ironies that a Government
bent only on winning the war, and meeting with
none too much luck in its latest venture, should thus
indirectly have been made to contribute to the con-
solidation of all the revolutionary elements in
Britain.

Consider the situation. Throughout the early

part of 1918 the greater part of the Labour movement had been watching events in Russia with
sympathetic but puzzled curiosity.   Lenin had been
at particular pains to snub the official British Labour
party, indicating that he did not consider its international activities to maintain the principles of the
" Internationale " and forbidding the more moderate
Russian Socialists to share them.   The ill-judged
attempt of the " United Socialist Council " to copy
the methods of the first (not the second) Russian
Revolutionary Government had been effectively
trounced by public opinion; and even the rank-and-
file movement in the spring of 1918 had declined to
broaden its policy in the direction of general revolution.   But the average Labour leader of 1918 was an
inveterate sentimentalist ; and when military action
against Bolshevik forces became necessary, the
crimes and horrors of Bolshevism were denied or
forgotten, and the Workers' Soviet Republic suddenly
became the much-maligned victim of an international capitalist conspiracy.

It is impossible to exaggerate the influence of this
misrepresentation upon the course of Labour opinion
in Britain.   Had the Russian campaigns succeeded,
or had the authorities surrendered to the opposition,
the effect might have been transient ; but the
Government could count on the support of a vast
majority in Parliament and the press, and the sheer
impotence of the Socialist opposition induced in
some of its leaders a state of mind for which the pace
of official Labour was altogether too slow.   It was
to such minds that Lenin's attitude was decisive.
Bolshevik policy aimed expressly at separating a
class-conscious minority from the central Labour
party in all countries ; and the mere sympathy of the
latter in the war Moscow affected to disdain.   The
only way, therefore, in which that sympathy, however passionately felt, could establish direct con-

nexion with its object was by definite revolutionary organisation ; and it thus came about that, while as a result of allied policy there arose an irrevocable and ever-widening divergence between the entire Labour party and the British Government, as a result of Russian policy there arose a sharper separatist tendency within the Labour party.

The working out of this complex situation as it affected the structure and the program of the party was to be determined largely by political and industrial circumstance. But the possibility was already apparent that when Providence, or the Coalition Government, let loose the full torrent of public opinion, the piers of the Fabian bridge might tend to diverge, and the foundations of the " house that we propose to erect " prove somewhat shaky.

CHAPTER III.

The Broad Highway.

§ 1.

Between the effort of the fighting services and the
effort of the munition shops there was this difference :
in the one case the enemy was materially and
actively present and menacing ; in the other his
reality was known mainly by report and his activity
felt only indirectly.   It was this difference, as much
as any, that resulted in an irascible reaction to periods
of abnormal strain in industry, and in an occasional
failure of the will-to-win among sections of munition
workers.   One could more easily believe in a peace
by negotiation when no resolute German was
" negotiating " day and night with stick bombs or
bullets from some neighbouring hole in the wilderness
of mud.   The difference did not affect the logic of the
general situation ; but it did affect the psychology
of the individual ; and the industrial " unrest " of
the late summer of 1918 was rather psychological
than logical in its nature.   It must be remembered,
too, that while the ordeal of the trenches was incom-
parably more severe and more deadly than that of
the workshops, there were few unfortunates for
whom it was quite as unintermittent.   It was the

cumulative strain of four years that told on the temper of the workmen.

The immediate cause of the engineers' strike of July, 1918, was an order of the Minister of Munitions limiting the numbers of skilled workmen which particular employers and firms might engage ; the ostensible object of the order being to prevent too unequal a distribution of what skilled labour was still available. The effect, however, was similar to a reimposition of the leaving certificate ; and in spite of the opposition of the trade union leaders, engineers in Coventry, Birmingham, and other centres struck work. The dispute was again organised by the shop stewards ; and on July 25th a conference of shop stewards committees at Leeds again called for a general strike against the Government policy. The movement was ended by an official announcement that strikers would be deemed to have " voluntarily placed themselves outside the area of munitions industries " and thus become liable to military service. Work was generally resumed after a six days' stoppage, and the only result was further to discredit the shop stewards movement in public estimation.

A series of industrial disputes followed throughout August and September. To the amazement of the general public, a large body of London police ceased work to secure better pay and conditions (which were generally admitted to be due to them), and the recognition of their union. Lancashire cotton spinners became involved in a dispute with the Cotton Control Board as to the method of spreading the unemployment caused by the reduction of the supplies of raw material. In this dispute also the inadequate advances given to the operatives, especially as compared with the large profits maintained in the industry, were a root cause of the trouble. Still more serious was the dispute over wage advances between the railwaymen and the Executive Committee of the companies, in which the men claimed a 10s. per week advance, and the Executive offered exactly half that amount. The dispute was settled at a meeting of the two trade unions concerned with the War Cabinet, when the Executive's offer was accepted by the leaders, and an arrangement was made for the future automatic regulation of wages in accordance with the cost of living. But so intense was the resentment of certain sections of the rank-and-file that meetings of protest were held throughout the country, and in South Wales and London strike action was threatened. A display of naval and military force by the Government forestalled an actual stoppage of the railways; but it may be noted that this dispute brought into prominence a sharp division of temper among the railwaymen and their leaders, as a result of which J. H. Thomas, who was primarily responsible for the settlement, temporarily resigned the secretaryship of the National Union.

§ 2.

From the historical standpoint, however, the industrial unrest of 1918 is less important than the measures that were taken in regard to the future conduct of industry and society. Apart from emergency arrangements, the year witnessed an important attempt to establish over a wide industrial field some more permanent machinery for regulating the terms and conditions of employment. In the ship-building, cotton, woollen textile, flax, and leather industries, joint bodies were already in existence which it was hoped would continue to deal with general questions of industrial reconstruction after the war; and the principle of joint action by representatives of em-

ployers and employed was further rapidly extended
by the adoption of the scheme recommended in the
Whitley reports. During the year Joint Industrial
Councils were set up in 19 industries. In addition to
these, joint bodies with similar functions, but formed
on an *ad hoc* basis, were set up by the Ministry of
Reconstruction in several of the smaller industries.
Considerable time was necessary to get the various
Councils and Committees in working order ; but
before the fighting ceased, several of them had
embarked on serious attempts at the co-ordination
and stabilisation of wage-rates and conditions of
employment in their industries, and one or two
had evinced an intention of dealing with the more
general objects indicated in their constitution.

The statutory regulation of wages had also been
extended as to minimum rates outside the area of
munitions employment. Under the Corn Production
Act of 1917 an Agricultural Wages Board for England
and Wales was set up on December 3rd, 1917, and
in the following five months 39 District Committees
were established by which legally enforcible rates
were prescribed for adult labour, payable at the age
of 18, varying from 30s. to 36s. for a specified number
of hours per week. For general industry the procedure for the establishment of Trade Boards was
expedited by an Amending Act passed in August,
1918, and the functions of the Boards were
somewhat extended in accordance with a recommendation of the Whitley Committee. With a view
to a wide use of the statutory powers thus obtained,
the Ministry of Labour initiated enquiries during the
latter part of the year into the conditions prevailing
in 26 of the less organised industries. Seeing that
coal-mines, railways, and the bulk of the engineering
trades were now under direct Government control,

the various measures thus outlined were calculated
to lay the foundations of reconstruction over almost
the entire industrial field.

§ 3.

Most fundamental of all enactments of the year
were the two great measures of social reform by which
the worker as citizen, not merely as wage-earner, was
affected.

Though the Franchise Act was but a due acknowledgment of the national service demanded and
received from the men and women of Britain during
the war, its enactment in February, 1918, was a
wise and courageous piece of legislation. In two
respects the new measure bore the mark of the
emergency that brought it to birth; youths of 19
who had served in the war were enfranchised, and
men who had maintained a conscientious objection
were denied the vote for five years unless they could
convince a tribunal that they had undertaken
alternative work of national importance. These,
however, were anomalies that would in time automatically disappear; and in general the Act brought
the basis of British Government within measurable
distance of simple adult franchise. "The more
you trust the majority of the people, the better, I
think, will be your new England," the Prime
Minister had said early in 1917; and in 1918 the
electorate was raised from 8 to 21 millions, the
addition including 6,000,000 women. The size of
the raw electorate thus added made the nature of
its first vote an attractive speculation; and, according
to their various lights, leaders of all parties vigorously
engaged in the task of political education.

For any improvement, however, in the quality of
British representative Government, it was less the

Franchise Act than the Education Act of 1918 that encouraged hope; since the beneficence of the former would in the long run obviously depend upon the efficacy of the latter. The mere extension of the franchise automatically tended to depress, rather than to raise, the level of intelligence displayed in general elections; and while it was a necessary step towards political democracy, there neither was nor ever had been any inherent guarantee that the latter would of itself ensure good or even tolerable government.

"Let us remember (said Mr. Fisher, on the second reading of his Bill) what we have been asking our young citizens to do, and what we intend to ask them to do. We have been asking them to fight and work for their country; we have been asking them, not only to appreciate the force of great political arguments and the significance of grave political emergencies, but to try to turn their appreciation of those arguments and emergencies into acts of renunciation and sacrifice. We have been asking them to die for their country, to economise for their country, to go short of food for their country, to work overtime for their country, to abandon trade union rules for their country, to be patient while towns are bombed from enemy aircraft, and while family after family is plunged into domestic sorrow. We have now decided to enfranchise for the first time the women of this country I ask then whether the education which is given to the great mass of our citizens is adequate to the new, serious and enduring liabilities which the development of this great world-war creates for our Empire, or to the new civic burdens which we are imposing upon millions of them. I say it is not adequate.

Any competent judge of facts in this country must agree with me."

The general sense of Parliament and of the country was undoubtedly in agreement with Mr. Fisher ; for the pre-war standard of education, inadequate as it was, had been rendered still lower during the war by the curtailment of even the normal minimum of schooling in several thousand cases. In this respect the Education Act had an important bearing on the industrial situation. There were at work by October, 1917, mostly in the munition trades, some 93,000 more boys and 258,000 more girls under 18 than were employed in July, 1914. A difficult problem of juvenile unemployment was therefore to be expected on the cessation of hostilities. Many of the girls might return to domestic life ; but for the boys the problem was rendered the more serious by the large proportion employed in " blind alley " occupations. At the age of 16-17 the boys were frequently discharged and replaced by children of 13-14, whom employers found equally suitable to repetition work and more amenable to discipline in the workshops. The older boys, having acquired no special skill, none the less demanded high wages in view of their previous earnings on piece-work ; and being liable to military service on reaching 18, they frequently spent twelve months or so out of work, with results detrimental alike to training and character. In view of these facts steps were taken during the latter part of 1917 to reduce the number of boys employed on repetition work ; and a recurrence of the difficulty was to some extent guarded against by the abolition under the Education Act of all exemption from school attendance below the age of 14, and by the power given to local authorities to raise the compulsory age of attendance to 15. Similarly the proposal to enforce at least 280 hours continued education per year on children of from 14 to 16 would tend not only to raise the level of ability, but to retard the future exploitation of juvenile labour. Among other provisions of the Education Act were the prohibition of all employment of children under 12, and strict limitation set upon the employment of children of from 12 to 14. The enabling provisions of the Act empowered local authorities to provide physical training centres, holiday camps, and nursery schools for children of from 2 to 5. A very large part in fact of the benefit obtainable under the Act was dependent on the initiative of the local authorities ; and an increased incentive was thereby given to the activity of the Labour party in the sphere of local politics.

Some allusion must be made, before quitting the subject of education, to the views of Labour as to the ideal curriculum. Official Labour policy (in strong contrast to the attitude of most working-class parents) was opposed to any specialisation before the last year of the secondary school course ; and arising from this liberal attitude, sharp opposition was manifested to the recognition of works schools as centres of continued education under the Government scheme. Schools maintained by employers, the Labour party argued, must necessarily tend to the diffusion of a " capitalist " point of view, and to the training, primarily, of wage-earners. In practical comment on this contention it was perhaps irrelevant to point out that some of the works schools attained a very high standard of efficiency ; but it was relevant that, although working for the most part on general lines, by the very fact of their connexion with employment they frequently secured a much higher degree of interest and attention from their students than the independent centres. It is in this latter respect that continued education of children of from 15 upwards has come so near failure ; and it may be argued that the Labour objection to specialisation, whether or no connected with the actual sphere of employment, has yet to overcome this difficult question of maintaining the interest of children through the intermediate years.

Among the extreme Socialist sections of the Labour movement it is held that all education, juvenile or adult, whether under State or private supervision, in the existing state of society, tends of necessity to a bias in favour of the " capitalist " order; and, in both adult and juvenile spheres, efforts have therefore been made to educate with a compensatory bias. The Central Labour College, maintained jointly by the Miners' Federation and the National Union of Railwaymen, is " based upon the recognition of the antagonism of interests between capital and labour " ; and it exists to provide working-class students with

> " the training necessary to equip workers to propagate and defend the interests of their class against the dominant ruling class ideas and theories prevalent in capitalist society."

Other industrial organisations, more especially the Iron and Steel Trades Confederation, have taken steps in recent years to secure for their members facilities for adult education, and the Workers' Educational Association and the University Tutorial Movement have achieved valuable results in organising and meeting the demand of the workers for fuller education. The Central Labour College is, however, unique in circumscribing the culture of the workers by the limitations of Karl Marx, and its endeavours have met with considerable success among the miners.

On the Clyde, in Sheffield, Manchester, Coventry, and some other strongholds of extreme opinion, efforts have also been made to inculcate socialist doctrine in the children by means of Sunday schools. The lay Sunday school is very far from being a novelty, and the recent excitement of the Conservative press anent the discovery of this development was somewhat overdone. The nature of the teaching given in some of these centres may perhaps be judged from the following extract from a lesson on " Communism for Children " (*Workers' Dreadnought*, March 12th, 1921) :

> 1. (Under Communism) the land will belong to everybody . . Everybody will be able to grow food on the land There is enough land in the British Isles to feed all the people on them. So everybody will have food.
> 2. All the buildings on the land will belong to everybody. . . . Everybody will then have a house to live in.
> 3. The railways, the canals, the docks—everything will belong to the people.
> 4. Everything will be free. Therefore there will be no money to be paid as wages. Nobody will want wages when they can have all they need for nothing. There will be no rent, no rates, no taxes, no profits.

This is preceded by a brief rehearsal of the fact that while a factory hand may make £20 worth of boots in a week, he may only get £2 a week in wages.

> The £18 left over after paying the workman is called profit It is used to pay rent for the factory, to pay taxes and rates, and to be divided amongst the people who form the Company.

*   *   *

In December, 1920, the Government, in the interests of national economy, decided on an indefinite postponement of the operation of the Continued Education clauses of the Fisher Act.

CHAPTER IV.

"Look Now Upon This Picture."

No similar period of modern history can show such drastic changes in the condition of Britain as were wrought in succession by the past four years of war and three of peace. Likely enough, when the generation that wrestled with the fate of Europe has told the tale of its bitter days to the end, the legend of the Britain it knew in war-time will be lost in the gloomy palimpsest of three years later. It is worth while pausing therefore at the point of victory for a brief survey of the general war-state of the country; the more so as such a survey may perhaps disclose the broad lines of its inevitable sequel.

To begin with, the very landscape was changed. Not only had the great army camps developed miniature cities, with well-laid roads and railway sidings, on spaces of field and moorland throughout England; but new towns had grown up about the national munitions factories with acres of timber and concrete housing, and in some cases well-built cottages planned on garden city lines. In and about the existing industrial centres also, armament works had been vastly extended by state subsidy, and new dwellings for workpeople erected. Taking it as a whole, what was left of the civil population had undergone a thorough "urbanisation": to such an extent, in fact, that it had been necessary to form special quasi-military corps of volunteer workers, largely women, for work on agriculture and the countryside. The extent of the redistribution of the men is perhaps sufficiently indicated by the statement that by the date of the Armistice, out of every 100 men employed in civil life on the outbreak of war, 41 were in the fighting services, and 29 on war-work of various descriptions ; leaving the diminished volume of ordinary business to be carried on by about 30 per cent., with the aid of any additional labour that could be utilised, plus the women. The magnitude of this change, and the introduction of additional labour, is clearly shown if it be expressed in round numbers. During the period of the war some $5\frac{1}{2}$ million men were enlisted in the fighting services ; but the total number of men actually employed in the country was reduced by rather less than $2\frac{1}{2}$ million, while the number of women so employed increased by over $1\frac{1}{2}$ million. In all it is estimated that there were about $7\frac{1}{2}$ million women occupied at the date of the Armistice, of which number over three million were in industry and transport, and some 61,000 in the various war-services. Of all the women employed, nearly two million were replacing men ; and more than half the replacement was in industry and transport. In the munition trades between 700,000 and 800,000 women were at work out of a total of about two million persons. The children, too, had been mobilised for industry, the numbers of boys and girls at work having risen since July, 1914, by 13 and 73 per cent. respectively. In the metal trades over $1\frac{3}{4}$ times the number of boys, and over $2\frac{1}{2}$ times the number of girls, were employed at the date of the Armistice, while in the chemical industries the increases were not much lower, though part of the expansion represents a corresponding loss to peace-trades.

The herding movement had entailed migration from their scattered homes of many thousand men, women, and children ; and in the armament centres, despite all that private and State enterprise could do, was such congestion as only the absence of leisure rendered tolerable. Day and night workers were sleeping turn about in beds that scarce grew cold between them. Every cottage in the great centres had its male or female lodgers, while large numbers of the women, married and single, whose lives were spent in housekeeping before the war, had joined the army of munition-makers. To some extent, more especially for the women, hostel accommodation had been provided, in which a very high standard of communal living was attained ; while within the larger factories excellent canteen arrangements had been made by or with the assist-ance of the responsible Ministry, and in the new workshops a model standard of light, ventilation, cleanliness, and safety was established. To the general well-being of munition workers special attention was devoted by the Ministry of Munitions, and the work of the Health of Munition Workers' Committee laid the beginning of a general and permanent improvement in the conditions of employ-ment. During the early years of the war practically all limits to the hours of labour, including the provisions of the Factory Acts, had been suspended ; but from the summer of 1917 a general revision set in ; women and children were employed on 8-hour shifts wherever possible, and Sunday labour was officially discouraged.

" The feeding of the industrial worker (stated the Committee above referred to) and the necessity of sufficient rest were in former times largely ignored. The employer assumed that such matters lay outside his purview, forgetting that the underfed and unrested workman is a

wasteful worker, unable when at work to yield
his value in wages, and too often on the sick
list. . . . There is a natural rhythm between
activity and rest, and if this principle be ignored
and work continued for too long hours or with
insufficient rest pauses, output declines and the
worker degenerates."

Accordingly the scientific study and mitigation of
industrial fatigue were undertaken, and the sphere
of the welfare officer extended beyond the limits of
the workshop over as many aspects of the life
of the woman worker as time and tact made possible.
And the success of the welfare officers of the great
factories was in fact a signal tribute both to the
knowledge and sympathy of those appointed and
to the selective skill of the various officials and
managements who appointed them.

But granted the utmost goodwill and the most
enlightened management there were certain secondary results of the herding process that could not be
avoided. To some of its effects upon working-class
opinion we have already alluded ; but there were
other psychological consequences to which the
women in particular were liable. For them the
general migration out of their natural environment
meant more than to the men. It involved as a rule
greater sacrifice, greater inconvenience, and greater
risk, and not even the finest welfare work could
altogether counteract the disadvantages. It needs
no showing at this date that the women made good,
and more than made good ; the war could hardly
have been won without them. On more than 500
processes in the munition shops, the filling factories,
and the shipyards, they proved their capacity.
Granted reasonable skill in selection and care in
supervision, they succeeded in work of the most
delicate and accurate character ; while for light
repetition piece-work they were considered by many

employers more suitable than men. To their tenacity, their courage, and their patriotism no record can pay too high a tribute. And while it is necessary to limit the inferences that can be drawn from their success, the recognition of that success need never be stinted.

It is necessary in the first place to remember that the major part of the women's success was made possible only by the minute sub-division of processes, and the extreme specialisation of plant and skill ; these in their turn being rendered economical only by the magnitude and the continuity of production. On a smaller scale, as the A.S.E. pointed out, it might be found that such methods would not pay, and that therefore there would no longer be the same wide field after the war for the employment of women on repetition work. Apart, however, from the financial point of view, and in the long run more important, is the effect of such extreme specialisation on the worker. Munition work saw the closest correlation between the machine and the human being that industry had yet achieved ; and the human being in the majority of cases was a woman. Up to a point there is no harm in the connexion ; but the safety point was necessarily passed when girls were working over 60 hours a week. Such work so continuously pursued is not merely deadening in its psychological effect. The insufficiency of mental interest is apt to demand abnormal compensation in the intervals, and the rational regulation of elementary impulse tends to be impaired by the constant circumscription of the intellect. Monotony in the workshops is twin brother of irresponsibility outside ; it may eventually appear that more harm than gain accrues from extreme specialisation of process and occupation unless it be accompanied by a most drastic curtailment of the hours of labour. Moreover, in the present stage of

society, the herding together of large numbers of
women tends always, except where counteracted by
a strong degree of precedent training and tradition,
to deterioration. If therefore the great munition
centres witnessed some modification of the conven-
tional standards of feminine manners and morality,
it is not necessary to impute more than the usual
degree of original sin to the exponents of the change.
That was part of the appointed price of war.

There was a further item. The sub-division of
processes in the munition shops enabled the very
children to earn adult wages on piece-work ; and
far larger numbers of boys and girls accordingly
dropped all attempt at training to become " a kind
of precocious labourer." Physique, intelligence, and
character alike suffered. " The increase in the
employment of children and young persons in
munition work or otherwise," wrote Sir George
Newman, " has demonstrated beyond all question
or doubt that many boys and girls are being spoilt
mentally, physically and morally "

" Parental control (stated the Committee on
Juvenile Employment) has been relaxed, largely
through the absence of fathers from their homes.
. . . Even the ordinary discipline of the workshop has in a varying degree given way, while the
withdrawal of influences making for the social
improvement of boys and girls has in many
districts been followed by a noticeable deterioration in behaviour and morality. Gambling has
increased. Excessive hours of strenuous labour
have overtaxed the energies of young people,
while many have taken advantage of the extraordinary demand for juvenile labour to change
even more rapidly from one blind alley employment to another."

Thus was the war adding to the future problem of
unemployment ; thus were developing the youths

who were to figure in the street riots of two or three years later. This also was part of the price of the liberty of Europe.

The general course of wages during the war is almost impossible to summarise, and average estimates are liable to wide variation. In general the time-rates (distinct from earnings) of wage-earners as a whole may be taken to have increased by between 100 and 110 per cent.; and in the engineering and shipbuilding trades the total increases ranged from about 91 to 98 per cent. for the highly skilled grades to 154 or 156 per cent. for labourers, with a general average rather less than half-way. In these trades the increase of women's wage-rates was not less than 150 per cent., reckoning the general pre-war wage at 15s. The difference between wage-rates and earnings is well illustrated in the following average returns relative to over 18,000 workers in 45 National Shell and Projectile Factories for April 1918 :

		Shell Factories.						Projectile Factories.					
		Rates.			Earnings.			Rates.			Earnings.		
		£	s.	d.	£	s.	d.	£	s.	d.	£.	s.	d.
Male average	...	2	19	3	4	6	6	2	19	1	4	14	8
Highest	...	4	16	6	6	13	4	5	5	10	6	12	7
Female average	...	1	12	8	2	2	4	1	14	8	2	16	8
Highest	...	2	2	1	2	10	10	2	9	8	3	4	2

Much has been made of the rise in the actual standard of living of the working classes that resulted from the war earnings ; but the improvement was of a somewhat limited nature and needs careful consideration. If a better standard of living be taken to include an increase of leisure and an improvement in accommodation, it must be recalled that for the vast majority of munition workers these prime desiderata were out of the question, no matter what money was brought into the family. A great and fundamental improvement would certainly have

resulted had the conditions of housing and employment remained normal ; but as it was, much of the
extra money was almost of necessity dissipated in
non-essential expenditure, and the sight of it simply
encouraged a hope that after the war, when industry
had settled down again, the workers might be able
to maintain better homes, and get better meals, and
better clothes, and better furniture.   Some of them
saved, no doubt ; many bought War Loan ; many,
too, spent part of their earnings on goods of some
permanent value.   But the broad result of the whole
experience was not so much an improvement in the
standard of living as the hope of it, and the determination to secure it, after the war.   If in the meantime expenditure was often prodigal, and sometimes
foolish, the circumstances of their case go far to
excuse the munition-workers ; and censure comes
with an ill grace from classes who never worked as
hard, or spent as little.   But in considering the later
history, these two psychological factors must be
borne in mind : namely, the widespread habit of
ill-considered expenditure, and the hope of a permanent advance in the standard of living—which
in too many cases was understood to be precisely
the same thing.   .

Evidently,   therefore,   apart from industrial or
political matters strictly so called, two things would
be urgently and immediately necessary to redeem
the future of the workers—houses and education.
During 1918 the Government had made provision
for both ; but only the wildest optimist would have
expected to find the way easy.   On the one hand,
any provision that could be made was dependent on
the financial situation of the country, that again
very largely on the handling of the peace negotiations
and on general policy—both matters of violent
contention   On the other hand, the exigencies of
the war had stimulated the expression of crude mass

impulse, thereby rendering a peaceful and gradual solution of difficult national problems less easy ; and it was doubtful whether the leaders of any political party—save one—would be able to disregard the attractions of an appeal to the war temper in favour of the remoter ends of policy. The physical ordeal was over. The spiritual ordeal was about to begin.

PART FOUR.

FROM JANUARY, 1919, TO THE SETTLEMENT OF THE MINERS' DISPUTE, JULY, 1921.

	1919.
Coal Industry Commission Act	Feb. 26
National Industrial Conference	Feb. 27
Ministry of Transport established ...	
Restoration of Pre-War Practices Act	
Coal Mines Act (reducing hours of employ- ment)	Aug. 15
Trades Union Congress	Sept. 8-13
Ironmoulders' Strike begins	Sept. 22
Railway Strike ... ...Sept. 27 to	Oct. 5
Industrial Courts Act	Nov. 20
Special Trades Union Congress	Dec. 9-10
Railway Wages Board set up	Dec. 30
	1920.
Ironmoulders' Strike settled	Jan. 12
Manchester Building Guild formed ...	Jan. 20
Transport Workers' Inquiry begun ...	Jan. 22
Trades Union Congress on Nationalisation	Mar. 10
" Dockers' Report " published	Mar. 31
Miners' Conference (2s. wage demand) ...	July 7
Unemployment Insurance Act... ...	
Council of Action formed	Aug. 9

CHAPTER I.

Vox Populi.

The "great munition feat" was ended. For four years industry, organised for war, had achieved what in time of peace it had found impossible—the abolition of unemployment, maximum production, effective State supervision of health and welfare, a statutory living wage for all engaged in the national service, and a practical unity of purpose from top to bottom. From the single task of winning the war the country had now to turn to the far more complex task of salvage and resettlement ; a task in which patience, fortitude, wisdom and sincerity could alone avail.

§ 1.

The termination of hostilities found organised labour in the strongest position it had ever attained in the community. "A century ago," says Mr. Beer,* " the working classes, treated as helots, were forbidden to volunteer ; in the years 1915-1918 the representatives of Labour were Cabinet Ministers, members of the Government, official envoys, and Controllers of the nation's food." Time after time

---

* *History of British Socialism,* Vol. II.

the trade unions had entered into agreements direct with the Government, had been consulted upon proposed legislation, had been called to assist in administration. They had in fact established a claim to represent organised labour which had in some degree competed with the claim of Parliament to represent the community in general ; and by its adoption of the Whitley Report the Government had acknowledged the importance of the unions to reconstruction of industry. In numerical strength the Trade Unions had increased between 1914 and 1918 from roughly four-and-a-fifth to over six-and-a-half million members; that is, from 30 to 50 per cent. of the total of employed workpeople. Among the clerks, especially those of the railways and the Civil Service, among the teachers, among the shop assistants, in agriculture and sea-transport, among the women, and in the occupations classed as general labour, increases ranging from 30 to 400 per cent. on the 1914 membership had taken place. Concurrently, the efficiency of organisation had improved, and the policy of centralised control had resulted in important rearrangements. New and highly interesting forms of national federation or close unity had been brought about during the war-period in the building trades, the iron and steel trades, the foundry trades, the boiler-making and shipbuilding trades, the textile trades, the Post Office societies, and general labour. All these new centralisations, like those already existing among the railwaymen, the transport workers and the miners, were more or less based on the principle of industrial unionism ; and as such they have their significance in policy, since by modern Socialist theory the industrial union is not only the most efficient instrument of direct action, but a necessary basis of industrial democracy. How far this increase in the corporate organisation of the workers had engendered a consciousness of political solidarity, events were soon to reveal.

§ 2.

The decision of the Coalition Government to go to the country in December, 1918, was on the face of it logical enough. Originally elected in 1910, the War Parliament had extended its own life no less than five times, and for five years even by-elections had been uncontested. The existing House of Commons, it was argued, was out of touch with the old electorate, let alone with the 'new. And from the point of view of the Coalition, no such favourable opportunity for a general election could be expected to recur. Outside the Coalition both Tory and Radical groups protested. The notice given was too short ; the soldiers were not home, and in spite of the postal vote large numbers of them would probably be disfranchised ; the Government—this, if you please, from both the Labour press and Mr. Bottomley—was engineering a "spoof election," trying to get a "blank cheque" on the strength of the military victory. Asquithian Liberals and official Labour cut adrift from the political truce ; the Coalition, formerly a pact, became a party.

The election campaign may fairly be described as feverish. The Government program—efficient de-mobilisation, encouragement of industry, health and housing schemes, national electricity supply, and (according to Mr. Churchill) nationalisation of the railways—was somewhat broadly sketched, accompanied by a vigorous and somewhat indiscriminate attack on any and every interest that could be called "Socialist," and reinforced at the eleventh hour by the prospect of "hanging the Kaiser," and

" making Germany pay." The Labour Press remained bitter and implacable—to the grave concern of even the Unionist *Observer*, which, taking a Coalition victory for granted, found cause for serious apprehension in the prospective dissociation of Labour from post-war reconstruction policy. Socialist opinion viewed the issue as a straight fight between Capitalism and Labour, and pitched its voice in an appropriate key. On the extreme left was vague talk of revolution, of " the complete destruction of the existing economic and political machinery " (*Workers' Dreadnought*), " rooting out of capitalism and the classes " (*Solidarity*), " rallying to the red flag " (*The Call*), and so forth. More warmth than light, doubtless ; but there was, in fact, as Mr. Lloyd George reminded the country, a decidedly revolutionary element for which, small as it was, accommodation could but with difficulty be secured inside the four walls of " the house that we propose to erect."

The official Labour program suffered in fact from the disease of compromise, and the strongest appeals for unity within the party were necessary to secure a united front in the " Great Labour Offensive."

361 Labour candidates of various political complexions took the field ; 63 were returned to lead His Majesty's Opposition. The Coalition victory passed all expectations. Labour's " Great Offensive " was broken : the left-wing leaders, Snowden, Macdonald, Jowett, and even the moderate Henderson, were unseated, along with the Liberal Premier of 1914. In leadership of any sort in fact the new Labour group was weaker than its predecessor in the House of Commons, though stronger than any other section of His Majesty's Opposition. The prospect of any alternative Government, Labour or other, was thus indefinitely postponed ; and the advocates of political as against industrial action

in the Labour world passed under a cloud which was soon to rain disaster.

It was alleged on behalf of both defeated parties that the tactics of their opponents gave them less than a fair chance in the election of 1918 ; that in fact the victory was secured by methods that were barely admissible in honest politics. The mentality, however, from which such argument proceeds is out of date in the twentieth century. There have been, it is true, phases of British history in which the duties of a Government have been regarded as partly tutelary in character ; but the steady progress of democracy has left those periods long behind. No practical politician would now maintain that a Government is under any obligation to take the masses of the modern electorate otherwise than as it finds them—particularly when its prospects might perhaps be impaired by so doing ; or that there are any limits of dignity and decorum within which merely abstract principles confine the pursuit of political expediency The fine art of politics requires that the leaders of parties as well as nations shall emulate, if possible excel, the success with which popular favour is solicited by the press, the music-hall, the cinema, and the patent medicine ; since failure in that respect might imperil the security of established persons, parties, or even institutions. The election of 1918 was therefore a perfectly fair election ; and the Labour party had no logical ground for protest, least of all protest of an " unconstitutional " character. Unfortunately—but inevitably—there were sections that failed to view the matter in such a reasonable light ; among whom there existed a pent-up antagonism, not of opinion merely, but of sentiment and even passion, to the governing body of the country.

§ 3.

For aspirants to revolution, " bloody " or otherwise, the choice of means seemed to have come to a
head in December, 1918. In reality, as the sequel
was to show, neither the vote nor the strike were
entirely satisfactory weapons ; both were unreliable,
on occasion treacherous ; but the patent failure of
the one was naturally and inevitably followed by a
reaction in favour of the other.

A fortnight before the election there occurred a
minor incident which seemed to constitute an object-
lesson. A Labour demonstration had been arranged
to take place in the Albert Hall, but a few days
beforehand the hire of the hall was cancelled by the
directors on the score of the alleged objectionable
character of the resolutions proposed for endorsement. Other political parties, however, had used
the Hall, and the workers cordially resented the
distinction. By way, therefore, of demonstrating
the value of Labour to a community desirous of
enlightenment, the electricians suddenly removed
the fuses, and quitted the building. Expostulation,
negotiation, and a hasty appeal from the directors
to Downing Street failed to get them back again.
In the event the demonstration was held, and the
victory celebrated in the Labour press as symbolic
of the coming bloodless revolution. When a fortnight later the vote was tried and found most
sadly wanting, the lesson was duly noted.

With the new year there began a period of industrial warfare unequalled in the history of British
labour. The 1919 total of disputes had once, in
1913, been passed ; that for 1920 not at all ; while
in respect of the number of workpeople affected,
both years exceeded all previous record. 1919
opened with a series of strikes that dislocated entire

sections of the community.   Shipyard and engineering workers claiming a shorter working week backed
their case by direct action over the north of England,
the Clyde Valley, and Belfast.   In the Irish city
municipal employees struck in support of the demand.
Gas and electricity supply ceased, and mills and
factories were brought to a standstill, along with the
city bakeries and the tramway system.   In Glasgow
the movement for a general stoppage culminated in
an attempt to cut off the power supply, followed by
a general fracas in the city square with overturning
of tramcars, smashing of shop windows, mounted
police charges, sundry arrests, and reading of the
Riot Act.   Delegates from the Clyde strike committee urged a conference of London engineers to
compel the Government to come to terms in Glasgow
by taking sympathetic action ; and a general strike
was accordingly announced by the Electrical Trades
Union to commence on February 6th.   The threat was
parried by the Government with a new regulation
under the Defence of the Realm Act, and little
more was heard of it ; the Clyde venture also col-
lapsed in mid-February.   But in the meantime
London had its own experience of direct action in the
sudden stoppage of the Tube railway system early
in February by a dispute as to motor-men's meal-
times.   150,000 Yorkshire miners struck work over
a dispute of which the ostensible cause was equally
fundamental.   Welsh electricians left the shops
over a proposed standardisation of wage-rates ;
serious trouble was threatening among the Metro-
politan police ; each of the constituent bodies of the
Triple Alliance was pressing a national program—
the miners to the point of a strike ballot ; while
demonstrations and riots both of service and of ex-
service men created a certain liveliness in Whitehall
and Westminster.   The little drama of the Albert
Hall was, in fact, being rehearsed on a wider stage ;
and the *dénouement* was still to come.

CHAPTER II.

VIA MEDIA.

§ 1.

To measure the importance of a dispute by the amount of inconvenience it entails on the public is a plausible but fallacious proceeding. To several of the strikes of 1919 first-rate individual importance need not be attached. Apart from the mere reaction to the discipline of the war-period, they are to be regarded rather as manifestations, on the first opportunity, of a new self-consciousness in the essential services, to which the sense of responsibility had still to be added, than as the abortive stirrings of revolution—this in spite of the fact that their technique owed something to the continental tradition of industrial violence. But of the industrial unrest as a whole the significance was profound. It indicated in the first place that only the paramount necessity of avoiding national defeat by a foreign power had been holding the country together in a semblance of unity. The military truce in Europe was the signal for the instant termination of the social truce in England. Disruptive forces came into operation with accumulated and irresponsible violence, and it could no longer be maintained that communal or national consciousness was predominant over group or class feeling.

The outbreak of 1919 may also be regarded as the culmination of the unofficial movement of the two preceding years within the trade unions. The national executives had become ever more and more distrusted as the exigencies of the military situation impelled them to fresh concessions to the Government. The shop stewards movement had focussed much of the revolutionary feeling stimulated by events in Russia ; and when the prospect of successful political action was finally disposed of by the election results of 1918, it was to the unofficial leaders that many of the men looked for a vigorous policy. Moreover, the appearance of a united front given to the Labour movement by the national program of 1918 was in fact fallacious, and the occasion for it seemed to have passed. The Fabian panopticon was not at all the kind of house that some sections of the workers proposed to erect, and the method of slowly adding brick to brick was not suited to their temper. What was necessary, said the Socialist left wing, was in the first place to clear the site ; and the old political as well as the industrial structure was marked for demolition. It is, of course, not uncommon in such cases for the demolition and the subsequent reconstruction processes to be undertaken by different contractors.

Especially significant in this connexion is the emergence of the Triple Alliance in the sphere of general policy. Almost from its inception the influence of the Alliance had been directed to matters —Industrial Conscription and the Capital Levy for example—in which the Labour movement as a whole was concerned ; and the mere existence of so large a fighting organisation tended to turn the heads of the more impetuous trade unionists towards direct action in the political sphere. In fact, the power of the Alliance was closely circumscribed by its own constitution and very cautiously invoked by its own leaders. But it stood none the less for the ultimate resort to force, and, like all fighting weapons, it served to stimulate the energies of those to whom force was inherently attractive.

Apart from the more psychological sources of the Labour unrest of 1919, some of its more immediate causes were indicated in a speech of the Minister of Labour (Sir Robert Horne) on February 27th, 1919 :

"We are emerging from a great conflict, which has left to this country, nay, to the whole world, tasks of a magnitude and complexity sufficient to test the whole resources of our civilisation. We have got to make a great change over from the problems of war to the problems of peace. Hundreds of thousands of people who have been devoting themselves for the past four years to the production of war material have now to find jobs in making articles of commerce. Millions of demobilised sailors and soldiers have got to be re-absorbed into the life of the industrial community. There is less employment, and there is a fear of greater unemployment ; there is a higher cost of living, and there is doubt with regard to the dwindling of wages ; there is a certain weariness of work after the strain of war, and a desire for rest ; there is a lack of enterprise and a hesitation to adventure ; and combined with all these factors there are fresh aspirations kindled in men's breasts by the power of war and a new sense of the value of the human spirit, which demand for the toilers better conditions of life and more adequate opportunities of leisure."

§ 2.

The audience to which Sir Robert Horne addressed

himself was a remarkable one. The Government, faced with a labour situation of increasing danger, had summoned a General Conference of employers' associations, trade unions and industrial councils, to give it "the best of their advice and assistance" as to "the root causes of these troubles." The Conference having heard Sir Robert and the Prime Minister appointed a joint committee of 60 members to consider certain detailed aspects of the situation ; and the report of this committee, adopted by the full Conference on April 4th, was forwarded to the Prime Minister. If the Government, as Lord Askwith averred, lacked a labour policy, the Industrial Conference hereby offered it a substantial instalment, of which the following were the leading items :

(1) The legal enforcement of a maximum working week of 48 hours for all employed persons, with certain exceptions.

(2) The establishment by legal enactment of minimum time-rates of wages, such rates to be universally applicable.

(3) The extension of State provision for both unemployment and under-employment.

(4) The establishment of a permanent national Industrial Advisory Council of 400 members.

It will be convenient from this starting point to trace the main lines of subsequent Government policy. In so doing, the general basis of that policy, as indicated at the close of 1918 by both the Minister of Labour and the Minister of Munitions must be borne constantly in mind.

Mr. Churchill four days before the Armistice had told a meeting of representative employers : " I am very anxious for you to realise that, although it will undoubtedly be necessary for some time to come for the Government of this country to intervene in industry, and to control and regulate aspects of industry . . . our only object is to liberate the forces of individual enterprise, to release the controls which have been found galling, to divest ourselves of responsibilities which the State has only accepted in this perilous emergency, and from which, in the overwhelming majority of cases, it had been far better to keep itself clear." The policy of " getting-out " was thus early clearly foreshadowed ; and in the succeeding years it was followed with a certain tenacity, and in spite of a good deal of opposition.

In fairness, the Government must be credited with having already provided, by the end of 1918, a good deal of machinery by which it was hoped industry would be able to take over an increasing share of the State responsibility. 20 Whitley Councils and 21 Interim Industrial Reconstruction Committees had been set going, with every encouragement to manage their own affairs ; joint machinery had been extended in the coal industry, and Pit Committees established by the Act of 1918 ; Joint Boards were in existence on the railways ; National and District Maritime Boards had been established during 1917 by the Ministry of Shipping ; National Wages Boards and District Committees in agriculture had been set up under the Corn Production Act of the same year ; and a considerable increase in the number of Trade Boards was being prepared for as a result of the Trade Boards Amendment Act of August, 1918. Joint Control Boards were at work in the woollen, cotton, flax, and leather industries ; and a host of Local Advisory Committees had been called into existence throughout the country to assist the Employment Exchanges in securing work for men discharged from the Army, and in co-ordinating the supply and demand for labour through the difficult period of resettlement.

§ 3.

It was perhaps to be expected that the process of demobilising several millions of men and women from the fighting and munitions services would not be entirely unattended with difficulties, no matter how much allowance were made for that irrational factor—the individual soldier in a hurry to get home. If, however, the best-laid plans of Ministers and men went somewhat awry it was not because they were altogether unsound. The prospect of dumping several million men in industry at a time when there would be dislocation enough and to spare from other causes was certainly forbidding ; and the first Government scheme was to regulate such demobilisation as the military situation warranted by the absorbent capacity of industry. Individuals were selected for demobilisation according as they were needed to assist in demobilising the rest, or were " pivotal " to trade and industry, while Local Advisory Committees and Employment Exchanges acted as channels by which definite offers of work for individuals were communicated and the men concerned given priority. But a certain amount of trouble, aggravated by extremist agitation as well as by minor difficulties of transport and allocation affecting the men on leave, resulted in the supersession of the original Government plan, at the risk of increased unemployment, by a looser scheme of demobilisation based on the grouping of men by age and length of service. Under the new arrangement over three and a-half million men had been released within twelve months of the Armistice. At the same time the demobilisation of munition workers was being dealt with ; the problem in this case being mitigated to some extent by the mainten-

ance of work on standard orders or on other pro-
ducts for which armament machinery could be
adapted, and by curtailment of the hours of labour.
To displaced munition workers special unemployment donation was made payable for a maximum of
13 weeks in the following 6 months, at the rate of
29s. per week for men and 25s. for women, with
additional allowances for children. For ex-soldiers
below commissioned rank the periods of relief were
doubled. These donations were adversely criticised
later in the year as tending to modify the willingness
of those in receipt of them to accept work ; but in
view of the distress that might have fallen upon
folk who of all others deserved well of the country,
and of the liberal scale on which munitions expenditure had been conducted without any such popular
criticism, the Government policy was on the whole
the only fair course to follow. In so far as it gave
the workers some little power of resisting the inherent
tendency of the situation towards the re-establish-
ment of depressed conditions of employment it
might be unpopular but was not necessarily unsound.

On the constructive side of its policy, for which
the Ministry of Labour was mainly responsible, the
Government showed both energy and enterprise.
Foremost among the problems to be dealt with were
the training and placing of untrained, partly trained,
and disabled men. For this purpose the industrial
training arrangements made by the Ministry of
Munitions and the technical training schemes of the
Ministry of Pensions were developed, and new State
instructional factories organised up to a total of 59
by the end of 1920. By these arrangements, 45,600
men, the majority more or less disabled, had been
trained, and 23,600 more were in training at June
30th, 1921. By way of ensuring subsequent
work for such men a King's Roll of employers
undertaking to find places for the disabled up to at

least 5 per cent. of their establishment was compiled. On this Roll, in addition to some 26,800 employers by June 30th, 1921, were entered all Government departments and industrial establishments, and both Houses of Parliament; 293,518 disabled men were thus guaranteed employment. At the same time arrangements for the completion of interrupted apprenticeships were made in the principal industries with the assistance of advisory committees of employers and trade union representatives, the general basis of such schemes being an agreed scale of progressive remuneration for the apprentice, with the State paying a decreasing maintenance allowance until the adult standard wage was payable on the completion of training. 44,343 ex-service apprentices had been accepted for training by private employers up to the end of June, 1921. For officers and men of higher educational attainments financial assistance was given in University, professional or business training, and large numbers of such found the possibility of residence at a University among the unexpected consequences of the war. Other grants to meet the civil liabilities of ex-service men, or to enable a start to be made in business life, were paid to the extent of some £3,000,000. All these arrangements of course were liable to minor abuse here and there, and in several respects they involved entirely novel methods of administration that acted none too perfectly. On the whole, however, they represent a very creditable State effort to grapple with a very formidable problem, and as regards their main objects—the mitigation of unemployment, the avoidance of a general deterioration of skill, and the re-equipment of those disabled in the struggle of war for the struggle of " peace "—the Government deserved and achieved a substantial measure of success. Perhaps its best ally was the temporary quickening of industry during 1919 by the partial re-opening of foreign trade and the pressure of re-placement orders. The fact that the real cost of four years' destruction did not come home to Britain until two years after the Armistice was in many respects a piece of sheer good fortune. That it was not generally recognised as such was apparently due to folk having almost forgotten by that time that there was any price to be paid for the ruin of half Europe.

§ 4.

Apart, however, from the special problems of demobilisation, the outbreak of peace revealed certain matters in the sphere of industrial relations as urgently in need of attention ; first among them, of course, being the prospective cessation of the Munitions Acts, and the reversion of industry to its pre-war practices.

In the Treasury Agreement of March, 1915, the Government had accepted the responsibility of ensuring the restoration of the *status quo ;* and before hostilities terminated, the draft of a Bill for giving effect to the Government guarantee was laid before the employers' associations and the trade unions. The precise terms of the proposed legislation were not agreed upon until August, 1919, in which month the Restoration of Pre-War Practices Act was passed by Parliament. This Act made it obligatory for employers concerned with work to which the Treasury Agreement or the Munitions Act applied to restore or permit restoration of any pre-existent trade practice suspended during and in consequence of the war, by October 15th, 1919, and to maintain it for twelve months after ; and employers failing to comply with this obligation were made liable to prosecution before a munitions tribunal.

> " In nearly every case (says the Ministry of Labour Report on Conciliation Proceedings for 1919) " the practices departed from were restored where the workmen so desired. More than 5,000 establishments supplied records of changes, and many of the 30,000 records collected contained details of more than one change of practice ; yet after the Act had been in operation for over a year, in only 22 cases had proceedings been instituted against firms for breaches of the Act. In four of these cases proceedings were withdrawn, and in only four of the remainder did the prosecutions prove successful."

In the light of the Labour distrust of the suspension of the trade practices, the absence of trouble arising from this source is not without honour to the State and the employers.

The post-war history of wage-regulation involved a longer period of transition, which was covered by the operation of the Wages (Temporary Regulation) Act (November, 1918). This Act repealed the Compulsory Arbitration clauses of the Munitions Acts except in respect of matters arising from the prescribed rates of wages, and provided that these rates should remain as legal minima for a period of six months after the Armistice (subsequent legislation extended the period to September, 1920). The Act also set up an Interim Court of Arbitration —which was virtually the old Committee on Production enlarged—to which wages disputes might be referred by either party. The effect was, broadly speaking, that the prescribed rates of wages ruling at the time of the Armistice, or such variations of them, reached either by agreement or by arbitration, as were approved by the Minister of Labour as "substituted rates," continued to be statutorily enforcible throughout the whole of the industries to which they applied. Although, therefore, no general legislation was introduced, as suggested by the Industrial Conference, for a universal minimum wage, statutory minimum wages were thus maintained for a limited period throughout the greater part of industry; and the principle was extended both by the action of the Agricultural Wages Boards and by the Trade Boards. The establishment of the latter was greatly facilitated by the Trade Boards Amendment Acts of 1918; and the wage-regulating machinery thus set up in the less organised industries was of a permanent character. This was not the case, however, in regard to the operation of the Wages (Temporary Regulation) Acts; and at the end of 1919 the Government policy of non-intervention was clearly asserted.

The Industrial Courts Act (November, 1919) replaced the Interim Court of Arbitration by a permanent Court of Arbitration; but whereas to the former body wage disputes could be referred on the application of either party and settlements be secured that were legally binding, to the Industrial Court disputes could only be referred by both parties jointly, and the awards were not legally enforcible. The responsibility for the settlement of the conditions of employment was thus virtually returned to those directly concerned, the State discarding its coercive powers in favour of an appeal to industrial and general opinion. This change was clearly indicated in the authority given to the Minister of Labour to conduct an enquiry into any existing or threatened dispute and make public an impartial account of the issues. In connexion with this change of policy, the Ministry of Labour Report on Conciliation and Arbitration for 1919 points out that a partial revision of the basis of wage-advances was actually in progress.   During the war the four-monthly awards of the Committee on Production, which acted as a general standard of wage advances, had been based on the increase in the cost of living. After the war the workers realised that this principle afforded no real improvement on the "fodder basis," and advances were claimed with reference to profits, the state of trade, the scarcity of labour and other matters.   In this more complex situation it no longer appeared desirable that the State should remain a direct party to industrial agreements, since such settlements obviously involved questions with which State machinery was unsuited to deal. After 1919, therefore, the only industries in which the State was a direct party to agreements and disputes were those which remained for the time being under full Government control—the mines and the railways.   For the rest, industrial affairs were left to those engaged on the several industries, and apart from the confirmation of agreements made by the Trade and Agricultural Wages Boards, the only positive action taken by the Government was to facilitate the formation of Joint Industrial Councils.

§ 5.

Although after the first months of 1918 the Whitley scheme ceased to figure in the foreground of public attention, its application to the industries of the country was steadily extended, and by the close of June, 1921, Joint Industrial Councils were functioning in 60 industries employing some $3\frac{1}{2}$ million work-people.   The principle had been applied to all Government industrial establishments, to the Civil Service, and throughout practically the entire field of municipal industry ;   and a large amount of unostentatious but important work had been accomplished by the various joint bodies. By far the greater part of this work naturally had reference to wages and conditions of employment. It was in these matters that the principle of collective bargaining had become most firmly established, and the Whitley scheme was thus a development of an existing practice to which the majority of organisations were already well used. But it must also be remembered that the period was one in which the necessity for dealing with these questions arose with abnormal frequency and in circumstances of abnormal difficulty, and it may safely be said that in the absence of the Joint Industrial Councils not only would many of the agreements made have been much more difficult of attainment and accompanied by a far greater measure of industrial unrest, but some of the most important would not have been reached at all. In several cases the Councils were instrumental in securing the first general standardisation of rates throughout their industries, and the arrangements frequently included the determination of a normal working week and the concession of an annual holiday with pay. Practically all the Councils acted, with considerable success, as conciliation and arbitration courts for the settlement of disputes, and in this connexion the local machinery set up by many of them proved its value.

It was, however, in the reference to the Joint Industrial Councils of a wide range of matters outside the immediate sphere of the cash nexus that the essential novelty of the Whitley scheme resided ; and in this field also, while there is less activity to record, results of considerable promise were secured by certain of the Councils. Some of the more general problems of industry—safety and welfare, workmen's compensation, and unemployment insurance, for example—were referred by the

Government to the Councils as occasion arose ; and the preparation of supplementary schemes of unemployment insurance in several industries gave the trade unionists an opportunity for demonstrating their fitness for a fuller measure of general control. Several of the Councils formulated standard schemes for apprenticeship and some prepared reports of considerable value on the general education and training of young persons. The Pottery and Wire-Manufacturing Councils also instituted general enquiries into the whole financial position of their industries—a task which must at least have resulted in extending the acquaintance of the workers' representatives with the economic problems of the employers. It cannot, however, be said that the trade union delegates as a whole displayed any remarkable initiative in respect of such matters.

By a few Councils requests were made to the Ministry of Labour for financial assistance—and wisely declined. A more general, though by no means unanimous, demand made by the Councils was for the grant of powers, such as were lately possessed by the Ministry of Munitions, by which the decisions of a majority on either side of an industry could be made legally binding upon the whole of it.* The principle involved in this proposal had been rejected by the Trade Union Congress in 1912, and by the Labour party in 1913. More recently it was again opposed by the trade unions at the time of the Industrial Courts Act, in view of the fact that any statutory force applied to industrial agreements would be held by the Government to be equally binding upon both sides. It may also be suggested that any such decision, apart from administrative difficulties occasioned by the loose definition

* This power has been conceded in the case of the Agricultural Conciliation Boards established on " Whitley " lines to replace the Wages Boards set up under the Corn Production Act.

of some of the Joint Industrial Councils, would necessitate some more definite provision against action of an anti-social character than the constitution of these bodies provided. In hardly any case have the relations between the two sides been intimate enough to render such action practically possible ; but in any statutory authority given to joint bodies composed exclusively of employers and employed in a given industry the contingency would require careful consideration.

Broadly speaking, and assuming the continuance of the pre-war economic system, the Whitley Councils may be said to have succeeded in providing a means of securing "a permanent improvement in the relations between employers and workmen." In so far, of course, as the measure of possible improvement was limited by the nature of that system, neither Whitley Councils nor any other form of joint organisation could remedy the inherent defects of the *status quo*.

§ 6.

We are now in a position to survey the extent to which the leading recommendations of the Industrial Conference were met by Government action. Towards the establishment of a universal 48-hour week no general legislation was passed. An Hours of Employment Bill was introduced, as Mr. Lloyd George had promised in October, 1919 ; but other urgent business prevented its passage that session, and the proposal got into difficulties in regard to agricultural workers, seamen, and others whom it might be necessary to except. Further action was postponed pending the report of the International Labour Conference at Washington (November, 1919), and finally the 48-hour week was referred to the

International Labour Office under the League of
Nations at Geneva, where for the present the matter
rests Considerable progress, however, was made
piecemeal in the several industries. In the engineering and allied trades the working week was reduced
from 54 to 47 hours shortly after the Armistice;
on the railways the 48-hour week was established
by the Government in March, 1919, with guaranteed
payment; the miners' working day was reduced
from 8 hours to 7; transport workers secured the
48-hour week by Industrial Council agreements;
and in several other industries a standard working
week of from 44 to 48 hours was instituted by the
Industrial Councils.

Towards a standard minimum wage progress was
also made piecemeal and not by general legislation;
though except in the case of the Trade Boards,
standard rather than minimum rates have been
determined. Throughout 1919 and 1920 the general
movement of wages was rapidly upward.

"It is estimated (says the *Labour Gazette*
for February, 1921), that the average increase
up to the end of December, 1920, in the weekly
full-time rates of wages of adult workpeople
in the industries for which particulars are available was equivalent to about 170 to 180 per
cent. on the pre-war rates. As the length of
the normal working week has been considerably
reduced in the same period, the usual range of
full-time working hours in industry generally
being about 44 to 48 weekly at the end of
December, 1920, as compared with 48 to 60
before the war, the percentage increase in
hourly rates of wages would be considerably
greater."

The above increase, however, is stated to be probably
above the true average for all industries, including
the unorganised trades; and it is pointed out

that as a result of short-time working and unemployment during the latter part of 1920, the average increase in earnings at the end of the year was at least 40 per cent. below the increase in wage-rates. It must be recalled, too, that the wages movement shows only one side of the medal; the other being the increase in the cost of living, which at the end of 1920 was officially estimated at 165 per cent. above the pre-war level; the increase in the cost of food alone being 178.

Of the fourth recommendation of the Industrial Conference respecting the establishment of a general and permanent Council of Industry no more has since been heard; and the functions which such a body might have been expected to perform have remained scattered between the Ministry of Labour, the Industrial Court, and the Board of Trade, the parliamentary committee of the Trades Union Congress, Fleet Street, Downing Street, and the committee rooms of the House of Commons. Which of these agencies best focusses the general sense and intelligence of the country the reader will determine as he lists. But of the third recommendation of the Conference as to unemployment the relevance became painfully apparent towards the autumn of 1920.

§ 7.

For eighteen months after the Armistice unemployment on the whole kept within the average limits of pre-war years. The pressure of replacement work, the anticipation of foreign trade, and the dissipation of a good deal of purchasing power by the home community, had maintained industry in an artificial semblance of prosperity. But about September, 1920, the reality of the world situation began to assert itself, while at the same time the endless rise in prices seemed to be discovering a limit to the effective demand of the community. Significantly enough, the textile, clothing and leather trades were the first to resort to general short-time working. Then came the coal strike ; immediately after the Bank Rate rose to 7 per cent. , and there was every prospect of a black winter.

The unemployment donation—"dole," as it was called—granted for the demobilisation period, and subsequently extended, ceased as regards civilians on November 22nd, 1919 ; for ex-Service men it remained in force until March 31st, 1921. But in the summer of 1920 the Government turned its attention to the question of some general provision against unemployment ; and on August 9th an Unemployment Insurance Act received Royal Assent, the effect of which was to extend insurance on a basis of joint contribution by the workers, the employer and the State, to a total of some 11,900,000 people as from November 8th, 1920. The benefits payable were 18s. for men, 12s. for women, and half rates for juveniles during a maximum of 18 weeks in a year, the qualification being the payment of 12 contributions in normal times, but for the first twelve months four only. In February, 1921, the normal benefit period* was extended, the qualifying period modified, and the payment increased to 20s. for men and 16s. for women ; but in consequence of the abnormal drain on the fund, these amounts were reduced in July to 15s. and 12s., and the contributions increased. Provision was also made under the 1920 Act, by which industries could "contract-out" of the State scheme ; but the financial position of the latter entailed the indefinite suspension of this clause in July, 1921.

The provision of State relief, however, did not tend to mitigate the growth of unemployment ; and

* *i.e*, after July, 1922, prior to which date special conditions apply.

the winter of 1920-1921 saw the most distressful period within memory—mills, factories, workshops driven first to short-time working and then to complete stoppage, coal-mines closed down, ships laid up for want of cargoes, and such armies of unemployed as the towns had never witnessed. Already at the close of 1920 the proportion of workers unemployed (6.1 per cent.) was greater than for ten years past ; by the end of the following March it exceeded all previous records (11.3). Nearly 1½ million people were registered as unemployed, while approximately one million more were working systematic short-time. Trade union funds were exhausted in many districts, large numbers of workers had drawn their last penny of State relief, and even local authorities' Poor Law funds administration— the last desperate resort of the unemployed—were in some cases threatened with bankruptcy.

The situation had called for emergency measures of relief. The Ministry of Transport made special grants for road and other construction ; a special State fund of £3,000,000 was allocated to the assistance of approved relief works administered by Local Authorities ; and the Government adopted and encouraged the system of organised short time working with a view to the more equal distribution of what work was available. But of genuine remedial measures the situation allowed no quick development, and the Labour party at its conference in January, 1921, failed to produce any. It advocated the immediate resumption of trade with Russia and ex-enemy countries ; the extension of international credits ; and, of course, an increased provision of public works and of unemployment relief. It also succeeded in quashing the particularly hopeful suggestion of a general strike. From other quarters came various suggestions, of which the most practical, for the future, was that each industry

as a unit should make provision for the maintenance
of its own unemployed. This principle met with a
certain amount of sympathy in official circles, as
well as elsewhere, and it had in fact been partly
subscribed to in the guaranteed week's pay for the
railwaymen, and in the Government negotiations
with the builders. The suggestion may be taken in
fact as marking an important approach to the
principle that the maintenance of the worker should
be the first, and not a subsidiary charge on industry.
But of immediate remedy there was none available,
for the whole world was sick of the same disease ;
and as to ultimate remedy—for which drastic surgery
of the body politic might perhaps be necessary—
there was agreement neither among the doctors of
the Labour movement nor the more experienced
general practitioners of the nation. "The old
world," wrote Mr. Lloyd George in September, 1919,
" where unemployment through the vicissitudes of
industry brought despair to multitudes of humble
homes . . . must, and will, come to an end."
The end was patently approaching.

CHAPTER III.

Homes for Heroes.

§ 1.

There are few periods in history more significant than those in which great and highly developed societies begin to fail in respect of the supply and distribution of the cardinal necessaries of life. Of such failure recent British history furnishes at least two examples—coal and housing : cases, each of them, in which the requisite material, labour and skill are undoubtedly available in the country, and in which the war period has merely accelerated without initiating the breakdown. And as if to clear away any illusion we may cherish, the housing problem supplies a case in which the failure is in no appreciable measure due to the much-canvassed economic law of diminishing return. Its scope therefore is a matter of some interest.

In October, 1917, the Advisory Housing Panel of the Ministry of Reconstruction, guided by the results of a detailed enquiry addressed to local authorities, estimated the housing shortage then due to the war at 175,000 for England and Wales, plus an additional 50,000 cottages urgently needed as an instalment in rural areas. Putting the necessary yearly increase of houses not exceeding £20

annual value at 75,000, the committee cited a total
of 300,000 houses as actually requiring erection
during 1918.   On this basis the shortage in England
and Wales alone at the end of that year would be
375,000.   Allowing for replacement of insanitary
dwellings, a very moderate estimate brought the
total up to 500,000.*   For Scotland the corresponding estimate was 150,000.

These totals, it must be clearly understood,
referred to the provision of such additional accommodation as would reduce the general average to not
more than two persons per room—living rooms
included, and two children reckoned as the equivalent
of one adult.   And this two-per-room standard
implied more than a mere return to pre-war conditions :   the pre-war standard was much lower.
The estimate of the Registrar General published in
January, 1921, stated that "as the estimated
population for 1919 is 700,000 in excess of that at
the last census, it would only require (apart from
replacement of defective houses) a net addition of
140,000 houses for the whole period 1911-1919 to
maintain the 1911 average—that is, if the new
census shows the present population estimate to
be fairly correct."   This statement was interpreted
in several prejudiced quarters as an authoritative
contradiction of the official estimate of half-a-million.
But all that it establishes is the truism that the 1911
standard (*a fortiori* the 1913 standard) was deplorably
lower than that underlying the Government scheme :
since it included some two million persons living under
overcrowded conditions, while 178,876 houses in
England and Wales alone were unfit for habitation.
What in fact the pre-war standard of accommodation
meant in, say, Glasgow or the East End of London—

* A survey of England and Wales undertaken by local authorities
in the spring of 1920 resulted in a total of about 800,000, from which
79,000 may be deducted as due to overlapping, etc.

what, for example, was involved in a woman's confinement where she, and her husband, and two or three children, had one room between them—it is unnecessary to describe ; but it may be pointed out that seven out of the eight Commissioners on Industrial Unrest cited the inadequacy of accommodation as one of its main causes in June, 1917.

To trace the development of the post-war situation in detail is beyond our present purpose. For years before the war, working-class property, for a variety of interesting reasons, had been failing to attract capital ; even during the years 1911-1913, when the annual value of new factories and workshops erected increased by 50 per cent., there was a decrease in the corresponding figures for new dwelling-houses of roughly one-tenth. In fact the question came before Parliament in July, 1914, when a proposal that the Board of Agriculture should be empowered to provide 15,000 cottages in rural areas was vetoed. Something was done, however, for the industrial employees of the Government by the Housing Act of August 10th, under which the Office of Works itself, or the Local Government Board by means of authorised societies, received power to provide urgently needed accommodation up to the value of £2,000,000. A month later, by way of meeting the war-unemployment, a second Housing Act was passed, by which the Board of Agriculture in rural areas and the Local Government Board elsewhere were empowered to provide, indirectly or directly if other means failed, for the building of new houses wherever needed to a maximum cost of £4,000,000. But the wave of unemployment passed, and the Act, which was in any case limited to a year's operation, had little or no effect on the main problem. Such building labour as remained in the country was increasingly drawn to Government work—to the munition factories or the camps ; and both the

War Office and the Admiralty, acting in some cases through the armament firms themselves, began building houses in the more congested areas of production. Then came the positive restrictions on private building in 1916; while the Ministry of Munitions, supplemented at Rosyth by the Scottish Local Government Board, and at Woolwich by the Office of Works, "ran up" accommodation—permanent or temporary, but in either case tolerable —for over 30,000 war-workers. An incidental result of this very necessary procedure was to create a sort of vested interest in the munition centres after the Armistice; particularly at Woolwich, where the demand of both the "town" and the munition workers for the allotment of civil work to the Arsenal was strengthened by the fact that even if the thousands of "munitioneers" could be dispersed with a fair prospect of finding employment, other accommodation they certainly could not find.

All this, however, touched but the fringe of the national housing problem; and by the time Parliament was invited to deal with that, another year's deficiency had accrued. The acquisition in December, 1918, of a new lease of life by the Coalition nerved the Government to set about it in earnest; and in the following session proposals were introduced by Dr. Addison which became the Housing Act of July 31st, 1919. By this Act compulsion was laid upon local authorities to take stock of their areas and submit to the Ministry of Health housing schemes to meet their respective needs; which should they fail to do, the County Councils or the Ministry might act in their stead, and charge the cost.

The Government undertook to indemnify the local authorities for any loss on approved housing schemes in excess of the product of a penny rate—save where the State acted in default of the local body, which might then be made liable for the full expenditure.

A group of miscellaneous provisions of the Act enabled the Local Authorities to acquire the necessary sites and rights with a minimum of delay, and gave additional powers in regard to finance and the employment of public utility societies ; and with a view to the more distant future, local authorities with populations above 20,000 on January 1st, 1923, were charged to submit town-planning schemes within the next three years.

Unfortunately, it did not appear that local authorities were eager to incur even the limited liabilities of the Act ; and with the cessation of the restriction upon private building and the continuance of Excess Profits Duty, contractors found many more attractive openings then " small property." Something more was needed to start housing operations ; and in the Housing (Additional Powers) Act of December, 1919, the Government undertook to provide it.

Subsidies up to a total of £15,000,000 (for England and Wales £12,000,000) were now made payable by the Ministry of Health to private builders in respect of approved houses begun and completed within the following twelve months. The original amounts offered were from £120 to £160 per house, according to size ; but in May, 1920, the offer was increased to £230 to £260, and at the end of the year the time limit was extended by another twelve months. By the same Act local authorities were authorised to issue local bonds, secured upon local rates and revenues, of amounts from £5 to £100 bearing interest at 6 per cent. They were also given power to prevent the demolition of habitable dwellings within their areas, and—here enters the labour problem—to restrict the amount of counter-attraction offered to labour by " luxury building."

As a result of the general speeding up, the number of houses in schemes for which tenders were approved increased during the first six months of 1920 from

19,175 to 120,405. A vigorous propaganda for the local loans was carried on from the spring, and during the year about $15\frac{1}{2}$ million pounds was subscribed. Unfortunately the number of houses actually put in hand was sadly lower than these figures might suggest, and infinitely lower than the popular anticipation.

By the end of March, 1920, 1,239 houses were completed by local authorities, and plans had been approved for a total of 161,837; in addition, 96 houses had been built by public utility societies and County Councils. Twelve months later, the plans approved for local authorities had reached a total of 275,868 and the houses completed by them numbered 25,878. In addition, public utility societies and County Councils had built 2,012, and private persons 13,703.* This result, considerable in itself, was insufficient to affect the general situation, and public opinion was castigating the traditional scape-goats — Government and Labour. In respect of the trade unions, criticism was particularly bitter. A ca'canny policy was undoubtedly prevalent; and there were other factors of the situation of which some account must be given.

§ 2.

The nature of the industry had always rendered the Building Trades peculiarly liable to fluctuations in employment; and during the three years pre-

* By mid-July, when the scheme was foreclosed, the number of houses built, building and approved under local authorities and public utility societies' schemes was 176,000, and under the private subsidy scheme about 23,000. Of the total, about 60,000 were then completed. (Hd. H/C, July 14th, and statement to Press by Ministry of Health. *Times*, July 21st.) For full statistics see Second Annual Report of the Ministry of Health. (Cmd. 1446, 1921.)

ceding the outbreak of war this disadvantage had
been increasingly manifest. According to the ideas
then prevailing, the one practicable remedy for this
state of things lay in the strict enforcement of
those provisions of Trade Unionism which tended
to control the supply of available labour. This
policy culminated, as we have seen, in the protracted
disputes of the summer of 1914, of which the fundamental issue was the principle of Trade Unionism.
But, further, the recruitment of the Building Trades
had been steadily declining ; apprentices were
being increasingly attracted to other industries where
the prospects were more certain ; and in the view of
the Trade Union leaders this decline could only be
counteracted by the improvement in general conditions and security of employment, to be achieved
through trade union action. During the first year
after the war it was evident that the industry would
be faced with a further serious decline in the labour
forces available ; it appeared in fact that between
1914 and 1919 a deficiency of nearly 200,000 workmen had accrued. The national housing programme
thus gave the trade unions a stronger position than
they had ever known ; and they came to the natural
conclusion that if ever a permanent improvement in
the status of building labour was to be achieved,
now was the time for it.

The extent to which housing schemes were actually
retarded by scarcity of skilled labour, is a highly
controversial question. The spokesmen of the
Government alleged, with increasing insistence as
public criticism of the progress made on housing
became more urgent, that the labour shortage was
a determining factor. The operatives, in reply,
pointed time after time to the trade union statistics
which showed that even at the end of 1920 as many
as 50,000 skilled men in the building industry were
yet unemployed. It will be recalled that a similar

argument was put forward by the engineers in 1915, when it proved inconclusive. And in 1920, as in 1915, the necessity of the work was made the basis of a request by the Government for dilution of the skilled trades, the Government case being now reinforced by the necessity of finding employment for very large numbers of ex-service men. The negotiations on this question focussed in the Resettlement Committee of the Building Trades Industrial Council, which during the greater part of 1920 conducted an intricate and apparently interminable controversy with the Ministry of Health as to the labour requirements of the national housing program and the estimated cost of certain of the proposals put forward by the operatives. In August the Government proposals were formulated as follows :

(1) That the numbers of skilled workmen in the industry should be augmented by the intensive training of labourers to the level of skilled men, the admittance of both juvenile and adult apprentices for special terms of training, and the intensive training of ex-service men.

(2) That a system of payment by results should be adopted.

(3) That in return a guaranteed week, including payment for time lost through bad weather, should be granted to workmen on housing schemes.

In reply the operatives indicated a firm objection to payment by results, and put forward an alternative scheme, agreed on by the Industrial Council, for adult apprenticeship ; at the same time the estimates on which the Government proposals were based were exhaustively criticised.

To cut short a somewhat intricate story, it may be stated that in the following December what were described by the Minister of Labour as the " definite and final proposals of the Government " were submitted. In these proposals the Government's offer was amended as follows :

(1) That the skilled unions should absorb for intensive training not less than 50,000 ex-service men.

(2) That in return the proposals for a guaranteed week should be applied.

(3) That the Government should pay £5 per head to the Trade Union funds for every dilutee accepted

The offer is of so unique a character that the words in which Dr. Macnamara, on December 21st, 1920, explained it to a somewhat critically minded House of Commons, deserve quotation :

" We say ' Take these men. Train them to be skilled craftsmen so that they can permanently earn hereafter the decent subsistence they so richly deserve.' We also say, ' Here is £5 for their training, £2 when they enter training, £3 at the end of the three years' course.' The building trades say' in a sentence, ' Well, but pre-war we suffered grave periods of unemployment.' That is true. They say in effect, ' When the housing arrears are made up are we to go back to all that ? ' We say, ' Your fears we think are really unfounded even when housing arrears are made up. What is here proposed will do no more than recruit your ranks to their normal strength. But if you have any genuine anxieties on that point, we suggest to you that you should use the training grant as the nucleus of a fund upon which you can build a really effective insurance scheme for your members, old and new.' That, I think, is a perfectly fair offer and involves a perfectly square deal. The next word, as I say, is with the building trades."

The next word was decisive. A ballot of the trade unions held in January, 1921, resulted in 310,000 votes against the Government scheme and 2,500 in favour. This marked the end of the negotiations between the Unions and the Government. The latter approached the Employers' Federation with the request that the Master Builders should consent to take 50,000 ex-service men ; and by a vote of employers the request was accepted. The move was interpreted by the operatives as a further challenge, and was countered by the adoption of a policy which may best be described as one of passive resistance. Employers in many districts proved unwilling to force the issue, and apart from the Office of Works, the number of dilutees actually employed was negligible. With the trade depression of the summer of 1921, and the abandonment of the national housing programme, the prospect of enforcing dilution on the building trades sank unnoticed out of sight.

The whole episode, it may be remarked in passing, was interpreted—not only in quarters normally hostile to the idea of State enterprise—as a significant object-lesson ; and a considerable section of the community began to wonder whether, in view of subsidies to the builders for building the houses, and subsidies to the unions for allowing the extra labour, the Government might not have been better advised to let the whole business alone.

§ 3.

Meanwhile, however, the operatives had not confined themselves to merely negative action ; and in this respect also the story goes back to 1914. During the London lockout of that year important work had successfully been executed by direct labour. The memory of the experiment survived with effect, and among its results was the advocacy of the same method of work by the labour organisations in connection with local housing schemes. A considerable number of housing contracts were, in fact,

successfully carried out on these lines ; and one of
them, as of special significance, is worth describing
in some detail.

At Camberwell, where special difficulties arose in
respect of the local housing scheme, the Ministry of
Health invited the assistance of the Office of Works ;
and at the request of the Borough Council direct
administration was resorted to. The Council claimed
that this method would eliminate a good deal of the
cost and, by arousing the public spirit of the workmen, would also secure better work and higher output.
Accordingly the Office of Works entered into close
relations with the local Trades and Labour Council.
The latter undertook to recruit the necessary labour,
and foremen were appointed by a small Joint
Committee of the two bodies. The result was a
distinct success.

> " It certainly must be said (states the journal of the
> Ministry of Health Housing Department) that these
> claims have undoubtedly been substantiated. The general
> progress of the work has been rapid and excellent ; the
> amount of skilled labour has been increased in accordance
> with the requirements of the three jobs ; while the output
> of the labour has been above that of the normal output in
> other works in London. The men show the keenest
> interest in furthering the progress of the work, and act
> throughout as recruiters for the necessary labour required
> as the job opens up. . . .
>
> " The relations between the Office of Works and the
> Borough Council and the Trades and Labour Council are
> of the most cordial nature. The Office of Works Labour
> Officer attends meetings of the Trades Council and hears
> all grievances at those meetings, and acts in conjunction
> with their officers and also with the manager of
> the Employment Exchange. The local feeling between
> the union officials and the manager of the Employment
> Exchange is excellent, and has proved very helpful through-
> out the progress of the work. One of the most convincing
> signs of satisfaction with the job is that practically no
> labour has left the site since its first engagement, with the
> exception of a very few men dismissed for inefficiency, etc.
> Further, the Labour and Trades Council have agreed with

the Office of Works to the principle of dilution of the skilled operatives by utilising trainees and improvers who are disabled ex-soldiers and also, under certain conditions, apprentices. . . .

There can be no question that by the execution of this work by direct administration with sympathetic help from labour the progress is excellent, and the scheme will be economical and rapid in execution."

But the ideal of the advance guard among the workmen went further than this. In the original proposals that led to the formation of the Building Trades Parliament there was foreshadowed the formation of two codes, one compulsory, the other voluntary, on which the industry might be organised as "a great national service." Both these codes, developed in the meantime by the influence of Guild Socialist ideas, were elaborated by a committee of the Building Industrial Council during 1919 and 1920. As formulated in the much discussed "Foster Report" they provide, broadly speaking, for the collective control by those, and only those, engaged in the industry, of both capital and means of production , they provide for the remuneration of all grades of workers upon fixed and guaranteed scales ; for the decasualisation of labour ; the regularisation of employment , the superannuation of operatives , and the devotion of surplus revenue to the common good of the industry The ideal explicitly aimed at was the increased efficiency of the industry as an organised public service, combined, with democratic control and improvement in status. A draft scheme for a National Building Guild appeared as an Appendix to the "Foster Report."

It is not surprising that these proposals failed to secure the support of the Building Trades Council. Such a body, on which all differences of opinion on either side are concentrated while the opportunity for persuasion is reduced to a minimum, is seldom in a position even adequately to criticise experimental schemes of such a nature. But the discussion had at least the indirect effect of advertising the constructive ideals in the industry ; and when at Manchester, in January, 1920, a definite scheme for the formation of a Guild was drawn up by the local trade unions, the ground was to some extent already prepared throughout the country.

The leading spirit in the Manchester movement was S. G. Hobson, a prominent exponent of Guild Socialism ; and it was fortunate for the trade union leaders that they were able to reach at Manchester an embodiment of their ideals which was sound both in practice and in law. The direct labour movement was now brought to a point at which the trade unions themselves were able to administer contracts from start to finish. For this purpose a small limited company with a nominal capital of £100 was formed and registered under the No Profit Clauses of the Joint Stock Acts ; and to this Company the local Guild Committees which rapidly sprang up were affiliated. Payments were to be made to and through the central body thus incorporated, and questions of general finance, administration and management were allocated to it. The actual carrying out of contracts was, however, relegated to the local Guild Committees, which were to choose their own managers and foremen, to arrange for the purchase of their own plant, control their individual accounts, and to take responsibility for the supply and efficiency of labour. Guild Committees on these lines were formed during the first half of 1920 in over fifty centres, mostly in the Midlands and the North of England. Meanwhile, in London a second Guild of Builders was established in May and registered as an Industrial Society under the Industrial and Provident Societies Acts, with Malcolm Sparkes as Secretary. As at Manchester, control was vested in a body of representatives elected by the functional groups in the industry ; and

the principle of industrial democracy has been so
consistently applied that even the labourers on guild
contracts elect their own " gangers."   A feature of
the London experiment was the call for volunteers—
a call extended to and answered by professional
as well as manual workers.

The placing of guild contracts by local authorities
brought up the question of purchase of materials,
for which neither the latter nor the trade unionists
were as a rule equipped with the necessary experience.
The difficulty was solved by the association in the
contracts of the Co-operative Wholesale Society,
which placed the services of the Building Department
at the guilds' disposal.   The Co-operative Wholesale Bank also assisted the formation of the London
guild, and subsequently arranged to insure local
authorities against loss in respect of guild contracts.
These provisions formed part of an agreement as
to contracts concluded between the guilds and the
Ministry of Health in July, 1920, on the basis of
which the Ministry, in face of considerable criticism,
undertook to sanction up to 20 guild contracts—of
which, however, only 13 were actually placed.   The
whole guild movement was reorganised on a
national basis at Manchester on July 23rd, 1921 ;
the scheme provided for a tripartite system of
local committees, regional councils, and a National
Board, and the guild announced its readiness to
undertake work of any description.   " We are now
prepared," said the chairman of the National
Building Guild Ltd., " to step into the field
and capture the control of the whole building
industry."

§ 4.

The fundamental principles underlying the guild

organisation are thus indicated in an early report issued by the Manchester group :

(1) " The abolition of the existing wage-contract in favour of a system by which labour shall be the first charge upon the industry. . . . Since dividends take priority over labour the Guild declines to issue any shares or stock of any description. It gives effect at the same time to the principle of the industrial maintenance of the unemployed." Guaranteed continuous payment, irrespective of time lost in bad weather, was a cardinal condition of Guild service.

(2) " The Guild declares (and acts upon its own belief) that industry must be conducted not with accumulated capital mostly stolen from labour, but upon the group credit inherent in industrial organisation."

(3) " The Guild further declares that democratic principles are at least equally desirable in industry as in politics. It therefore provides the machinery to compass that end."

(4) " The Guild declares that it has a definite duty to the community. . . . This duty is best accomplished by returning to the community all and any surplus over the cost of production "—cost being reckoned to include the maintenance in bad times as in good of Guild labour.

(5) " The Guild declares that true craftsmanship must be revived. There is no reason, save only the profiteering greed of modern capitalism, why building guildsmen should not equal or surpass the triumphs of the mediæval period. But to attain this the National Building Guild must control not only its mature but its immature labour. All technical instruction and training must come under the Guild's jurisdiction."

It is indeed a remarkable and significant progress from the first enunciation of " organised public service " as an ideal in Malcolm Sparkes' proposals of 1916 to the proclamation of that watchword on notice boards up and down the country behind which many thousands of operatives are actually working : and working with a will, so that their output is not infrequently two or three times as great as that of

the men working under the old profit-making regime.*
To what ultimate end that progress will lead it is
as yet too early to say. The ability of the guild
system to cope with fluctuations in demand arising
from general causes, and the adaptability of its
financial arrangements to the normal economic
position of the industry and the working of the general
credit system, have yet to be demonstrated. This
much at least may be said already—that the pioneers .
of the building guilds have succeeded in inculcating
a spirit in industry which no profit-sharing, co-
partnership, industrial council or other scheme has
hitherto made possible ; and that they have demonstrated, in a difficult time and none too promising a
field, the possibilities of a new social ideal.

* See Report on Building Guilds by Mr. Ernest Selley, *Garden Cities
and Town Planning Journal*, June, 1921   By July 1921 work valued at
£300,000 was stated to have been completed by the guild committees,
of which 115 were then in existence. (See Report of Manchester Conference, *Daily Herald*, July 25th, 1921)

CHAPTER IV.

" A Conservative Sort of Animal."

§ 1.

In the general record of the three years following the election of 1918 it is impossible sharply to distinguish the political and the industrial aspects of the Labour movement. The term itself ceased in fact to have any clear and single connotation, and while its use remains an unfortunate necessity— in the absence of any satisfactory alternative— the plural form is really more applicable than the singular to the tangle of tendencies we have now to unravel.

Despite the growth in size and influence of the trade unions during the war, and the reconstitution of the enlarged Labour party directly after it, the year 1918 found the Labour movement as a whole rather worse off in respect of co-ordinating machinery than it had been four years earlier. By the Trade Union Act of 1913 the political and industrial activities of the trade unions had to be kept at least formally separate ; but taking labour as a whole, the separation was much more than formal. The Labour party—now definitely Socialist—while it exceeded the scope of trade union organisation, was not coterminous with the whole trade union membership. The Trade Union Congress—the parliament, or "talking" of the unions—annually registered an incredible number of resolutions on general policy; but its Executive Committee could do no more to enforce them than deputise Government departments or pass them on for constitutional action by the Labour party. It could neither call nor administer a general strike, and the increased industrial strength of the unions thus remained without any effective centre of concentration and direction. The Triple Alliance had come into being as a partial remedy for this state of affairs, ousting in its rise the conservative "General Federation of Trade Unions"; but neither on the political nor on the industrial side was there room as yet for a third directing party, and the Alliance had to bide its time and place. Meanwhile it was easy to see that should any specific issue arise on which Labour opinion was so strong as to demand united and positive action the movement would probably fall back on its original method, or no-method, of improvisation. Such an issue arose over Russia.

For the effective expression of its views, which were emphatic, on this aspect of Government policy, the Labour party was under the disadvantage that the measures to which it objected were not matters of Parliamentary decision. Had the leaders of opinion been content to accept the situation all would doubtless have been well; but as time and military action in Russia went on, the official labour opposition was reinforced by an extra-official *ad hoc* body called the "Hands off Russia Committee." This Committee, which was by no means exclusively composed of pro-Bolsheviks, conducted a vigorous agitation against the Government policy, largely by street meetings; and getting more desperate as its apparent impotence was revealed, at last issued a manifesto (May, 1920) on its own account " to the

organised workers of Great Britain," calling for a
national labour conference and a general strike. This
action, it may be noticed, was resented as an interference by the officials of the Transport Workers'
Federation. By this time, however, the question
of Allied action in the Russo-Polish war was exciting
general attention, and sporadic instances of direct
action were breaking out against the transport of
munitions from England. It was plain that the
occasion for whatever general and drastic protest
labour could compass had arrived. Some looked
to the Triple Alliance, others to the Trade Union
Congress for a lead ; since for such a lead there was
no extant machinery. At length the Parliamentary
Committee of the Trade Union Congress, the
Executive Committee of the Labour Party, and the
Parliamentary Labour Party (the names are less
cumbrous than the reality) were brought together
in a Committee Room of the House of Commons ;
where on August 9th, 1920, they proceeded to
appoint a special " Council of Action " representing
the entire Labour movement (singular or plural).
A conference of over 1,000 delegates was assembled
four days later at the Central Hall, Westminster, at
which the Council of Action was enthusiastically
approved. If, as Frank Hodges once remarked, the
average British workman is " a conservative sort
of animal," he was on this occasion much misrepresented. The Council was instructed to remain
in session until it had secured an absolute guarantee
of British non-intervention in Russia, and the
recognition of the Soviet Government ; and it was
authorised to call for " any and every form of withdrawal of labour which circumstances may require
to give effect to the foregoing policy." Whether
or no the Council could have called with effect
remains a moot point, since the necessity was
obviated by negotiation with the Government.

It was claimed that the decision actually prevented a declaration of war by Great Britain, and expedited a Russo-Polish peace. More relevant to the present study is the fact that an attempt had been made to mobilise the whole force of Labour on a political issue, and the precedent was subsequently recalled on more than one occasion. No attempt was made, however, to wield the power conferred upon the Council of Action, and no subsequent issue arose on which there was so thorough a unanimity in the Labour movement. General opinion was that the power of a general strike could not, even at the time, have been evoked by the Council of Action with success. The onus of a lead in the direction of a general strike thus devolved on the Triple Alliance.

An important advance, however, was made towards a better organisation of trade unionism as a whole by the adoption of the " general staff " scheme in September, 1920. It was then decided that from the Trade Union Congress of 1921 central control should reside in a General Council of 32 members, elected to represent 17 specified groups of industries in a proportion based upon the trade union membership in each group. The General Council was to take charge of industrial policy and propaganda generally, to promote the settlement of inter-union disputes, to act with the Labour party on political questions, and with the trade unions concerned on industrial questions. It was also to constitute the only official means of affiliation with the international trade union movement. This decision was by way of discarding the machinery of the old General Federation of Trade Unions, a body which had never covered more than a small proportion of the total trade union membership, and that the most conservative.

§ 2.

The more positive effect of the reaction to Russian affairs is a longer story, to which, for clue, the avowed and consistently-pursued policy of Lenin must be borne in mind. That policy, outlined by the executive of the Third (Communist) International was, in brief, the deliberate splitting up of the Socialist and Labour parties in all countries so that a compact revolutionary nucleus might emerge. The nucleus was to act as the revolutionary advance guard of Communism, attacking both Parliamentary and old trade union organisations from within and without, by means legal or illegal as occasion demanded. The immediate aim was the establishment of a proletarian dictatorship as the only means to the workers' revolution. A majority in elections was not a primary necessity : the majority was to be obtained by the dictatorship, not the dictatorship by the majority, and the prospect of physical as well as merely dialectical or verbal war must be faced. At least the first item of this program met with considerable success throughout Europe.

During the war, as we have seen in previous chapters, the rank-and-file and the shop stewards movements received their impetus from what were mainly industrial questions. The unofficial movement attained in June, 1917, a central organisation, and the National Administrative Council then established acted as a centre of co-ordination for the Shop Stewards Committees, Workers' Committees, Vigilance Committees and other local unofficial organisations. During 1918 and 1919 the general drift of the movement had become more and more political and revolutionary ; and from " industrial unionism " and " control by the workers " it progressed towards frank Sovietism.   At the same time, however, the scope and the coherence of the movement diminished, and its membership underwent a certain purge ; so that by 1920 the unofficial committees had largely lost touch, had ceased to function in some cases, and were seeking affiliation to Moscow in others.   It was on the basis of what was left of the Workers' Committee movement that the British Socialist Party, the Socialist Labour Party, the Workers' Socialist Federation, the South Wales Socialist Society, and certain other minor revolutionary groups set to work.   The " Hands off Russia " agitation was in some cases contributory to their aim ; in others local organisations of unemployed or of ex-service men supplied converts and assistance.

Throughout the winter of 1919-1920 attempts were in progress to combine the various societies above referred to in a united Communist party ; but differences on the question of tactics proved insuperable up to April, 1920.   The question immediately at issue was that of affiliation to the Labour Party, and the Workers' Socialist Federation (Sylvia Pankhurst) maintained a solitary stand against any connexion with reformist movements.   To this attitude the other organisations demurred ; and Lenin, to whom Sylvia appealed, also opposed it on the ground of expediency.   Minor differences separated the B.S.P. and the S.L.P., and in the event not one but three Communist parties were announced, all claiming affiliation to the Third International, and all criticising each other in public according to the established tradition of British working-class politics.

Acting on the Moscow policy, the new " Communist Party of Great Britain " (formed on the basis of the erstwhile British Socialist Party in August, 1920) applied to the Labour party for affiliation ; and was promptly refused.   The Labour party had just assisted in setting up its own " Council of Action " which no wilder a revolutionary than J. H. Thomas described as " a challenge to the whole constitution of the country." During the war, moreover, as the Communists pointed out, " the I.L.P. had a policy absolutely opposed to the declared policy of the Labour party, and they were not expelled nor was their annual application for affiliation questioned." But to admit this avowedly revolutionary organisation, with its anti-bourgeois policy, its advocacy of the Soviet and the proletarian dictatorship, and unconstitutionalism, and violence, and the devil (or Lenin) knew what else—that was demanding too much of the Labour party. Clearly there could be no room in " the house that we propose to erect " for tenants of this sort. Local branches of the Labour party were therefore instructed to follow the lead of the National Executive in excluding the Communists.

This decision of the Labour party solved for the Communists the dispute as to tactics ; but personalities as well as principles stood in the way of co-ordination, and a direct instruction from Moscow was necessary to set the unity negotiations going again. At last (January 29th, 1921) representatives of the three parties and of various local Communist groups met in conference at Leeds and accepted a basis of common action on the lines of the Moscow policy.

A considerable part in these negotiations was taken by the National Council of Shop Stewards and Workers' Committees which by this time were largely permeated with Communist elements. But as an industrial movement they did not form a part of the unified Communist party, though their policy of industrial action and workers' control was used as a spur to Communism in workshop propaganda. The Shop Stewards and Workers' Committees constituted in fact the industrial arm of the Communist organisation, and it was largely by their action that the attack on "reactionary" trade unionism was made from within the unions.

The manœuvre of September, 1920, was repeated by the left wing group of the Independent Labour Party, and in March, 1921, a resolution favouring affiliation to the Communist International was submitted to the delegate conference at Southport and decisively rejected; whereupon the Communist section of the membership decided to withdraw and to join the official Communist party. It was asserted by *The Communist* that some 5,000 or more new members were thus added *en bloc*. On the political side the bifurcation was thus completed. But on the industrial side confusion still remained, and members of the Shop Stewards and Workers' Committees continued their propaganda within the unions. This propaganda, in addition to its strictly industrial aspect, was increasingly directed towards affiliation to the Trade Union Section of the Third International (the "Red" Trade Union International); and although the Workers' Committee movement as such remained outside the Communist party, it became an active recruiting agency. In the mining industry the unofficial reform committees were co-ordinated on a national scale in February, 1921, when Communism was definitely adopted as an aim of industrial policy, it being interpreted to mean "the ownership and absolute control of the means of livelihood by the working classes." A manifesto issued by the "British Miners' Reform Movement" called for concerted agitation within the unions to secure a new constitution for the Miners' Federation; rank-and-file control of officials and policy; and affiliation to the Red Trade Union International. Reform Committees were at that date organised in South Wales, Yorkshire, Fifeshire,

Lanarkshire, and the north of England; but they were not as a whole formally affiliated to the Workers' Committee movement. On the industrial side, therefore, the revolutionary elements were still unsegregated; and the possibility of a Triple Alliance strike tended for the time being to postpone a division.

Of the importance of the Communist revolutionary movement as a whole, it is impossible to speak in any save the most general terms. Where, as in South Wales, its adherents were fairly numerous and in close touch, its influence was considerable; where, as in Yorkshire and in London, its adherents were scattered through various localities and industries, it could encourage unrest, but not to the point of any general action. The expulsion from the Labour party of the Communists was probably a good thing for both sides. The former was faced with a coherent and vigorous opposition, and compelled to a more definite exposition of its policy and tactics than it had been used to putting forward; the latter were forced into the open, relieved of any motive for political dissimulation, and aided, both by their isolation, and by the imprisonment of some of their leaders, to achieve a compact revolutionary nucleus. In industry the conflict was waged chiefly in the local branches of the unions, many of which were captured by the extremists. It was frequently alleged, and with truth, that branch decisions of a revolutionary character were engineered by Communist minorities; but the fact was no reproach to these latter. If the Communists were more attentive to their lodges than the Moderates, they earned any results that might be secured; the apathy of the latter, not the energy of the former, was responsible if the lodges "went red" and the position of moderate leaders became difficult. Probably South Wales was the only district in which a majority of the rank-and-file were more advanced than their official leaders as a whole. In other industries the extremists constituted only a small section. But it must be recalled that by Communist doctrine—which in this instance at least corresponded to fact—a numerical majority was not a necessary preliminary to revolution.

CHAPTER V.

DE PROFUNDIS.

As a study both in the direction and control of mass impulse, and in the strategy of present-day trade unionism, the post-war history of the miners is of peculiar significance. It furnishes a central clue to both the ideals and the policy of the modern Labour movement, and as regards either theories or tactics it calls for careful examination.

As with other things not always so apprehended, the sources of the nationalising movement in the coal industry are psychological. For nearly 50 years nationalisation of the mines has been an annual aspiration of trade unionism ; but in Wales, where idealisms are prone to fever, the doctrine was held with a difference, in an other than Fabian temper : as witness the most famous of Welshmen asking his Limehouse audience years ago, " who was it laid the foundations of the mountains and placed this precious thing beneath the everlasting hills ? " You do not dispose of men for whom nationalisation follows on the answer to that question by arguing that nationalisation is not a " business proposition."

But as a business proposition nationalisation had much to recommend it to the miners. The capacity of industry to earn a profit is a factor of employment to which in more cases than this the men have

objected ; but in .this case of the mines there are
special considerations. Labour and capital both
being largely " fixed," fluctuations in the profit-
earning capacity react sharply on employment in
the mines on the economic margin.   By regulating
wages in accordance with the market value of the
product the fluctuations could to some extent be
counteracted before the war.   But the main cost of
counteraction thus came out of the miners' pockets,
and living was little cheaper for the miner in the
worst mine than for the miner in the best ; moreover,
inasmuch as there was a downward limit (varying,
it is true, from district to district) there was a point
at which counteraction became inaction—for the
miner.   Alternatively, you could pool the profits of
all the mines, as was done under Government control
from February, 1918—better mines thus subsidising
worse ones, and paying economic rent as cost of
counteracting the fluctuation ; and since at the back
of this arrangement was a State guarantee of standard
profits, counteraction thus became assured—at the
possible cost of the Exchequer.   Which, said the
miners—coal being a natural asset and a national
necessity—was a perfectly reasonable arrangement,
giving the men, who served this national necessity
by their daily dangerous labour, good wages and
secure tenure of employment.   But, obviously, under
such a system, some substitute would be necessary
for the working of the economic laws suspended :
there would be, in the extreme case, no sense in
producing coal that nobody wanted ; and nationalisation—taken to mean both national ownership and
national unification of the industry—became the
issue of the general dilemma : which were we to
maintain—a " natural " system in which profit-
earning capacity determined the working of the coal-
mines, or an " artificial " system under which labour
could be reckoned a standing first charge on the

industry, and social control take the place of economic regulation ?

§ I.

The second Coalition Government of Mr. Lloyd George had been in the saddle barely a week when the Miners' Federation (of which Robert Smillie was now permanent President, and Frank Hodges permanent Secretary) decided to demand of it a reduction of the underground working day from 8 to 6 hours, an increase on standard wages of 30 per cent., nationalisation of the mines, and other small matters. The Government offered in reply an increase in the war-wage from 18s. to 19s.—and an enquiry. This was duly refused in February, 1919, and a ballot taken on the question of a strike. The ballot has been cited as an example of the policy of so framing an issue as to anticipate a result desired for strategical use by the executive. The ballot paper, it was stated,* " asked the voter whether he was in favour of a national strike to secure

(1) a 30 per cent. increase in wages ;
(2) a six-hour day ;
(3) Full maintenance at trade union rates for mine workers unemployed through demobilisation ;
(4) Nationalisation of the mines.

The miner was not to write yes or no to each of the questions, but yes or no to all of them. . . . The public were told that the vote was for nationalisation." At any rate, it was effective in arming the executive with the strike weapon ; and if the miners' leaders used the material promises as a means to an ulterior end in policy, they were but profiting by a recent conspicuous example. In fact, strike notices were

* W. A. Appleton in *The Democrat.*

duly tendered, and with difficulty restrained from taking effect; while under the threat of a stoppage the Government proposal for a Royal Commission on the industry was embodied in an Act of Parliament (February 26th, 1919), and the Miners' Federation were persuaded to take part in the enquiry. A determining factor in the decision was the following statement made by the Home Secretary in the House of Commons on February 24th :

" It is a pure business proposition, and if it turns out on investigation that it is for the good of the country as a whole that the mines should be nationalised, that the people of the country would be better off if the mines were worked under a national system rather than under private ownership, then it is a good business proposition, and we should accept it "

That statement was understood by the miners to mean that if the Commission reported in favour of nationalisation, nationalisation there would be.

The Commission under Mr. Justice Sankey, whatever else it did, provided the finest example of a public enquiry into any industry that the country had yet received. The proceedings received very adequate publicity, and were followed with intense interest—while they lasted. Whether or no public opinion was any nearer a decision at the close is another matter , at least if it were not; it was not for want of information.

The Interim Report (or Reports, for the miners, the owners, and the independent members reported separately) of the Commission was presented, as it had been promised, on March 20th. The principal recommendations of the Chairman and the independent members were :

That an increase of 2s. per shift should be granted ;

That the underground working day should be reduced from eight hours to seven ; and

That " even upon the evidence already given, the present system of ownership and working in the coal industry stands condemned, and some other system must be substituted for it, either nationalisation or a method of unification by national purchase and/or by joint control."

The Leader of the House, Mr. Bonar Law, told the House of Commons on March 20th :

> " The Government is prepared to adopt the report in the spirit as well as in the letter, and to take all the necessary steps to carry out its recommendations without delay."

Five days later he informed the miners :

> " If this Commission is allowed to continue, Interim Reports will be issued dealing with subject after subject in which you are vitally interested, and not merely will these Interim Reports be issued, which in ordinary circumstances might be put in the waste-paper basket, but it is part of the Government's undertaking to deal with these Reports in the spirit as well as in the letter, and steps will be taken to enable these recommendations to be carried into effect."

After which assurance the miners, by ballot, decided that they also would accept the recommendations of the Interim Report. The Commission continued, now with explicit reference to the issue of nationalisation. Not unnaturally, the miners' hopes ran high, and higher as point after point was scored by their very able representatives on the Commission. On June 23rd, the final Reports appeared. The Chairman's report opened as follows :

(1) I recommend that Parliament be invited immediately to pass legislation acquiring the coal royalties for the State and paying fair and just compensation to the owners.

(2) I recommend on the evidence before me that the principle of State ownership of the coal mines be accepted.

With these conclusions the Labour members were in substantial agreement ; there being thus a majority of 7 out of the 13 members reporting in favour of the principle of nationalisation. Sir Arthur Duckham, reporting independently and against nationalisation, decided " that the private ownership of minerals has not been and is not in the best interests of the community," and that " the whole of the mineral rights of Great Britain should be acquired by the State," to be administered by a Ministry of Mines through a series of District Boards of directors on which the workmen should be represented ; and that the State should retain the right to take over any Board which for four years out of seven failed to pay its way. The remaining members of the Commission agreed " that it is clear that the present economic condition of the industry cannot continue " and that full nationalisation would not improve it. They recommended that the State should acquire the ownership of the coal in the mines, and supervise both working and labour conditions ; they also emphasized the importance of the decline in output.

On August 18th Mr. Lloyd George reminded the House of Commons of the pledge as to the Interim Report given by Mr. Bonar Law, and continued :

" In that Report there is a recommendation in favour of the unification and reorganisation of the industry. In his final Report Mr. Justice Sankey proceeded with his interpretation of that principle. We accept the principle, but we cannot accept Mr. Justice Sankey's final interpretation. His scheme for carrying that out we cannot accept."

At the same time the Prime Minister outlined proposals for " unification and reorganisation " of the industry on lines somewhat similar to those of Sir Arthur Duckham's report. The " unification " was to be, not national, but by districts ; and a

subsequent Mining Industry Act (August 16th, 1920)
provided for the establishment of joint district and
national boards. But the miners would have none
of the Government schemes.

Since 1882 the Trade Union Congress had passed
42 resolutions in favour of nationalisation. On
September 10th, 1919, it passed one more : condemn-
ing the Government proposals, pledging itself to help
the miners in coercing the Government to accept
nationalisation, instructing its Committee to see
the Prime Minister and insist on compliance, and in
case of refusal arranging for a special congress to
decide " the form of action to be taken to compel the
Government."

§ 2.

The Prime Minister was duly interviewed, and, as
anticipated, declined to go beyond the Government
unification scheme based on the Duckham report.
The action of another member of the Triple Alliance
had furnished the Government with an additional
argument. For nine days in September-October
the railwaymen had held up the transport system
over a wage dispute with the Government.* The
issue had been attended with the novel feature of
rival propaganda by poster and advertisement on
both sides. But the railwaymen had acted with a
cavalier disregard not only of the general public,
but of their partners in the Triple Alliance. Public
feeling, irritated at the inconvenience, and confused
by the figures, had been against the strikers ; and
the demonstration that national control afforded no
remedy for industrial unrest was turned to account
against the miners. Congress, meeting in December,
had now to answer its own question as to the next

* For a full account see Webb: *op. cit.*

step ; but all that it was asked as yet to do was to sanction an intensive educational campaign agreed on by the united Labour executives.

The "Mines for the Nation" campaign was accordingly inaugurated. During January and February the Labour party, by meetings, demonstrations, leaflets, pamphlets, advertisement, conducted a grand frontal attack on public opinion—and failed. Unaided by the popular press, the assault left public opinion unconverted, almost unmoved. Circumstances were against the miners ; the tide was setting in the opposite direction. The experience of the war and of the past year could be quoted against as well as in favour of nationalisation, and the reaction against every form of control made the idea vaguely repugnant even to many trade unionists. Bitterly Hodges remarked that the opposition experienced made them feel sometimes that it would be " better to start with the children, and drop all this high-falutin' talk about the intelligence of the working classes." Quite evidently the prospect of vigorous trade union action for a principle was no nearer than it ever had been ; and when, in February, 1920, the Congress met to decide the fate of the forward policy, the issue was a foregone conclusion that Hodges' incisive harangue could not change.

" We have seen the inertia," said he, " in regard to profits in the wool and cotton trades, and we have seen industrial action taken for advances in wages. But when we have said that we do not desire increases in wages, the cynicism with which we have been greeted appals us. We are not believed. . . . If there is not to be any great movement for nationalisation, where do you thrust the miners to ? Into the vortex where all of you appear to be swimming. Wages, wages, wages ! An endless and futile race after prices, instead of tackling fundamentally the whole problem."

But the Philippic was unavailing. Called on at
last for a clear choice as to method, trade union
delegates rejected the policy of a general strike for
nationalisation by 3,870,000 votes against 1,050,000.
There was no mistaking that answer.

Ca'canny is the sulk of labour; and ca'canny set
in at the coal mines. More; since the country would
have none of their nationalisation, why then the
miners would join the rest in the wage-scramble,
and damn the profits of the industry. More wages
they got, after another strike ballot, in April—a
further 2s. per shift. Then in May the Government,
in face of the miners' opposition, advanced the price
of coal by 14s. 2d. a ton, as a first step towards putting
back the industry on a " normal basis "; and the
crest of the wave was in sight.

§ 3.

The crucial phase of the movement began at
Leamington on July 7th, 1920, when the Miners'
Federation decided upon a dual demand: for a
wage increase of 2s. per shift and a reduction in the
price of domestic coal by 14s. 2d. per ton. The wages
claim was based on the cost of living and backed by
the miners' disapproval of the Government scheme
for buying out the royalty owners with the excess
profits of the industry; the price reduction on the
contention that the industry as a whole could well
afford it, and also perhaps on the desire of the
miners emphatically to disclaim the onus of gain at
the expense of the community. This " one and
indissoluble " claim was duly presented to the Board
of Trade, and criticised by its President (Sir Robert
Horne). Sir Robert averred that the miners' wages
had now increased at least as much as the cost of
living; that the price of British domestic supplies

was considerably lower than the world price, and that
in fact the high profit on the export trade alone
made possible the home figure ; and further, that
whereas at present the bulk of the profit went direct
to the Exchequer, the miners were in fact demanding
that 27 millions of it should go in wages, 36 in reduction of prices, and only about 3 direct to the State.
Excess profits of other industries were going to the
Exchequer, indirectly therefore to the community ;
why should the coal industry be made the exception ?

It was in fact unfortunate for the miners that their
bonâ fide claim for a price reduction met with very
little welcome from the general public. Perhaps the
nature of the demand was still too novel ; certainly
the miners' determination to press it was doubted ;
and when at a later date the miners were induced to
waive the price demand in favour of an " enquiry,"
and were left clinging to the wage demand only, their
bid for general support definitely failed.

Both sides now took a stiffer attitude. The miners
by ballot decided in favour of strike action, and
tendered notices to expire on September 25th. The
Government maintained in effect that while the
wage question might be dealt with by arbitration,
the price question was ultimately a matter for
Parliament, to which neither the miners nor anybody
else could dictate. Even yet, however, the miners
stuck to their principle—to the point at least of
stipulating that their wage increase should not be
put on the price of domestic coal ; and they further
proposed an investigation into the causes of declining
output. With this new element a prospect of settlement seemed to open, the Government indicating a
much more favourable attitude to wage demands
when made contingent upon output. Meanwhile the
question of continuation of control had been
broached ; Frank Hodges had pointed out to the
Government how the national treatment of the

industry safeguarded the workers in the least profitable districts. For the present, however, no trouble was anticipated on that score, since, said Sir Robert Horne, nobody suggested decontrolling prices now or at any near period (September 9th).

On the principle of wages-per-output negotiations continued during the early part of September, the miners still sticking to their demand for 2s. per shift increase as a preliminary. But strike notices were in and due to expire on the 25th; the matter was getting urgent. At which point enter on the men's side the Council of the Triple Alliance with an endorsement of the miners' claim; on the Government's side, the Prime Minister. Two days before the threatened strike a saving " formula " was drawn up; and on the 24th Mr. Lloyd George persuaded the miners' executive to consent to the suspension of the strike for a week in order that the " formula " might have due consideration. The formula embodied the " datum line " proposal—which, as finally defined, meant an increase of 1s. to correspond with an output at the rate of 240 million tons a year, with an additional 6d. for each 4 million tons. To secure the increased output, the mine-owners promised their hearty co-operation.

Strike notices had now been suspended a second time, and during the second week of October the datum line proposal was put to the vote of the miners. The situation seemed, to the uninformed, distinctly hopeful. The ill-starred price demand had disappeared; the 2s. had not been conceded unconditionally, but apparently fair means had been devised by which an even greater interest might soon accrue; into the bargain, there was a prospect of more coal getting to the surface. The decisive rejection of the scheme by the miners' ballot was a shock to more than the general public. Robert Smillie had advised the men to accept.

P

Something of tragedy lurks about the sequel.
On October 18th work ceased in all the coal mines
of Great Britain ; what was probably the widest
and most disciplined strike in British history up to
that date began—and with it probably the last phase
of the British mining industry. Older leaders of
the men looked on with grave misgiving ; it seemed
as if the strike threat, once let loose, had insisted
despite all efforts on its own fulfilment. In truth,
the pent-up dissatisfaction of five years was behind
the movement, reinforced by the vague revolutionary
ardour of South Wales and the disappointment of
the whole trade over its repeated failure to enlist
public sympathy. In some districts the men had
come out early in October without waiting for the
national order. And yet—greatest pity of it all—
the issue had narrowed down during four months'
negotiation to nothing better than the old-type wage
demand.

There was a momentous sequel. The support of
the whole Triple Alliance of miners, railwaymen and
transport workers was discussed, and the railwaymen, led by C. T. Cramp, delivered a 48-hours'
ultimatum threatening sympathetic action. The
Government replied with the most drastic measure
in modern legislation. The Emergency Powers Act,
introduced on October 22nd, authorises a Government to " proclaim " a " state of emergency " if it
appears that " any action has been taken, or is
immediately threatened, by any person or body of
persons, of such a nature, or on so extensive a scale,
as . . . to deprive the community, or any substantial portion of the community, of the essentials
of life " ; such action being envisaged to include
interference with the supply and distribution of food,
water, fuel, light, or the means of locomotion.
Under such circumstances, by this Act administration
may in effect be conducted by Order in Council

conferring undefined and unlimited powers on the executive departments and establishing, if necessary, courts of summary jurisdiction. The move was fairly interpreted by the *New Statesman* in a remark that since the Triple Alliance by its evident power to threaten the life of the community " promises the action of unconstitutional forces " the Government in reply " can hardly do less than demand the power of abrogating constitutional principles." The effect on public opinion of the new Act, which received royal assent on October 29th, was immense ; but whether or no it contributed to the suspension of the railwaymen's threat is debatable. The influence of J. H. Thomas, hastily returning from Geneva, was probably more responsible—in the phrase of one organ of the extreme left " Thomas had sabotaged the railway strike." But in fact the issue was not one on which the Triple Alliance could have maintained solidarity in action ; the influence of Thomas, Brace, Hartshorn, and others—reviled as they were for it by the extremists—probably averted not revolution but the collapse of the Triple Alliance. The immediate result was to intensify the efforts for peace. The basis on which the dispute was compromised was first outlined by William Brace, a right wing member of the South Wales Miners' Federation, in Parliament on October 19th ; it led to a settlement on the following lines. The men were to have their 2s. advance on resumption of work ; and during the period January 3rd to March 31st, 1921, the advance was to be liable to fluctuation in accordance with the value of the amount of coal produced in excess of a fixed annual rate of output of 219 million tons. Owners and men undertook to co-operate with a view to obtaining increased output, and also to produce for submission to the Government by March 31st a new scheme for the regulation of wages " having regard, among other considerations, to the profits of the industry, and to the principles upon which any surplus profits are to be dealt with." The proposals thus broadly summarised were put to the vote of the men on November 1st and 2nd ; practically all their leaders advising acceptance. The result showed a slightly adverse majority—346,504 against, 338,045 in favour. By Federation rules a two-thirds majority was necessary to a continuance of the strike. The men were therefore advised to resume work—which they did on November 4th, with less reluctance, even in South Wales and Lancashire, than the heavy adverse votes of those areas had indicated. The eighteen days' struggle was suspended ; it only remained to count—and pay—the cost.

§ 4.

The immediate effect of the stoppage had not been as severe as was anticipated ; partly because large reserves of coal had been accumulating, partly on account of the Emergency Orders of the Board of Trade, limiting the consumption of fuel, light and power. But the fall in employment due to complete or partial stoppage of factories was considerable. By November 3rd the Ministry of Labour reported 95,000 discharges due to closure of works, 148,000 due to reduction of staff, while 348,000 workers had been placed on short time ; 13 or 14 million tons of coal were lost to the country, and 14 or 15 million pounds lost to the miners in wages. But that was not all the loss to either party. Foreign markets, from which the large surplus on the export trade had been derived, were given an additional impetus to seek supplies elsewhere than in England. In something like panic, Continental buyers placed huge orders in America, where, as prices were beginning to fall, they were eagerly welcomed and executed.

The policy of surcharging foreign buyers to subsidise the British consumer, by which no small amount of resentment had been raised abroad, thus ended in a disastrous recoil ; and the additional deliveries of German coal to France, under the terms of the Peace Treaty, finally disposed of this source of profit to the British industry. On the new financial situation thus brought about, and precipitated by the trade depression at home, the new year opened.

CHAPTER VI.

ZERO.

§ 1.

It is as well, before embarking upon the calamitous last phase of the coal industry, to pause for a brief survey of the general position in which it was left by the settlement of November, 1920. That position was one of fundamental instability. State control acting under circumstances in which there was an effective (but temporary and artificial) demand for maximum output, had fixed export prices at a level that savoured of exploitation, and inland prices below the actual cost of production. Standard profits were guaranteed to the owners from a profits pool administered by the State. Wage advances had been awarded to the miners on a flat rate based on a maintenance principle that had nothing to do with the economic position of the various coalfields; and to these was now added a bonus on output-value which was really dependent, not on the work of the miners, but on the continuance of the artificial effective demand. Certain concealed possibilities were inherent in all this. Pits were working, even in 1920, that did not yield the standard profit; and obviously when the artificial demand ceased—a contingency that the Peace Treaty alone had done much to ensure—the number of such pits would enormously increase. What then would be the position of the Government in respect of the guaranteed profits? Further: with inland demand stifled by the trade depression, what means would remain by which the economic position of the industry could be retrieved? An increase in the price of coal would only contribute to the dilemma and was admitted by all parties to be undesirable; and for a decrease in wages—which were estimated as amounting to over 75 per cent. of the cost of production—no machinery whatever had been left in existence. Was the profits pool arrangement to degenerate into a plain subsidy? If so, what was to be the end of it? If not, what was to happen to wages?

One by one, these contingencies were realised—as inevitably they must be. Early in 1921 the Government estimated that by the end of March the profits pool would be exhausted. On February 28th the Secretary for Mines announced that from that date on—in consequence, be it remembered, of the loss of export trade and the industrial depression at home which had already resulted in almost universal short time working and as much as 50 per cent. unemployment in some coalfields—no further output wage would be payable under the November agreement. Pit after pit was closing, unemployment increasing week by week, the profits-pool steadily draining. Then came the "bomb shell": financial control of the industry was to cease on March 31st.

It is doubtful whether so drastic a purge had ever before been administered to any industry. Owners and miners alike protested—the former at the prospect of being compelled to resume management at a moment when the industry was losing at the rate of over £50,000,000 a year; the latter at the prospect of the cessation of unification, the abandonment of all progress towards nationalisation, and a probable return to the pre-war status. The Government replied that no industry ought to be carried on by subsidy, and that since export prices and home prices were now almost identical, the necessity for control—protection of the home consumer—had disappeared.

Now during the preceding weeks two sets of negotiations had been going on. The coal-owners and the Government had been considering a revision of the arrangement as to guaranteed profits, and had agreed that in view of the decline in the pool, owners should waive their claim to any surplus over pre-war profits for the period March, 1919, to December, 1920, and in return should be guaranteed nine-tenths of the pre-war profit for the first quarter of 1921. The owners and the government were also alive to the possibility of serious industrial trouble should both mines and railways be decontrolled simultaneously in August; and the owners' opposition to the earlier cessation of control was subject to the possibility that should the State be compelled to continue control through a period of loss, control might be maintained through the subsequent recovery until at least the national account were squared again. By these considerations the owners were induced to accept decontrol on March 31st.

A second set of negotiations between masters and men with a view to providing a new wage-basis for the industry had been proceeding in accordance with the previous strike settlement ; and by the beginning of March agreement had been reached as to the following principles :—

1. Wages must conform to the capacity of the industry to pay them.

2. The receipt of a standard wage should justify a corresponding minimum profit. (The miners suggested that the profit should be 10

per cent., the owners that it should be 17 per cent. of the wages total.)

3. Any surplus remaining should be divided in agreed proportions. (The miners suggested that 10 per cent., the owners that 20 per cent., should be allocated to profits.)

4. Joint audit of the owners' books.

This was not an altogether hopeless position ; but the sudden imminence of decontrol when there was actually not only no surplus, but not enough proceeds to pay the existing wage-bill, precipitated the inevitable crisis. In the new situation all hope of agreement rapidly disappeared. The fundamental issue had in fact already emerged in the discussions on the standard wage to which the minimum profit was to correspond. The owners proposed " to take the district base rates including percentage additions (or their equivalent) prevailing in July, 1914." The Miners' Federation demanded " the national settlement of wage and profits problems " to be brought about by means of " a National Wage Board which would have the right to levy a small sum per ton on all the coal raised to be used to keep the poorer collieries in production as long as they were required." To this demand for a National Wage Board and a National Profits Pool, the mine-owners emphatically demurred. " We maintain," they said, " that to adopt such a principle would be suicidal to the industry. Where is the incentive to the individual to manage efficiently his own colliery so as to produce the greatest output at the lowest possible cost, to improve methods of working by introducing machinery, and to expend capital to get the best results, if he knows that in the event of a loss it will be made up, and if he makes more than a certain profit it will be taken from him ? It is this unsound, pernicious economic doctrine that the coal-owners are determined to reject at all costs." Here, in other words, was the

naked issue : which were we to maintain—a
" natural " system under which profit-earning capacity determined the working of the coal-mines, or
an " artificial " system under which labour could
be reckoned a standing first charge on the industry,
and social control take the place of economic
regulation ? Whether or no nationalisation as formerly understood was involved in the pooling
arrangement was now a secondary issue.   The miners
maintained that it was not essential—that the
national regulation might be voluntary ; the owners
pointed out that inasmuch as they were determined
not to accept it voluntarily, legislation would be
required to make them.   But whether or no national-
sation were a necessary corollary the issue was
fundamental ; and it involved the fate of the
competitive " capitalist " system.

Decontrol being fixed for March 31st, the mine-
owners gave legal notice to terminate the existing
wage-contracts throughout the coalfields and published new wage-lists for the various districts at
which they were prepared to offer future employment. These lists, which were presumably based on
the real economic situation in the districts, showed
reductions in average wages of all workers in 13
districts ranging from about 40s. per week in South
Wales to 6s. in Cannock, and in the cases of South
Yorkshire and Leicestershire average increases of 1s.
and 6s. 5d. Averages, however, are in this case
of even less than their usual relevance ; for the
uncontested fact was that in the case of certain
classes, after allowance made for the increase of
141 per cent. in the cost of maintaining the pre-
war working class standard of life, the new schedules
meant a considerably smaller real wage than was
paid in July, 1914. In several cases the new wage
was less than that of unskilled labourers ; in some
it was less than was being paid to men engaged on

road construction by way of unemployment relief. On this score considerable sympathy was felt with the miners. The latter did not dispute the necessity, under any system, of a fall in wages ; but they were prepared to discuss it on the national basis only, and claimed temporary financial assistance for the industry from the Government to prevent its present economic condition driving real wages below the 1914 standard. Settlement district by district they were not prepared to discuss at all. Throughout the negotiations the principle of national settlement was not merely adhered to, but made preliminary to any negotiation on the actual figures. The Government sternly refused either an extension of control or a subsidy ; and thus with chaos and bankruptcy in the industry and masters and men lined up for devastating warfare, State control of the coal mines came to an end on March 31st, 1921. On the same day, for the second time in six months, work ceased in all the coal-mines of Great Britain

§ 2.

Such was the issue, narrowly defined, that in April brought Great Britain to the gravest industrial crisis of its history. But to comprehend that in which it proved potent to concentrate the fighting strength of organised labour on what was apparently a point of economic principle a somewhat wider view is necessary.

In the first place there was the broad position, in regard to the general state of trade, of the coal industry itself and of one or two other essential services. Britain was organised on a scale that made world trade essential to her internal prosperity. Under the present system, therefore, any general improvement in the internal economies of the country was primarily dependent on such a fall in the relative cost of produce for the world market as would enable British industry to meet foreign competition. Which meant, in condensed cold fact, that a fall of the cost of production in industries which lay at the very basis of British trade was a precedent condition of any real improvement in the economic welfare of British workers. It was thus probable that for a limited period wages in certain cardinal industries—of which coal mining was the chief—would in the absence of special regulation tend to decline faster than the cost of living. Short of an economic revolution there was no escape from this limiting consideration.

Secondly, the general fall in wages had begun. In several industries it operated automatically by sliding scales based on the cost of living. In others agreement had been reached by collective bargaining. In others again the reduction was proceeding piecemeal, firm by firm. In several of the smaller industries lower rates were in operation by the end of March, the decrease varying as a rule between 10 and 20 per cent. of average wages. But in regard to the greater trades of the country the general fall was as yet only pending. In both shipbuilding and engineering trades a drop of 6s. per week in time-workers' wages, 15 per cent. in piece-rates plus the cessation of the $12\frac{1}{2}$ per cent. bonus on earnings, was proposed by the employers as from the end of April; but no agreement had as yet been arrived at, and the issue was being awaited by many trades in which changes in engineering rates were generally followed. Transport by rail, road and water was affected; cuts of from 4s. to 27s. a week were proposed in various branches of the two last-named, while on the railways a sharp dispute over the interpretation of a sliding scale agreement occupied the first fortnight of March. More significant to the railwaymen was the question as to what would happen when control of the railways came to an end in August. Alarming rumours were circulated according to which the companies intended to abolish national settlements and to make further drastic cuts in basic wages. With a view to the contingency the National Union of Railwaymen reaffirmed, early in March, its insistence on the principles of nationalisation of the railways and full partnership of the workers in their management ; while among the various grades and districts a strong movement was afoot for strengthening the machinery of the union, and more effectively using the power of the Triple Alliance. In the building trades also the operatives were balloting on the adoption of a sliding scale by which wages would be reduced in the immediate future. During the first four months of 1921 arrangements for reduction of wages were made, and in the majority of cases put into practice, in 51 industries affecting $1\frac{3}{4}$ million workpeople. It was of course inevitable that the initiative in reducing wages should come from the employers ; but it is safe to say that a majority of the workers and of their leaders, in view of the falling cost of living and of the unprecedented decline in the commercial prosperity of the country, acknowledged the force of the *prima facie* case. Extremists, however, took the opportunity to foment class feeling, and by the Socialist press, especially the *Daily Herald*, the situation was represented as the " Employers' War on Wages."

As such the building trade operatives—who were threatened with forcible " dilution " as well as lower wages—at once took it seriously ; and with a view to united labour opposition they requested the Triple Alliance, early in March, to call a conference of the most powerful industrial societies. The Triple Alliance declined the request as not within its competence, and the matter passed on to the Trade Union Congress Committee. The Committee, as might have been expected, declined to mobilise the whole Labour movement, and recommended instead conferences by trade groups of the unions affected. The builders, determined on some sort of common action, accordingly decided at the end of the month to call a conference of the engineers and other kindred societies ; but their invitation met with a chilly response, and a plain " No " from the engineers. By this time, however, the coal dispute was dominating the entire situation, and calls for the Triple Alliance were many and insistent.

§ 3.

Throughout the catastrophic sequel it is necessary to recall the fact that the miners were fighting, not on a wage-question (as to which no small body of public opinion supported them) but for a principle relative to the control of the coal industry. Their action was thus made consistent with the policy which for four years, under the guidance of its permanent secretary, the Miners' Federation had pursued. On this issue, which practically, if not theoretically, involved legislation, they were opposed by the Government as well as the coal-owners ; and their antagonism to the former was strengthened by the conviction that in advancing the date of decontrol the Government had deliberately precipitated the crisis. The strike thus took on a distinct anti-constitutional bearing. While orthodox trade unionism backed it on the wage question, revolutionary Labour welcomed its wider aspect.

At the very outset a certain division of temper was manifest within the Miners' Executive itself. A decision to withdraw the pump hands and enginemen was reached by a narrow majority, and issued by the secretary under protest. It was a desperate decision, said Hodges ; a decision which would only have been taken in the most desperate circumstances. But the circumstances were desperate : " I think the Government means to starve us into submission. If it is a question of endurance we may go down If we go down, the nation is doomed." The decision was obeyed. The flooding of the mines began.

The Government apparently concurred in Mr Hodges' diagnosis of the situation as desperate. A " State of Emergency " under the Act of October, 1920, had been proclaimed on the eve of the stoppage. At the commencement of the following week naval and military leave was stopped, and movements of troops, tanks, and machine-guns began. On Friday, April 8th (by which date minor riots had occurred at the pit-heads in Wales, Lanarkshire, and Fifeshire), the Prime Minister announced that in view of the imminent flooding of the.mines and the necessity for armed protection of voluntary workers, a Royal Proclamation had been issued calling out the army Reserve, Class B of the Royal Fleet Reserve, and the Air Force Reserve : the Army Reserve being called for " permanent service." New Defence Units attached to the regular army were to be formed for " temporary military service not exceeding 90 days "; and " Loyal Citizens capable of bearing arms " were invited to enrol.

On the evening of this same Friday the Triple Alliance made its first declaration as a fighting body.

" Unless negotiations are re-opened between the Miners' Federation, the mine-owners or the Government, the full strike power of the Triple Alliance shall be put into operation as from Tuesday next at midnight."

Strike committees began organising up and down the country ; the wages issue was emphasised in propaganda, and the successful miners' strike of 1915 was recalled. Violence was everywhere deprecated by the Labour spokesmen ; but the issue was represented as a " frontal attack on the whole working-class " by " the Capitalists and their Government." Meanwhile inside the Alliance Executive the miners were being urged to negotiate.

The way was cleared by the Government waiving its prior condition as to the return of the safety-men, the miners agreeing not to oppose voluntary action. Negotiations were re-opened ; the general strike postponed. But the miners insisted that their principle must be conceded before wage negotiations could begin ; and an offer from the Government of temporary financial aid to the industry after economic wages for the various districts had been agreed on by the owners and the Miners' Federation failed to weaken them The Triple Alliance, it is important to notice, was now committed to a position in which a bare majority of the miners, by simply refusing to negotiate, could virtually compel the whole machine into action. The Alliance had in fact either to reaffirm the strike decision or to retreat ; and despite passionate efforts of its more moderate members to escape the dilemma, the strike decision was " unanimously " reaffirmed. J. H. Thomas, a man visibly racked by an almost insupportable ordeal, announced on Wednesday, April 13th, that at 10 p.m. on the following Friday night the general strike would begin.

§ 4.

With this momentous decision the whole issue took on a wider character. The Alliance was the supreme fighting machine of organised Labour. For five years its directors had hesitated on the brink of action, and time after time the insurgent elements in Labour had looked in vain for a fighting lead. Only

four weeks ago the building trades operatives had
sought help from the Alliance rather than the Trade
Union Congress, and the Alliance had again hesitated.
Now at last the vast machine was in motion, and the
whole civil and military force of the Government
was mobilised against it. "We are not proclaiming
a revolution," said the Triple Alliance ; but the
tactics of the opposing leaders had forced the issue
to nothing less ;* and the letter of the dispute was
overshadowed by the major question of fact—could
organised Labour successfully give battle to the
forces of the British constitution ? The prospect was
enought to appal bolder men than Thomas.

On either side the last stages of mobilisation were
hurried on. Kensington Gardens became an armed
camp. Hyde Park and Regent's Park were occupied
by quasi-military transport equipped for the emergency scheme of food distribution. Voluntary transport
was enrolled and organised. Disused military camps
of the great war were reoccupied ; and the country
was divided into eleven areas to which the Civil
Commissioners and their staffs were despatched. On
the Labour side the whole political movement—the
Parliamentary Committee of the Trade Union Congress, the Parliamentary Labour Party, and the
National Labour Party—pledged its support to the
Triple Alliance, and urged " every citizen who cares
for the well-being of the community to stand solidly
against this attack on the workers' position."
Union after union signified its adherence. The
Locomotive Engineers sank their quarrel with the
railwaymen and arranged to strike with the rest ;
the Electrical Trades Union in London promised a
simultaneous withdrawal of labour ; the executive
council of the 1,500,000 General Workers pledged

* " The Triple Alliance, had it but responded to the pressure of the
militants at the time of the most recent mining crisis, would have precipitated a revolutionary situation."—Robert Williams : *The New Labour
Outlook.*

its support whenever and wherever possible. Local
Labour councils up and down the country assisted
in the organisation of strike committees. The
Co-operative movement made special arrangements
for the disbursement of trade union funds ; and on
the left flank Communist parties and unofficial
organisations rattled the side drums and raised
their scarlet standard.

§ 5.

The miners had now been idle for fourteen days.
Over 8,000,000 tons of coal had already been lost,
and what damage had been done to the mines no
man could yet say. The weather had turned to
bitter cold and in many parts of England snow was
falling. The number of totally unemployed workers
had risen in the fortnight from 1,450,000 (12.1 per
cent.) to 1,693,238 (12.6 per cent.) in addition to
over 875,000 working short time. In many districts
the miners' funds were running low ; in at least
one county the second week's strike pay had drained
them dry. The prospect of actual starvation was
drawing nearer ; in all parties men were appalled
by the outlook, and the official leaders of the Triple
Alliance itself were advancing under pressure, in
horror rather than in hope.

So matters stood on the very eve of the general
strike. Debate in Parliament had been postponed
from day to day as likely to prejudice the success
of the negotiations ; but with success no longer
possible, members of the House of Commons,
braving the disapproval of the " Whips," took the
affair into their own hands ; and the general welcome
given by all parties to their action indicated a widespread sense of something previously lacking. The
coal-owners were invited to state their position to a

meeting of private members on the Thursday evening, at which meeting it was ascertained on the owners' admission that the new wages offered to the men were in fact no better than the miners had for some weeks been asserting. The impression made on the members was naturally profound ; and it was there and then resolved that the miners should be invited to state their case forthwith. The invitation was conveyed to Hodges and Thomas who happened to be dining together in the House ; and at 9.30 that evening Frank Hodges stood up to plead the cause of the miners of Great Britain before what, after all, appeared to be the supreme Tribunal (in undress) of the country.

Before such an audience Hodges was naturally at his best. His sensitive mind was instant to grasp the tenour of the meeting. By bitter experience he had come to despair of direct industrial action for an abstract principle ; but on the wages issue he had the manifest sympathy of the Parliamentary gathering as well as of the country, and by a decision of no small personal temerity he decided to stake all upon it. The miners, he said, would be prepared to consider a temporary settlement of the wages issue provided their fundamental demands were not ruled out of a permanent settlement. Thomas followed with a personal opinion that in the event of this declaration bearing fruit, there need be no Triple Alliance strike. The Prime Minister, " amazed and sceptical," was apprised of the turn in events at midnight ; and the miners were at once invited to open negotiations on the ground Hodges had suggested.

Such was the situation that broke the Triple Alliance. On the Friday morning—" Black Friday," as it came to be called in advanced Labour circles— Hodges was repudiated by a majority of two on the Miners' Executive. Leaders of the Railway and Transport Workers fell to wild recrimination as to the general position (which in reality had not changed), and the solidarity of their men ; and after a day that disposed of any credit that still remained to Labour strategy, the strike of the Railway and Transport Workers was called off, less than six hours before it was due to begin. The reason assigned was that the refusal of the miners to negotiate on Hodges' terms impaired the prospect of united action.

In point of fact, Hodge's unauthorised offer, whether designedly or no, had given the non-militant sections of the railway and transport executives an opportunity of escape from their dilemma. The strike order would have been obeyed by an effective proportion of the associated unions in the principal centres. On the wages issue alone it would have been obeyed without question ; but on any issue it is difficult for a trade-unionist in a well-organised centre to disobey an official order to strike. At the same time a bare majority of the miners had forced the Triple Alliance to adopt the weaker tactical position, in which majorities of their associated executives felt grave misgiving ; and the action of the Government overlooking the immediate issue, appeared (as perhaps it was meant to appear) as challenging those who desired a violent revolution to invoke it. If that were in fact the issue, among neither the transport workers nor the railway men was there a majority prepared to take up the challenge. It must remain a matter of the gravest doubt whether, even assuming a general strike to have been followed by a temporary re-control of the coal mines, ultimate victory in the national struggle would have rested with the miners.

§ 6.

The immediate sequel was a new effort at compromise. Revised terms were offered on a basis of unification by areas—a scheme which the miners had already refused to accept as the Mining Industry Act of 1920 ; a State grant of £10,000,000 was also offered, on certain conditions, for the mitigation and equalisation of the wage reductions. But the National Pool was defined by the Government as a political issue involving legislation ; and the miners' delegates replied " that this conference rejects the Government proposals, as they do not concede the fundamental principles of a National Wages Board and a National Pool, for which we stand." Complete deadlock was thus again reached over exactly the position on which it first arose. But within the other unions even the appearance of solidarity broke down. The headquarters offices of the Transport Workers were actually seized and held for two days by rebels of the rank-and-file ; branches and leaders complained bitterly and in public of the " great betrayal " which other branches and leaders struggled to justify. Unorganised action was taken in certain centres where dockers and other workers refused to handle imported coal, or coal lying at sidings, or to bunker vessels known to be taking sufficient coal for an outward voyage only. This " embargo " policy subsequently received official confirmation both by the N.U.R. and the T.W.F. ; and the latter body, through the International Federation of Transport Workers, attempted to secure the co-operation of dock labourers in other countries. But the general instruction did not secure sufficient adherence among the affiliated unions to be effective, and by one of them it was actively opposed. After the collapse of the major strike threat, little enthusiasm was displayed for the direct action policy on a smaller scale, and the embargo on imported coal was officially withdrawn, in view of the *de facto* failure, on June 1st. Mean-

while, unofficial conferences of railway and transport
workers, and of other unions, had been convened, at
which various means of reviving the militant movement were proposed ; and the National Workers'
Committee attempted to organise a general strike
for May 15th :* but without visible result. In
point of fact, even had the desire for such a policy
been general, the unprecedented unemployment
rendered sympathetic strike action almost imprac-
ticable ; and such positive assistance as the other
unions could render the miners was mainly limited
during the rest of the stoppage to grants or loans
to the funds of the various miners' associations.
Perhaps in this direction the most useful aid of all
was that rendered by the Co-operative Societies,
whose system of allowing credit to their members in
the affected areas enabled many a miner's family to
obtain at least food long after its removable assets
had found their way to the pawnbroker's. Mention
must also be made of the *Daily Herald* fund for the
miners' children, which by the end of June totalled
£76,797, raised almost entirely in small subscriptions.

For a sullen month, during which the weekly
totals of unemployed rose to still more ominous
levels, no official move towards a settlement was
made by either side. Informal conversations, however, were held, as a result of which the Government
on May 28th made further definite proposals. A
grant of £10,000,000 from the Exchequer was
offered, to be used in mitigating wage reductions ;

---

* The National Workers' Committee Movement (Miners' section) at
the end of April circulated a pamphlet among railway and transport
workers from which the following passage is quoted : " Your officials
have prevented action up to date. They will continue to prevent action
so long as you depend upon them. Disregard them. Set up in every
district unofficial committees, and set them up now. These unofficial
committees will do their best to secure as early as possible an official strike,
but failing that you must obey their call to action by May 15th at latest
and declare an unofficial strike." The pamphlet was subsequently the
subject of a prosecution and an appeal, as to which see the *Manchester
Guardian*, 23rd July, 1921.

to which end the mine-owners also volunteered to surrender their profits during three months in districts in which, and in so far as, Government assistance was necessary. The Government grant was made conditional on the conclusion of a " continuing agreement," and was coupled with certain proposals for a permanent settlement, which were understood, until the impression was officially removed, to refer to compulsory arbitration. It was also evident from the wording of the Government offer that district settlements of wages were contemplated. These suggestions were referred by the Miners' Executive to district conferences ; and in every case rejected. In reply the Government intimated (on June 3rd) that it had no further proposals to make, and that the offer of £10,000,000 would remain open only for fourteen days longer. Negotiations between the miners and the owners were at once resumed, and a week later further proposals were submitted to a national delegate conference. Definite terms as to standard and minimum wages, and a maximum initial reduction were now added to suggestions on the lines already indicated ; and it was then decided that a ballot of the men should be taken on the question of acceptance or fighting on " for the principles of the National Wages Board and National Pool." Again contrary to much popular expectation, the ballot resulted in rejection of the terms by the overwhelming majority of 435,890 to 180,724.

But the end was in sight. The powers of endurance not only of the miners' associations, but of the Co-operative Societies, were in many cases on the verge of exhaustion, and there was no prospect that success would be brought appreciably nearer by a protraction of the struggle. A curious incident revealed the pass to which the miners had now come. In March, as we saw, the building workers appealed to the Triple Alliance, to the Trades Unions Congress, and to other unions for some sort of concerted action against wage reductions. Now, three disastrous months later, the miners—who had hitherto, even in the counsels of the Triple Alliance, been a law unto themselves—appealed to other unions affected by wage reductions for a conference to discuss joint action. But even less than in March was joint action now practicable : no conference was held. Still more significant was Hodges' speech to the Labour party on June 21st :

> "The conclusion we have drawn," he said, "is that, industrially, the trade union movement is for the most part unhappily a mere grouping of close corporations with only the interests of a particular group at stake ; and as the British industrial movement develops we find that tendency more and more marked. . . . There are things in our programme which may not be susceptible of success in this stoppage. Maybe we shall have to bend, but we shall not rest content until we have achieved politically what we have failed to get industrially. We must achieve it ; we cannot help but do so. Our ultimate triumph is inevitable."

That was a frank and courageous admission of imminent defeat. A week later agreed terms of settlement were recommended by the Miners' Federation executive to the districts ; and on July 1st the terms were formally accepted and endorsed on behalf of the Miners' Federation of Great Britain, the Mining Association, and the Government.

§ 7.

In the general sense, among the trade unionists, of defeat, and among the remainder of the community, of relief, little critical examination of the settlement was made.

As regards " the fundamental principles of a National Wages Board and a National Pool, for which we stand " the miners were completely defeated. On this issue—and the miners had insisted that it was the cardinal issue—the whole of the three months' suffering was totally and absolutely wasted. A " National Board " was indeed provided by the settlement, but the only functions assigned to it were those of determining what items should be included as " cost of production other than wages," and of deciding the dates of wage revision after September, 1921. The district basis was re-established by a schedule of 13 areas, in each of which joint boards were to be formed on lines similar to those of the Mining Act of 1920. As regards wages, a new standard was defined on the district basis, consisting of the existing base rates plus the pre-war percent ages, war advances thus being dropped ; and the minimum wage was fixed at 20 per cent. above the standard. Immediate reductions were reduced to 2s., 2s. 6d , and 3s. per shift in July, August and September by the use of the Government grant of £10,000,000. In the view of Frank Hodges, a better settlement could probably have been secured in March, before the stoppage began, and certainly after the House of Commons' speech, had the miners' executive consented to negotiate. The settlement embodied the principles (agreed upon before the stoppage began) that the receipt of a standard wage should justify a corresponding minimum profit, and that any surplus should be divided in agreed proportions ; the standard profit being 17 per cent. of the standard wage bill, and the surplus being divided as to 83 per cent. wages and 17 per cent. profit. The principle of joint audit of the owners' books (also agreed upon in March) was incorporated.

Certain clauses of the final terms do, however, mark some advance in principle. In the first place, the regulation of wages is made dependent, not directly upon the price of coal as formerly, but upon " the surplus proceeds of the industry." A more interesting advance is implied in the following provisions :

" If the rates of wages thus determined in any district do not provide a subsistence to low-paid day wage workers, such additions in the form of allowances per shift worked shall be made for that period to the daily wages of these workers as, in the opinion of the District Board, or, in the event of failure to agree by the parties, in the opinion of the Independent Chairman, may be necessary for the purpose. Such allowances shall be treated as items of cost in the district ascertainments."

" In any district in which reductions in wages continue to be made after the first ascertainment, no part of the surplus proceeds shall be assigned to profits if and in so far as this would have the effect of reducing the wages below the level in the preceding month."

" In any district in which the wages calculated in accordance with the terms of this settlement are less than the wages payable under the maximum reductions aforesaid, the difference shall be met by the owners in that district during September to the extent of the aggregate net profits realised by them on the district ascertainment for July, and during October to the extent of the aggregate net profits realised by them on the district ascertainments for July and August."

In these clauses there is implied a definite, though partial, recognition of the principle that the " maintenance of the worker shall be the first charge on the industry."

The soundness of the general settlement remains to be tested. Under the profit-sharing scheme it is probable that variations between district wages may be at least as great as before the war. In so far as such variations were a cause of discontent the finality of the terms may perhaps be questioned. More certain is the prospect that for the financial provisions to prove stable the numbers employed in the industry must be reduced by at least as much, and probably more, than the absorption of labour during the war (estimated at 200,000). And even then, how long the standard wage will remain payable, and how long the miners will consent to accept it, remain matters of none too sanguine conjecture.*

* The following statement, issued on July 8th by the Secretary for Mines (Mr. Bridgeman) shows the average earnings per shift before the stoppage, the estimated earnings under the offer of March, and the settlement offer :—

	Average Earnings before stoppage.		Estimated Earnings.	
	June, 1914.	March, 1921.	March offer (for April).	Settlement offer until end of July
	s. d.	s. d.	s. d.	s. d.
Cumberland	6 11	17 11	9 11	15 11
Lancs and Cheshire ...	6 8	17 0	13 2	15 0
North Staffs	7 7	15 9	11 4	13 9
North Wales	6 4	16 4	9 8	14 4
Salop	5 1	15 9	10 9	13 9
South Staffs	5 3	15 0	9 5	14 0
Cannock Chase ...	6 8	16 0	14 2	14 7
Warwick	6 7	16 8	12 11	15 3
S. Derbyshire ...	6 10	16 8	15 4	15 3
Leicester	6 4	16 9	16 9	15 4
Yorkshire	7 8	18 5	17 2	17 0
Notts and N. Derby ...	7 2	18 6	16 2	17 1
Scotland	7 2	18 6	14 4	16 6
Northumberland	6 11	17 10	12 9	15 10
Durham	6 10	17 11	12 11	15 11
South Wales	7 4	19 5	12 5	17 5
Somerset ...	5 0	15 0	9 11	13 0
Forest of Dean ...	5 7	15. 8	9 3	13 8
Bristol	5 0	15 6	9 8	13 6

§ 8.

The three months' stoppage of the coal-mines, with the resultant increase of unemployment, and heavy drain on trade union resources, naturally accelerated the reduction of wages which the state of the industry, and the fall in the cost of living, seemed to demand. Statistics given in the *Labour Gazette* for July, 1921, indicate that during the first six months of the year the wage rates of 4,324,000 workers were reduced by amounts totalling £1,768,500 per week. A rough calculation suggests that this figure would represent an average reduction of from 10 to 15 per cent. on the wages for December, 1920. Seeing that during the same period the cost of living index declined by 46 points (that is, roughly, $17\frac{1}{2}$ per cent. of the figure for January), it may be argued that in theory the workers secured some economic advantage. But the unprecedented expansion of unemployment must be borne in mind. According to the trade union returns (which probably form the more relevant basis of comparison in this case) three times as much total unemployment prevailed at the end as at the beginning of the six months. Despite State and trade union benefits, it would thus appear that substantially less purchasing power was being distributed to the workers ; and it is certain that notwithstanding the theoretical advantage shown by the wage figures, and ignoring the plight of the miners, the actual average level of working class living as a whole was worse than in 1914. A proportion of the calamitous unemployment was of course a direct consequence of the mining stoppage. But the increase was well under way before the end of March, when the mining industry was losing at the rate of $1\frac{1}{2}$ million pounds per week. Had that loss continued to be borne entirely by the Exchequer the stoppage would certainly have been postponed, but the eventual result would have been to increase the general burden of taxation, thus merely spreading over a wider field and through a longer period the sacrifice represented by the proposed fall in miners' wages, while providing no surety of a revival of prosperity and an increase of employment. In fact the adjustment of industry to the post-war situation, by whatever means achieved, appears to admit of no alternative to a fall in real as well as nominal wages ; and it therefore remains highly problematical whether, while they retain a theoretical advantage of present-day real wages, the workers can escape the negating factor of a fall in the volume of employment. The provision of State employment or maintenance offers no escape from this prospect.

Some reference must be made in conclusion to the effect on general opinion of these developments. Whether or no the intention of the Government was to challenge the revolutionary forces in the country, such was in effect the issue of the policy of March, 1921 ; and in the result those forces were for the time dissipated. In each of the three constituent groups of the Triple Alliance the wrangle over the events of " Black Friday " ended in virtual majority votes of confidence in the officials. The faith of many trade unionists in the possibilities of direct action had suffered a lasting set-back ; and there was a natural reaction in favour of the political weapon. The Labour party, while protesting in accordance with its traditions against the imprisonment of some 70 Communists for seditious speeches, reiterated its refusal to admit them to membership, and commenced preparation for the next election on a larger scale than before.

All this might signify little more than the " swing

of the pendulum " were it not that in many sections
of the community a change, if not of opinion, of
disposition, was commencing. The events of the
past few years had raised the question of the social
status of the great industries. The battle over
the miners' wages suggested that the claim of the
worker to adequate maintenance should rest, not
on his capacity to assist in profit-earning for the
private employer, but on the social value of the
service he performed. The reaction (much of it
likely to be transient) against State enterprise, and
the confusion of the older political schools of thought,
left an atmosphere favourable to whatever constructive suggestions Labour could make ; and the manifest need of something more than palliative measures
deepened the doubt as to whether the pre-war
industrial system could ever return unmodified.

In respect of housing in particular, there arose a
dilemma which illustrates the temper of the moment.
The failure, and eventual abandonment, of the State
scheme, left the problem not merely unsolved, but
with no prospect of solution. House-room for those
who most needed it remained almost impossible to
obtain, and all rents—save those limited by statute—
soared to unheard-of levels. For what little living
room became available " premiums "—fantastic sums
demanded as the price of the privilege of paying an
exorbitant rental for indifferent accommodation—
were exacted in some form or other by almost every
species of property holder. In essence, the situation
only reflected the natural relation of price to supply
and demand ; but the intense indignation of all
except the vendors served to remind them that quasi-
mechanical economic law is simply brute earth for
humanity to set its feet on, and that there is no
particular reason why the feet should always move
in a circle.

Never in fact was national progress so much dependent upon careful thinking. The situation on which this seven years closes was one in which Britain could certainly "muddle" *ad infinitum,* but with small hope, as the phrase has it, of "muddling through." Nations may choose if they will the method of trial and error ; but the trial is apt to be long, and the error is punished. War, social and international, would seem to have been fore-ordained for this past decade ; but the meaning of such ordinance is not that war is a necessary phase of collective activity, but that society has to pay the full price of its own mistakes.

In the industrial field, the war of employer and employed, of capital and labour, is essentially a side-issue. The real campaign is that of just and intelligent men on both sides in quest of a better social system.

EPILOGUE.

Contemporary history, clutching at the flying skirts of the hour, is apt to fetch up breathless on a few loose ends that only some later survey can bind or bury. Yet all history, however essayed, consists not in an impossible recapture of the infinite vagaries of circumstance, but in the imposition of significant form upon the fluent chaos of experience. As such it is a species of action on the one hand and of art upon the other : both these, less by intention than by the sheer necessity of the mind. Even of events conveniently past, the record is never so much a catalogue as an interpretation ; and from the nature of things, or the nature of thought, or both (if indeed they be two, and not one) the interpretation appears to follow a broad rhythm of systole and diastole in which, with the regular irregularity of life, points of comparative pause seem to recur giving scale and significance to the endless sequence. And though the odds would lie against the accidental present falling on such a node, the summer of 1921 may mark in fact the close of a cycle.

So far, some future writer may discern, the violent eruption of the past decade—of which war was the climax, not the origin—has carried social and industrial affairs. At length the nation, having been blown high enough to glimpse in the clouds a land fit for heroes to live in, falls rapidly earthward, hoping in vain that the ground may prove no harder than it was in 1914. Like the inflated currency of the war. the inflated hopes of the peace shrink and subside. The cost of living declines by 46 points of the official index in six months—a swifter movement than in any such period of the past seven years; and the wage-rates of 4½ million workers suffer their first general reduction. So also the great reform projects of 1918 are left suspended in the region of aspiration. The national education scheme is indefinitely postponed, while the London County Council overrides the law in flight from its commitments. The half-a-million houses that figured in the national reconstruction scheme dwindle to a bare 176,000, which the workers may perhaps be able to rent on an improved standard of two families per house. Minimum wage legislation is perforce curtailed, while in at least one section of industry the hours of labour are extended. In vain does the Provisional Joint Committee of 1919 dissolve itself in protest against the non-fulfilment of government promises; more than the Provisional Joint Committee will dissolve before those promises become redeemable. Meanwhile the smoke of factory chimneys belching again into the unwontedly clean air suggests some normal breath of industry returning after a period of paroxysm; and employers innumerable, and 2½ million unemployed, watch eagerly for the first faint sign of a "trade revival." "Work and goodwill," chants *The Times*; "Increased output is essential," says Vernon Hartshorn to the miners; "Now for a good time," bellows *John Bull* as the pits re-open. Thus does the country settle down, late and painfully, on the edge of the financial crater, uncertain whether on the whole it is more likely to blow up again, or fall in, or by good luck remain comparatively stable; and those who were nethermost before find themselves nethermost again.

The worker, looking on with doubtful eyes and

lighter pocket, feels perhaps less jubilant than Mr. Bottomley. " It is not the intention of the employers," says with variations many a trade agreement, " to reduce the economic status of the worker to the pre-war level " ; but it is patently the intention of blind economic law, which human prescience will be hard tried in the long run to circumvent. Short of financial revolution, the " pre-war level " would seem the utmost limit of what can for many years be hoped for ; and the miner, the engineer, the builder, the textile worker and many another may not unnaturally wonder in ruminant silence whether that is what it is all to come to— whether the best the years can bring is the gradual and painful restoration of the *status quo ante.*

The question comes at a critical moment. For ten years past industrial organisation has been increasing in unprecedented fashion. Among the employers it has reached a degree not merely of magnitude, but of efficiency, of which neither the general public nor the vast majority of trade unionists is allowed to form any adequate idea. Power has been quietly encompassed with such success that in the industrial field, as far as organisation is concerned, a national lock-out is more feasible than a general strike ; while in the political field, in the very House of Commons, the interests of the Federation of British Industries are watched by a larger group of abler men than that which stands for labour. But the decade has also seen a determined attempt on the part of the workers to consolidate their hold on industrial power ; and the principle *si vis pacem para bellum,* formerly applied with such auspicious results in international affairs, is thus informing the social structure ever more thoroughly. In particular, for the past two years there has been a general move to strengthen the centralised control of the main industrial groups. In the printing, engineering, iron and steel, building, and transport industries, in general labour, among the clerks, the teachers, and the civil servants, the previous federations, affiliations or working arrangements between various sections are being steadily modified in the direction of complete amalgamation. The process has been accelerated by the wage reduction of the past six months ; but it is as yet far from the desired ideal, and the weakness of the present position is aptly illustrated in the following passage from the Journal of the Amalgamated Engineering Union for May 21st—a passage which provides an interesting commentary on the events of 1917 :

"Once again we are faced with the weakness of our position owing to sectionalism in the industry. We went into conference with the employers to put forward our views against the employers' claim for reduced wages with the knowledge that a few hours previous, officials representing an important section of our trade had agreed to recommend to their members a reduction in wages amounting to 6s. per week. This question must receive the immediate attention of the men in the shop. Neither officialism nor the question of benefits must be allowed to stand in the way. We therefore appeal to the Shop Stewards and local officials to make efforts with the members of other organisations to bring the matter before their respective branches with a view to inducing their officials to take action."

Thus do circumstances urge the complete integration of trade unions on a comprehensive industrial basis. To both defensive and aggressive action that is now clearly essential ; and we may look forward, along the line of present development, to such an array of rival forces as will render industrial disputes perhaps less frequent, but ever more extensive and

more devastating. Recent experience indeed suggests
that the employment of industrial coercion in other
than strictly industrial issues is if anything less
feasible on the larger than on the smaller scale ; nor
does it appear that the expansion of workers'
organisation has materially tilted the balance of
power in the workers' favour. But it does appear
that such industrial disputes as occur must jeopardise
the common weal to an ever-increasing degree ; and
it is possible that the functions of the State will
with increasing difficulty be confined to those of
" keeping the ring." It may well be that a policy
of non-intervention will fall permanently short of
the minimum duties of government, and that states-
men of whatever party will find themselves compelled
to adopt active rather than passive measures, in
defence of the common weal.   In such circumstances
the ideal impartiality of the State will be more and
more difficult of preservation ; and should the balance
of political power between the classes remain substantially unchanged, and the conduct of industry
suffer no great and drastic modification, a revolutionary situation must inevitably arise within the
next few decades even though there be no specific
resort to industrial coercion in political issues.

This process, it must be emphasized, is not
dependent upon the deliberate adoption of a
revolutionary policy by the trade unions, nor upon
any marked expansion of their present sphere of
action.   And the limits of that sphere are now fairly
apparent.   As custodians of the economic status of
their members, as instruments for stabilising, on
occasion bettering the terms and conditions of
employment, the trade unions have proved thmselves
indispensable to the workers.   But on the profounder
factors of economic welfare their influence is little
more than negative.   Despite Whitley Councils and
other such joint boards of employers and employed,

the trade unions are yet unable to lay hold on more of the reality of industrial control than is gratuitously offered them—nor have they proved their title. Except within the narrowest limits, they are unable to modify the rise or fall of the value of the wages they secure, or to stay the actual depression of such wages to bare subsistence point where industry demands, or to regulate the ebb and flow of the unemployment they insure against. And if in such cases *force majeure* be pleaded—as with reason it may—in the free territory of thought their prerogative is scarcely better grounded. Despite, or because of, their intimate acquaintance with the working of the present system of industry, the trade unions have made little contribution to current efforts at the solution of its more fundamental problems. The unexampled trade depression brings forth again from the Trade Union Congress the threadbare suggestion that each individual should do less work in order that more may be employed; as if the deliberate restriction of output by the workers were one whit less culpable than the deliberate curtailment of production by the employers. The most practical proposals for industrial maintenance have been worked out by employers rather than trade unionists, and thwarted in case after case by the internecine jealousy and mutual suspicion of the unions. The origin of the national guilds scheme lies in far other than trade union circles, and the name borne by the much discussed Foster report is the name of an employer. The pioneers of the building guilds were respectively manager and journalist; and the most searching criticism of the most fundamental aspect of modern industry—that contained in the Douglas-Orage credit scheme—has only with the greatest difficulty secured a bare hearing from the most prominent trade union leaders. Neither in deed nor in thought can it be maintained that the trade unions have made positive contribution to the reconstruction of the industry and productive capacity of the nation.

It will be argued that trade unions do not set out to do these things ; their responsibility is simply to their members for such advantages as they can secure, and to no-one else. That is precisely the point. It is forgotten in the constant struggle over the terms and conditions of employment that the ultimate concern of society is not with the fact or the conditions of labour, but with the product of labour and its distribution. The inequities of distribution do not absolve the trade unions from their share of responsibility for production ; the defects of the present social system do not justify the tacit denial of all allegiance to the community. The sanction now given by the State and by society to the extant industrial organisations—a sanction amounting almost to privilege in the case of the trade unions— entails a certain reciprocal obligation of service ; an obligation that is not to be shirked merely because the service is for the most part indirectly rendered. The natural sequel to four years unbridled destruction is many years increased effort for less reward ; yet ca'canny, which was an occasional policy before the war, is now over large areas of industry a mere habit, and bids to become a disease ; and it is not the kind of disease from which recovery can be made on a sudden, at will or behest. If in the future that is not to be regarded as a trade union matter, and an important one, so much the worse for labour. In sober truth, the trade union must either concern itself, here and now, with the quality and quantity of the service its members render to society, or consign itself to oblivion.

But if the sense of social responsibility is at times found wanting in trade union practice, it is infinitely farther to seek among the employers'

associations; for there are activities of these latter
in which the interest of the community is not
merely neglected, but positively jeopardised.
Individual employers, it is true, have in many
cases done their utmost to secure the good of their
workers and the fair service of the public; but
good and bad alike are bound by the limits of a
system that makes the ability of an industry to
earn a competitive profit for the private employer
the determining factor. That principle, abandoned
perforce under stress of war, has failed to meet
the most crying needs of society in time of peace;
and in at least some branches of industry a change
in the sphere of motive is essential.

It is on this score that the demand for workers'
control has gained many adherents. But those on
whom at present the *onus probandi* rests must
prove their case on more counts than one. In the
first place, it is by no means certain that a sense
of social responsibility, at present largely to seek
among trade unions, will be more easily inculcated
as their development proceeds; yet unless the
inculcation of that sense is timely begun, the
functional organisation of society implied in workers'
control would conceivably raise more problems than
it solved. But granted that a change in the sphere
of motive were thus satisfactorily effected, there is
a farther issue. "Workers' control," like many
another time-honoured phrase, is now thoroughly
cant-encrusted, and its implications are not so
simple as appears. Control of any sort implies
that the liberty of someone or other is to be
restricted; and the immediate practical point for
industry is whether or no the restriction carries
the voluntary consent of the controlled. In so far
as workers' control might secure the consent of a
larger proportion of the population it is *ipso facto*
desirable as tending to the smoother working and

increased productivity of industry. It is upon this initial advantage that the success of the building guilds has so far been secured ; but there is a second test. In the long run—*pace* Lenin—workers' control can only justify itself to society by proving intrinsically better control. The affairs of modern industry admit of no more bungling from the workers than from any other body ; and it is an open question whether, were some unforeseen turn of fortune to saddle the trade unions with the reality of workers' control at short notice, the gain in the sphere of motivation would outweigh for as much as six months the certain loss in practical efficiency. There is in many quarters a tacit assumption that the abstract justice of the idea of workers' control would in some way redeem that loss. We are too easily deceived. There are possible states of society which, while verging on the intolerable through social injustice, are yet liable to utterly disastrous collapse at too drastic and sudden an application of strict social justice. Let modern civilisation beware how it tempt the blind goddess.

In the advance towards any radical change in the conduct of modern industry the interests of society demand that the workers should seek always to widen the scope of the forces they take with them. An exclusive or jealous interpretation of their ideals could be justified only by the existence of a plethora of technical and directive ability within the trade unions which at present is not there. The process of " change in the sphere of motive " must for permanence be a conversion rather than a catastrophe ; and the conversion must include the largest possible proportion of those now engaged in industry. Every effort towards a wider basis of service may therefore contribute to the ultimate reorganisation The building guilds, the co-partnership schemes of private employers, the efforts at reconstruction made by the Joint Industrial Councils, the solid, quiet work of the Labour Research Department, the effort of every agency engaged in the education, and especially in aiding the self-education, of the workers, and, above all, the great co-operative movement, with its social and educational activities—these things are a surer ground of hope than reams of print and seas of agitation   In the present organisation of the trade unions labour has at least a ready-made opportunity of advancing not merely the economic status, but the intrinsic value, the moral and intellectual worth, of the workers ; and that opportunity is in the last resort more momentous and of fuller promise than the coercive force of industrial combination.

For it is in and through such educational effort, broadly conceived and patiently pursued, that the psychological revolution, the " revolution in the spirit of man " for which since Ibsen's day so many have called in vain, can be brought about.   It is the curse upon the present system that goodwill among men—of which there is far more, even in the industrial world, than the vulgar press discerns—is so largely _suppressed and thwarted.   Among the various groups of workers, despite much rivalry and jealous exclusiveness, there is a nascent consciousness of confraternity that is not to be regarded as an evil thing merely because its range is limited and its action sometimes misapplied.   The task of the future is not to suppress, but to educate and liberate that consciousness.   Membership of so large a community as the nation is seldom a dynamic, generally a potential factor of human motive.   Consciousness of smaller communities is, however, an ever-present and ever-active stimulus ; and in the light of recent history the sense of mutual service appears a more durable cement of the social fabric than the cash nexus.   Here it may be lies the compensatory ele-

ment for the deficiency of personal motive in modern
industry—in the consciousness of recognised public
service, rendered and acknowledged through the
industrial group

What modifications of constitutional theory and
practice that social revolution may entail it is
the task of the Labour party, not the trade unions,
to discover and prepare. The political movement
will have, as its constant preoccupation, the interpretation step by step of the labour ideals with a
view to their acceptance by, rather than their enforcement upon, public opinion ; since to their
realisation the support of a large measure of public
opinion is absolutely necessary. Ultimately the
political movement will be called on to solve the
anomaly by which at present the great industrial
groups have no existence as constitutional entities
nor any sort of constitutional connexion with the
executive organisations of government—an anomaly
by which the efficiency of government as well as
industry is impaired. And it will be called on—
it, or whoever else can—to solve the greater and
truly staggering discrepancy between real and effective demand : the discrepancy by which at present
appalling destitution and unprecedented productive
capacity can coexist in the same areas of the same
country. Before such tasks can be accomplished
the limitations of the present trade union outlook
must be exceeded—where necessary, over-ridden ;
and in the meantime labour leaders must regard
themselves as charged with the education both of
general and especially of industrial opinion. That
policy may seem slow ; but it is as swift as the
realities of labour organisation and the national
temper will allow, and its promise is surer than that
of any more drastic alternative.

For the central tradition of British history, the
very genius of the race, lies in plasticity and in the

power of assimilation. That tradition has persisted through many vicissitudes—thwarted sometimes, it is true, by interludes of violent struggle, but only to reassert itself when the noise of battle is ended and the captains and the kings depart. Over industrial history in particular the lesson is writ too plain for even the most doctrinaire reading to ignore. The greatest inequities have arisen not by sudden enactment but by gradual cumulation, and as concomitant by-products of positive material advance; and it is in the last degree unlikely that the ill-adjustment of the social balance will be firmly righted by any sudden kick of the beam. The one wise policy in national affairs is that of deliberate disinterested acquiescence in the main tradition; and persons or parties that run counter to it, with no matter how laudable intentions, work in the long run to postpone, to jeopardise, possibly to destroy the common weal. Great and tangible sacrifices, of power and privilege and possession, will ultimately prove necessary to the establishment of a better social order; but the demand must be made in the name of the community, and endorsed by an authority not less than national. The militant strength of labour will remain a last desperate and doubtful resource; but it is the interest of all who care for Britain that in due time the necessary sacrifices should be secured, not by the industrial power of labour driven to drastic measures of coercion, but by the general conscience of the community roused to a finer sense of what is just.

THE END.

SELECTED AUTHORITIES, ETC.

GENERAL.

The principal authority for the whole period is the daily and periodical Press, in which practically all important statements of the Government, Ministry of Munitions or other authorities were published as issued. The Trade Union Journals, particularly the Monthly Journal of the A.S.E. and the British Trade Union Review, supply valuable detail; and the official *Labour Gazette* contains statistics and reviews of labour legislation, important disputes, etc.

A note may be added on the Labour Press. The *Daily Citizen* was published from October, 1912, to June, 1915 Its pre-war circulation reached at one time 300,000, but it declined from the close of 1913. It represented moderate opinion and was not sufficiently individual to compete with the popular newspapers. The *Herald* commenced publication as a daily early in 1912, it was published weekly during the war, and was restarted as a daily on March 31st, 1919. It took up a decidedly left wing attitude and latterly became an organ of extremist opinion, supporting the "direct action" policy. Its principal financial support comes from the Miners' Federation and the N.U R. Its circulation in the years 1918-1921 has varied from about 230,000 to 330,000; during the railway strike of 1919 the circulation rose to nearly 500,000. The I.L.P. has been represented throughout by the *Labour Leader* (weekly), which during the war was extreme Socialist and pacifist. The *Labour Leader* republished the account of the Clydeside meetings of December, 1915, after *Forward* (Clyde Workers' Committee organ) was suppressed. Other left-wing organs to which reference should be made are:

The Call, Solidarity, and *Workers' Dreadnought* (the last originally a women's suffrage paper). The *Call,* formerly the organ of the British Socialist Party, was amalgamated with the *Communist* in the autumn of 1920. The circulation of the latter averaged 49,000 weekly during April, 1921, and over the Triple Alliance crisis rose to 60,000.

Among books of general reference the following may be mentioned :

Annual Registers, 1914-1920.
Labour Year Books, 1916 and 1919.
Webb : History of Trade Unionism.
Askwith · Industrial Disputes.
Gray . War-time Control of Industry.
Burns : Government and Industry.
Money : The Case for Nationalisation.
Dewar : The Great Munition Feat.
Ministry of Labour : Reports on Conciliation and Arbitration for
    1914-1918 and 1919.

Reference is also made to reports of Trade Union and Labour Party Conferences, etc., Acts of Parliament and Hansard. The following are among the authorities relating to special periods or aspects :

PART ONE.

Cole : Labour in War-time.
Report of Workers War Emergency Committee, 1914-1916.
Special Reports of Board of Trade on the State of Employment
    in October, 1914, December, 1914, February, 1915. (Cd.
    7703, 7755, 7850.)
Reports of Local Government Board on Distress Committees, etc.
    (Cd. 7603, 7763, 7756.)
Drake · Women in the Engineering Trades.
Report on Bad Time-keeping. (H.C. 220.)
On the munitions supply question, see (inter alia) ·

Repington : The Great European War
Caldwell Experiences of a Dug-out.
Arthur : Life of Lord Kitchener (Vol. III). ·
Hansard . H.C., LXX, 1277 ; LXXI, 277-329, 1642 *seq.* ;
    LXXII, 18, 1221-22 ; LXXVII, 96 *seq.*

On the influence and work of the Press, see especially:

Cook : The Press in War-time.

Ch XVII of Caldwell, *op. cit.*, is particularly valuable ; see also the Debate in H.C., March 11th, 1918 ; Hd. 104, 73 *seq.*

On recruitment :

Labour Year Book, 1916, and Cole, *op. cit.* (details relating to various industries)

Repington, *op. cit.*

War Cabinet Report, 1918, p. 95.

PART TWO.

Goodrich : The Frontier of Control (valuable bibliography).

War Cabinet Report, 1917.

Commission of Inquiry into Industrial Unrest : Reports. (Cd 8662-9 ; 8696.)

Labour Memorandum on War-aims

Union of Democratic Control : pamphlets—
    The National Policy
    War and the Workers.
    The Morrow of the War, etc.

Labour Press as indicated.

PART THREE.

War Cabinet Report, 1918.

Report on Clyde Munition Workers. (Cd. 8136)

Reports of the Whitley Committee. (Cd. 8606, 9085, 9099, 9153)

Industrial Reports of Ministry of Labour, Nos. 1-4.

Bulletins on Work of Joint Industrial Councils (Ministry of Labour).

Industrial Council for the Building Industry : Garton Foundation.

Month's Work (monthly record of Ministry of Labour).

Health of Munition Workers' Committee : Reports and Handbook.

Juvenile Employment during the War and After : Ministry of Reconstruction.

Report of Departmental Committee on Juvenile Education. (Cd. 8512.)

Findlay : The Young Wage-earner.

Report of War Cabinet Committee on Women in Industry. (Cmd. 135, 157.)

The Position of Women after the War : Report of Standing
   Joint Committee of Women's Organisations
L. K. Yates . The Women's Part.

PART FOUR.

Housing : Report on Emergency Problem. (Cd. 9087.)
Housing and Town-planning Report. (Cmd. 917.)
Housing in England and Wales (Ministry of Reconstruction).
Housing : Journal of Ministry of Health.
Report on Position of the Building Industry after the War.
   (Cd. 9197.)
Ministry of Health : Second Annual Report (1921).
Coal Industry Commission : Reports, Cmd. 210. (Details of
   disputes, etc., in *Labour Gazette* and Labour Press.)

On Socialist opinion generally :

Beer : History of British Socialism.
Labour and the New Social Order.
Labour and the Peace Treaty (Ministry of Labour).
R. W. Polegate : The International during the War.
R. P. Dutt : The Two Internationals.
Robert Williams : The New Labour Outlook.
Pamphlets, etc., of National Guilds League, British Socialist
   Party, Labour Party, Communist Party, etc.

STATISTICS OF LABOUR ORGANISATION.

1913–1920.

	Employed Workers.			Trade Union Membership in United Kingdom.			Affiliated to Trade Union Congress.
	Men.	Women.	Total Adults.	Men.	Women.	Total.	
1913	—	—	—	3,630,152	356,963	3,987,115	2,217,836
1914	10,600,000*	3,287,000	13,887,000	—	—	4,199,000	2,866,077
1915	—	—	—	3,896,000	492,000	4,388,000	2,677,357
1916	—	—	—	4,043,000	626,000	4,669,000	2,850,547
1917	8,232,000†	4,713,000	12,945,000	4,660,000	880,000	5,540,000	3,082,352
1918	8,163,000‡	4,940,000	13,103,000	5,423,000	1,222,000	6,645,000	4,532,085
1919	—	—	—	—	—	—	5,265,426
1920	10,739,000‖	4,146,000	14,885,000	6,695,000	1,329,000	8,024,000	6,494,707
1921	—	—	—	—	—	—	6,389,123

* Figures relate to July, 1914.
†　　,,　　,,　　October, 1917.
‡　　,,　　,,　　November, 1918.
‖　　,,　　,,　　April, 1920.

Compiled from 17th Abstract of Labour Statistics, Labour Gazette, Board of Trade Employment Statistics, Labour Year Book, 1919, British Trade Union Review

PERCENTAGES OF TOTAL UNEMPLOYMENT AMONG INSURED WORKPEOPLE AND TRADE UNIONISTS AFTER THE WAR.

End of	1919.		1920.		1921.	
	U.I.A.	T.U.	U.I.A.	T.U.	U.I.A.	T.U.
January	9.93	2.5	6.10	2.9	8.2	6.9
February ...	10.71	2.8	4.42	1.6	9.5	8.5
March	*	2.9	3.63	1.1	11.3	10.0
April	*	2.7	2.8	.9	15.0	17.6
May	*	2.1	2.68	1.1	17.31	22.2
June	*	1.7	2.62	1.2	17.81	23.1
July	*	2.0	2.73	1.4	14.80	16.7
August	*	2.2	2.88	1.6	13.15	16.5
September ...	*	1.6	3.80	2.2	—	—
October	*	2.6	4.10†	5.3	—	—
November ...	8.32	2.9	3.7	3.7	—	—
December ...	6.58	3.2	5.8	6.1	—	—

* Percentages not available.

† On 15th October, after which date no further statistics under the Acts of 1911–16 are available. The November figure relates to the Act of 1920.

The Trade Union percentages relate to from 3½ to 4 million workers, mainly of skilled workpeople: they understate the proportion of general unemployment, but are on a more constant basis than the Insurance figures. The latter up to November 8th, 1920, cover from 3½ to 4 million workers, skilled and unskilled, among whom the liability to unemployment was on the whole greater than the average among the 11,900,000 workers to whom since November 8th the figures refer. In the former period from two-thirds to three-quarters of the insured workpeople were demobilised men and women; and throughout 1919 an absolute majority of those registered were women. (*Labour Gazette*, 1919-1921.)

S

RISE IN THE COST OF MAINTAINING THE AVERAGE PRE-WAR WORKING CLASS STANDARD OF LIVING.

Weighted Percentage increase in cost of all items at beginning of month (July, 1914 = 100).

	1914	1915	1916	1917	1918	1919	1920	1921
January ...	—	10–15	35	65	85–90	120	125	165
April ...	—	15–20	35–40	70–75	90–95	110	132	133
July ...	—	25	45–50	80	100–105	105–110	152	119
October ...	10	30	50–55	75–80	115–120	120	164	—

From *Labour Gazette*, August, 1919, April, 1921 (*q.v.* for further detail).

INDEX.

S 2

Lightning Source UK Ltd.
Milton Keynes UK
29 November 2010

163612UK00006B/47/P